Occupational Stress:

Issues and Developments in Research

Occupational Stress:

Issues and Developments in Research

Edited by

Joseph J. Hurrell, Jr.
Lawrence R. Murphy
Steven L. Sauter

National Institute for Occupational Safety and Health, Cincinnati, USA

and

Cary L. Cooper

University of Manchester, England

Taylor & Francis
New York · Philadelphia · London
1988

UK   Taylor & Francis Ltd, 4 John St., London WC1N 2ET

USA   Taylor and Francis Inc., 242 Cherry St., Philadelphia, PA 19106-1906

Copyright © Taylor & Francis Ltd 1988

British Library Cataloguing in Publication Data

Occupational stress: issues and developments
  in research.
  1. Job stress
  I. Hurrell, Joseph J.
  158.7   HF5548.85

  ISBN 0–85066–418–7

Library of Congress Cataloging-in-Publication Data

Occupational stress.

  Bibliography: p.
  Includes index.
  1. Job stress. I. Hurrell, Joseph J.
HF5548.85.O26 1988   158.7   87–33567
ISBN 0–85066–418–7

Cover design by Ray Eves
Typeset by Chapterhouse, The Cloisters, Formby, L37 3PX
Printed in Great Britain by
Redwood Burn Limited, Trowbridge, Wiltshire.

Contents

Preface

Workers in increasing numbers are claiming that stress in the workplace has caused them some form of disability. A recent study by the US National Council on Compensation Insurance (NCCI, 1984), for example, indicated that claims involving mental disorders caused by stress accounted for nearly 11% of all occupational claims between 1980 and 1982. The severity of such problems are reflected in a recent study (Fischback *et al.*, 1986) which found that among US Social Security Administration disability allowances, mental disorders were the third most disabling condition preceded only by musculoskeletal injuries and circulatory diseases. However, despite the increased appreciation of stress as an occupational health problem, our understanding of causes and effects is far from complete. A major limiting factor has to do with our approaches to stress research.

Indeed, a variety of conceptual, methodological and measurement problems in this research area have been identified. Kasl (1978) has noted that survey studies of occupational stress often fail to distinguish between measures of stressors and measures of resulting strain. Likewise, record studies are not without faults. For example, over 40 different measures of absenteeism exist and it is clear that they do not represent a homogeneous set of behaviours (Muchinsky, 1977; Clegg, 1983). Conceptually, absence from work may reflect ill-health, personnel policies, and/or various socio-demographic, economic and occupational factors. Even in the controlled confines of the laboratory, there are pitfalls. Here for example, psychophysiological measures have presented difficulties. In the case of blood pressure, issues surrounding basal pressure variability (Schulte *et al.*, 1984), interactions of personality (e.g. Type A) with task demands (Dembrowski *et al.*, 1978) and regression to the mean (Shepard and Finison, 1983) represent a few contaminating factors.

This book addresses these research issues and aims to stimulate improvements in methods for assessing stressful job environments and attendant health, safety and performance consequences. The volume is divided into two parts. Chapters in the first part deal with *Stressors* while chapters in the second part are concerned with the *Physiological Consequences of Stress*. Chapter 1 provides an overview of work environment factors that have been identified as sources of employee stress while Chapter 2 provides a perspective on the specific methodologies needed to measure different types of stressors. Chapter 3 focuses on the content and psychometric properties of scales commonly used in occupational stress research. The next three chapters contain recommendations for improving methods and measurement in this research via situationally anchored scales (Chapter 4), epidemiological problem analysis (Chapter 5) and more precise operationalization of constructs (Chapter 6), respectively. Chapter 7 discusses the role of personality in dampening the negative impact of job stressors. The last chapter in Part I (Chapter 8) presents a social action model which, in contrast to traditional stress research paradigms, emphasizes worker involvement in the research process and self-definition of stressors.

Part II deals with physiological consequences of stress. Chapters 9 and 10 provide an in-depth critique of various methods and measures employed. Chapter 11 emphasizes the implications of cardiovascular hyper-responsiveness to stressful conditions while perceptual and physiological correlates of self-reported stress, physical symptoms and health are examined in Chapter 12. The last chapter (Chapter 13) proposes a triangulation approach to the study of stress incorporating both biomedical and behavioural measures.

We wish to extend our thanks to each of the contributors to this book for their thoughtful discussions.

The opinions, findings, and conclusions expressed in this volume are not necessarily those of the National Institute for Occupational Safety and Health, nor does mention of company names or products constitute endorsement by the National Institute for Occupational Safety and Health.

Joseph J. Hurrell, Jr.
Lawrence R. Murphy
Steven L. Sauter

References

Clegg, C. W. (1983). Psychology of employee lateness, absence, and turnover: A methodological critique and empirical study. *Journal of Applied Psychology*, **68**(1), 88–101.

Dembroski, T. M., MacDougall, J. M., Shields, J. L., Pettito, J. and Lushine, R. (1978). Components of the Type A coronary-prone behavior pattern and cardiovascular responses to psychomotor performance challenge. *Journal of Behavioral Medicine*, **1**, 159–176.

Fischback, T. J., Dacey, E. W., Sestito, J. P. and Green, J. H. (1986). *Occupational Characteristics of Disabled Workers*, 1975–1976. DHHS (NIOSH) Publication No. 86–106, Washington, DC.

Kasl, S. V. (1978). Epidemiological contributions to the study of work stress. In C. L. Cooper and R. Payne (eds), *Stress at Work* (New York: John Wiley).

Muchinsky, P. M. (1977). Employee absenteeism: A review of the literature. *Journal of Vocational Behavior*, **10**, 316–340.

NCCI (1984). National Council on Compensation Insurance Media Release, May 7, 1984, Deerfield Beach, Fl.

Shepard, D. S. and Finison, L. R. (1983). Blood pressure reduction: Correcting for regression to the mean. *Preventive Medicine*, **12**, 304–317.

Shulte, W., Neus, H., Thones, M. and Von Eiff, A. W. (1984). Basal blood pressure variability and reactivity of blood pressure to emotional stress in essential hypertension. *Basic Research in Cardiology*, **79**, 9–16.

Contributors

Dr Julian Barling

Dept of Psychology, Queens University, Kingston, Ont., Canada

Dr Paul M. Cinciripini

Behavioral Medicine Laboratory, Dept of Psychiatry, University of Texas Medical Branch, Galveston, TX 77550, USA

Professor Cary L. Cooper

Dept of Management Sciences, UMIST, PO Box 88, Manchester M60 1QD, England

Dr Richard S. DeFrank

Dept of Preventive Medicine and Community Health, University of Texas Medical Branch, Galveston, TX 77550-2777, USA

Dr Gerald R. Ferris

Texas A&M University, College Station, TX, USA

Dr Shirley Fisher

Stress Research Unit, University of Dundee, Dundee, Scotland

Yitzhak Fried

Dept of Management, Wayne State University, Detroit, MI 48202, USA

Dr Daniel C. Ganster

Dept of Management, University of Nebraska, Lincoln, NE 68588, USA

Dr J. Alan Herd

Institute for Preventive Medicine, The Methodist Hospital, 6565 Fannin, Houston, TX 77030, USA

Dr John M. Ivancevich

Dept of Organizational Behavior and Management, 312 McElhinney Building, University of Houston, Houston, TX 77004, USA

Dr Michael T. Matteson

Dept of Organizational Behaviour and Management, 312 McElhinney Building, University of Houston, Houston, TX 77004, USA

Dr Suzanne C. Ouellette
  Kobasa   Dept of Psychology, The Graduate Program,
                                City University of New York, 33 W 42nd Street,
                                New York, NY 10036, USA
Dr Vanja Orlans   Stress Research and Control Centre, Birkbeck
                                College, University of London, Malet Street,
                                London WC1E 7HX, England
Dr James W. Pennebaker   Dept of Psychology, Southern Methodist
                                University, Dallas TX 75275, USA
Dr Laurie I. Pratt   Dept of Psychology, Queens University,
                                Kingston, Ont., Canada
Dr Kendrith M. Rowland   Dept of Business Administration, University of
                                Illinois at Urbana–Champaign, 194 Commerce W
                                Street, Champaign, IL 61820, USA
Dr Patricia Shipley   Stress Research and Control Centre, Birkbeck
                                College, University of London, Malet Street,
                                London WC1E 7HX, England
Dr Arie Shirom   Dept of Labor Studies, Faculty of Social Sciences,
                                Tel Aviv University, Ramat-Aviv 69978,
                                Tel Aviv, Israel
Dr Valerie Sutherland   Dept of Management Sciences, UMIST, PO Box 88,
                                Manchester M60 1QD, England
Dr Charlotte D. Sutton   Texas A&M University, College Station, TX,
                                USA
Dr David Watson   Dept of Psychology, Southern Methodist
                                University, Dallas, TX 75275, USA

PART I
WORK STRESSORS

1

Sources of Work Stress

Valerie J. Sutherland and Cary L. Cooper

"We work not only to produce but to give value to time."
Delacroix

1. Introduction

For the past decade the unanimous call for a greater understanding of psychosocial and occupational stressors has echoed worldwide. At supranational level, the World Health Organization has undertaken studies on the psychosocial implications of industrialization, and the International Labour Office (1975) urged concern for psychosocial factors in "making work more human". There is also acceptance of an association between work experience and certain psychological disorders at government level (NIOSH, 1984); and concerned individuals continually emphasize the need to recognize people as an organization's most important resource (Flamholtz, 1971; Cooper, 1984; Womack, 1985). Informed and progressive corporations and companies are realizing that counting the cost of human resources has tremendous potential benefit. In many instances they have taken the advice "to engage in extensive stress audits" of particular jobs (Cooper and Payne, 1978) because occupational stress is acknowledged as *the* threat to work (Cox, 1978).

Our understanding of the nature of stress increases as the data from many different occupational groups begins to take on a definite pattern. Research findings generally support the idea that sources of stress in a particular job, together with certain individual/personality characteristics, may be predictive of stress manifestation in the form of job dissatisfaction, mental ill health, heart disease, accident occurrence, alcohol abuse and social/family problems, etc. (Cooper, 1985); and that one symptom may exacerbate another.

It is suggested that stress is inevitable, distress is not (Quick and Quick, 1984). Thus to optimize the stress that is the spice of life, essential to growth, development and change (Selye, 1956), it is first necessary to define, identify and measure sources of stress. These can be considered in three broad categories: organizational demands; extra-organizational demands; and the characteristics of the individual.

2. Organizational demands

Five categories of potential sources of psychosocial and occupational stress are identified within this classification, and include factors intrinsic to the job; the role of

3

the individual in the organization; the relationships and interpersonal demands of the work environment; career development; and the organizational structure and climate (Figure 1.1). No significance is placed on order of presentation and the categories are not necessarily independent or discrete. A situation may also be perceived as a threat because of the interaction or additive quality of two or more stressors and it is the perceived imbalance between a threat and the ability to cope which is crucial to the understanding of the state of stress or distress. This is the basis of 'person–environment fit' theory (French, 1973; Caplan, 1983). The stress associated with lack of 'fit' between the person and the job, either in skill, ability, capacity, needs and/or values will lead to job dissatisfaction, anxiety and depression.

Factors intrinsic to the job

Both the task demands and the physical demands of the work environment are considered within this category. Factors intrinsic to the job as potential sources of stress have been an issue of study for many years, and were a first and vital focus of investigation for early 'shop-floor' researchers (Cooper and Marshall, 1978). Kornhauser (1965) found that poor mental well-being was directly related to unpleasant work conditions, the necessity to work fast, expenditure of physical effort, and inconvenient hours.

Physical demands include: noise; vibration; temperature variation, humidity and ventilation; lighting and illumination levels; hygiene factors and climate. And the task factors discussed are: shiftwork/nightworking; work-load (including new technology and working long hours/overtime); repetitiveness, monotony and boredom; and the experience of risk and hazards.

Physical demands

Although the importance and significance of 'subjective reactivity' to physical environmental factors owes its origins to the Hawthorne studies of the 1920s (Roethlisberger and Dickson, 1939), the concept was not incorporated into models and definitions of stress until much later; for example, French and Caplan's (1973) person–environmental fit model; Cox and Mackay's (1976) transactional model of stress; and Cooper's (1981) person environment model of stress. The perceived ability to cope with a situation is the central feature in the balance/imbalance, stress/distress equation. For the researcher, it raises two major problems. Can demand be measured both objectively and subjectively? Can perceived control/coping be measured? The recent investigations into role overload and coping among police despatchers in the USA indicates the advantages of a dual approach (Kirmeyer, 1985). This is also evident in the study of 'noise' as a stressor. The perception of 'noise' in the work environment is a highly subjective experience, and the use of purely objective measurements would be totally inadequate.

NOISE

Jones (1983) suggests, "it is difficult to overstate the importance of sound to our well-being". Language and communication enriches human culture. Our concern is,

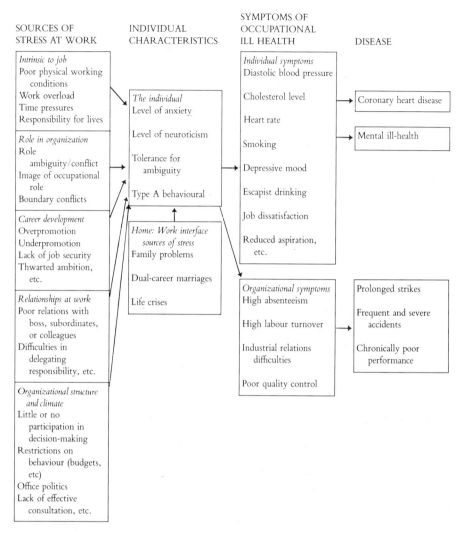

Figure 1.1 A model of stress at work.
Source: Cooper, C. L. (1986).

however, unwanted sound; this defines a sound as 'noise' (Jones, 1983). Exposure to noise can impede hearing ability, and may be problematic in that the detection of a wanted sound is masked. For example, an accident may occur if warning sounds are not observed (Poulton, 1978). The extent to which noise is a source of stress, causing an increased level of arousal and psychological imbalance, is still debated. Ivancevich and Matteson (1980) suggest that excessive noise (approximately 80 decibels) on a recurring, prolonged basis, can cause stress. The main psychosocial impact of excessive noise, and other physical demands, in the workplace is to reduce worker tolerance to other stressors, and adversely affect motivation (Smith, M. J. *et al.*, 1978); thus the impact is additive, not primary. In spite of this observation, noise is reported by many groups of blue-collar workers as a harmfully perceived stressor, for example, in the UK steel industry (Kelly and Cooper, 1981) and by blue-collar workers in Finland (Koskela *et al.*, 1973, cited ILO, 1986). Unpleasant working conditions due to noise (and other factors intrinsic to the job) was a significant predictor of job dissatisfaction among workers on drilling rigs and platforms in the North Sea (Sutherland and Cooper, 1986) and on an offshore installation in Norwegian waters (Hellesøy, 1985).

Many studies have observed the relationship between noise in the workplace and productivity, and noise and rate of error (Broadbent and Little, 1960). Of particular importance is the factor of noise in increasing vulnerability to accidents. Kerr (1950) found mean noise levels correlating significantly with accident frequencies, but not accident severity, among 12 000 employees on one site; and Cohen found accidents to be more frequent in noisy areas, that is, 95 decibels or above, particularly among the younger and less experienced workers: the introduction of ear defenders produced a significant reduction in accident rates (Cohen, 1974, 1976).

Although noise can be expressed in objective, physical terms, and it is necessary to consider many aspects of noise in the workplace—for example, intensity, variability, frequency, predictability and control—reaction to noise is ultimately a subjective experience (Kummer, 1983), and often the task itself (usually acting as a dependant variable) is also a source of stress; thereby confounding the measurements even further. Exposure to noise is associated with reported fatigue, headaches, irritability and inability to concentrate; the behavioural consequences are in terms of reduced performance/productivity and accident occurrence. Social behaviour is also influenced; for example, a reduction in helping behaviour, a more extreme or negative attitude to others, and more open hostility and overt aggression (Jones, 1983). Thus there are implications for impoverished relationships in the environment as a consequence of imposed isolation due to excessive noise (and/or the need to wear ear protectors), or poor interpersonal interactions resulting from an accumulation of physical frustration tensions (Keenan and Kerr, 1951). The problem of investigating any single source of work stress is therefore virtually impossible and essentially futile.

b) VIBRATION

Although less reported in the literature, vibration is acknowledged as a powerful source of stress resulting in elevated catecholamine levels and alterations to psychological and neurological functioning (Selye, 1976). Vibration from rotary or impacting machines could be problematic, for example, in steel casting (Kelly and Cooper, 1981): and this is also true for pneumatic drills, riveting hammers, aircraft propellers, helicopters, etc. Vibrations that transfer from physical objects to the body may adversely affect performance; hands and feet are particularly vulnerable but the 'annoyance' factor is also a major psychological consideration.

Frankenhaeuser and Gardell (1976) observed significantly elevated catecholamine levels among the assembly-line workers in a sawmill compared to the maintenance and repair men in the same plant. The differences are attributed to the perceived degree of control reported by the two groups of workers. It is, however, possible that the machinery in use, with a vibratory action, affected the hands, and could contribute to the physiological response observed.

In the offshore environment, on fixed rigs and platform installations, vibration is a potential source of stress. The activity of helicopters landing on helidecks positioned over living accommodation and the drilling operations cause vibration which may be significantly more damaging in the long term because the individuals must live and work in the same environment for 7–14 days, or more, without respite. Although the workers claim that "you get used to it", "unpleasant working conditions due to vibration" and disturbance in the living accommodation were rated as stressors by 37% and 27% of the workers, respectively. The long term effects of this exposure are not known (Sutherland and Cooper, 1986).

TEMPERATURE VARIATION, VENTILATION AND HUMIDITY

Physiological response to thermal conditions varies greatly between workers and within the same individual from one occasion to the next (Ramsey, 1983). The factory environment is too often characterized as too hot, too cold, too stuffy, too draughty etc., and thus creates both physical and attitudinal problems (Smith, M.J. *et al.*, 1978).

Work demanding critical decisions, fine discrimination and performance of fast or skilled action is impaired by thermal stress (Wing, 1965, cited in Ramsey, 1983). Manual dexterity is reduced in a cold environment and may be a factor in accident occurrence, due most likely to reduced sensitivity, slowed movement and interference from protective clothing, rather than the loss of impaired cognitive ability (Surrey, 1968). Again the subjective report of thermal comfort is all important. The inability to personally control one's physical environment could also be a significant factor in the perception of thermal comfort. As Ramsey suggests, there seems to be a correlation between 'comfort' and an individual's performance on perceptual motor tasks. A strong inverse correlation was observed between the perception of comfort and accident rates among shop-floor workers in a tractor factory. Keenan and Kerr (1950) suggest that heat and noise conditions leads to 'distractive' behaviour which results in reduced quality of work and accidents.

Noise, fumes and heat were the most commonly reported problems among casters in the steel industry (Kelly and Cooper, 1981). Most frequently mentioned by Norwegian workers on offshore platforms were the draughts, uncomfortable temperatures and the dry humid air (Hellesøy, 1985). More dissatisfaction was expressed about overheated working conditions (25%) than about the cold (12% of the respondents). The general effect of working in overheated conditions is a negative reaction to one's surroundings and, as already stated, the effect therefore becomes interactive, and additive. Unpleasant working conditions, due to heat, cold, noise and vibration, was a significant predictor of job dissatisfaction among rig workers in the UK and Dutch sectors of the North Sea (Sutherland and Cooper, 1986).

Again it is difficult to isolate out any single particular stressor. Workers forced to live and work in one environment, with a constant need for artificial ventilation, lighting and temperature control, report discomfort and sore throats from the dry air, and from the noise and constant whine of air-conditioning units and generators. As Smith, M.J. *et al.*, (1978) state, this will result in lowered tolerance to other stressors and affect worker motivation. The presence of these sources of stress 'uses up' some attention capacity (Hockey, 1970) and therefore limits the capacity to attend to task-relevant information.

d) LIGHTING AND ILLUMINATION LEVELS

The relationship between lighting/illumination levels and production was the concern of the Hawthorne Studies (Roethlisberger and Dickson, 1939). Adequate illumination is an obvious factor associated with safe working. Poor lighting and glare leads to eye strain, damaged vision, headaches, visual fatigue, tension and frustration because the task may be more difficult and time consuming (Poulton, 1978). Many work environments require constant artificial lighting. It is therefore important that a system creates a pleasant environment which facilitates performance and promotes safety (McKenna, 1987).

e) HYGIENE

Too many of the world's workforce are employed where hygienic conditions are poor, and exposure to accidents and disease causes a constant threat to health (ILO, 1986). Shostak (1980) reports blue-collar grievances of generally neglected working conditions, and the 'double standard' that exists. The 'all-glass', lavish front offices are compared to the noise, lack of windows and air conditioning in dirty factories and workshops. Workers in the steel industry describe dirty, dusty conditions, the poor accommodation provided for rest periods, and the lack of toilet facilities nearby (Kelly and Cooper, 1981). These stressors in the physical environment rated high on a list among the casting crews.

A clean and orderly environment is important for both safety and hygiene reasons and for the morale of the workforce, especially where a situation is already acknowledged as hazardous. However, theory (Herzberg *et al.*, 1959) states that although unsatisactory working conditions (hygiene needs) produce dissatisfied personnel in the workplace, the improvement of conditions usually means that the workers are no longer dissatisfied, but are not 'satisfied'. As Herzberg suggests, satisfaction and dissatisfaction are two completely different phenomena, and have different effects on behaviour.

f) CLIMATE

In the USA, a nationwide sample of workers polled in 1971 rated 'unpleasant working conditions' the third source of discontent (compensation rated first; health and safety hazards second). As Shostack (1980) states, "part of the problem is native to the setting, as in outdoor work". So, the worse thing is "the weather" and the need to work outside in all conditions. This affects many blue-collar occupational groups, including construction sites, dockyards, highways, seafaring, agricultural work, etc. Unpleasant climatic conditions affect physical well-being, morale and motivation, and thus vulnerability to accident involvement. If work routines and environments can not be altered, then adequate protective clothing is vital and attempts to address morale and motivational problems should be considered in alternative ways.

While it may be impossible, impractical or unnecessary to modify or eliminate the impact of some aspects of stress associated with the physical demands of a job, it is vital to understand the stress situation from a total perspective before any changes can or should be made. It is also necessary to realize that task demands may also be potential sources of stress.

2 Task demands

a) SHIFTWORK; NIGHTWORKING

It is estimated that 20% of the working population in Europe and North America is working some form of shift system (Tasto and Colligan, 1978; Cooper and Smith, 1986), not by choice, but of necessity. Despite considerable research effort, it is not possible to make overall generalizations regarding the 'best' shift system, but it is clear that shiftwork represents a major source of stress among blue-collar workers (Monk and Tepas, 1985). Shiftworkers complain more frequently of fatigue and gastro-intestinal troubles than day workers (Rutenfranz *et al.*, 1977) and the impact of shift-working on eating habits may be responsible for gastrointestinal disorders (Smith, M.J. *et al.*, 1982). Influences are both biological and emotional, due to circadian rhythm disruption of the sleep/wake cycle, temperature pattern and adrenaline excretion rhythm (Monk and Folkard, 1983).

Monk and Folkard (1983) state that shiftwork is a common aspect of contemporary society that must be consciously coped with. They believe that there are three factors which have got to be right for successful coping with shiftwork; sleep, social and family life, and circadian rhythms. These factors are interrelated, so that a problem with one can negate the positive effects of success achieved in the others.

Singer (1985) reports 487 different shiftwork systems operating in Europe, including permanent, rotating and continuous shift patterns, some of which demand nightworking; ultimately roster designs aim to maximize the positive effects and minimize the negative impact of shiftwork on health and social life caused by the disruption to circadian rhythms. Evidence from research in France (Reinberg, cited Singer, 1985) suggests that certain individuals, with steeper adrenaline curves than normal, are those who tolerate shiftwork best, that is, those with a pattern of very high adrenaline levels during the day, and very low levels at night; the steeper rhythm is less vulnerable to distortion, and the rationale is that non-adaptation is better than partial adaptation. Akerstedt's study of railroad workers supports this observation. Three weeks of daywork were followed by three weeks of nightworking, and very little adjustment in the pattern of adrenaline excretion was observed after three shifts of nightwork, with adrenaline remaining high during the day when the workers should be sleeping. Even after three weeks of nightworking no significant adjustment was observed. Akerstedt (1977) suggests that high adrenaline levels may be the source of the disrupted sleep patterns. In spite of the observation that some people may be physiologically better suited to shiftwork, many blue-collar workers have no choice. Therefore Knauth and Rutenfranz (1982) suggest that rapidly rotating shift systems with few nightshifts in succession may be best in terms of circadian rhythm disruption.

Other areas of study have focused on the relationship between shiftwork and accidents (Carter and Corlett, 1981). This review highlights the complexity and difficulties involved in understanding the causation of accidents. The authors conclude that not enough is known about psychological stressors among blue-collar workers, the effects of multiple stressors in the work environment, and the coping strategies used by the "army of shiftworkers who support our industrial society".

Although Selye (1976) suggests that individuals do habituate to shiftwork and it becomes physically less stressful with time, some work patterns might prevent habituation occurring; for example, the offshore rig worker who may work a mix of 12-hour day- and night-shifts for 7 or 14 consecutive days without a break, and then has 7 or 14 days at home on leave (Sutherland and Cooper, 1986).

WORKLOAD

Task factors intrinsic to the job includes the concept of workload as a potential source of stress. Both overload and underload are acknowledged as stressors (Frankenhaeuser *et al.*, 1971). The curvilinear relationship between the amount of work and health and performance is explained in terms of the Yerkes–Dodson Law (Yerkes and Dodson, 1908), the inverted-U hypothesis. Two further distinctions of workload are identified: 'quantitative' overload/underload results from the employee being given too many or too few tasks to complete in a given period of time; and 'qualitative' overload/underload is when the individual does not feel able or capable of doing the given task, or the task does not utilize the skills and/or potential of the worker (French and Caplan, 1973). Within these categories it is necessary to understand that the impact of new technology can affect both overload and underload, and that the pressure of both quantitative and qualitative overload can result in the need to work excessive hours, which is an additional source of stress.

Quantitative overload. Both physical and mental overload, that is, simply having too much to do, is a potent source of stress at work. Having to work under time pressure in order to meet deadlines is an independent source of stress. Studies show that stress levels increase as difficult deadlines draw near (Friedman *et al.*, 1958). An association between objective, quantitative overload and cigarette smoking, a risk factor in coronary heart disease and cancer, was observed by French and Caplan (1970).

Linked to the concept of overload is the issue of 'workpace'. Rate of working has been shown to be a significant factor in blue-collar ill health, especially when the worker is not able to control the pace (Frankenhaeuser, 1986). In a national survey in the USA, Margolis *et al.*, (1974) found that quantitative overload was significantly related to a number of symptoms or indicators of stress—poor motivation, low self-esteem, absenteeism, escapist drinking and an absence of suggestion to employers.

Quantitative underload. Underload may also affect one's psychological well-being. Boredom in the daily work routine, as a result of too little to do, may result in in-attentiveness. This is potentially hazardous if the employee fails to respond appropriately in an emergency (Davidson and Veno, 1980). Boredom was identified as a significant source of stress among crane operators (Cooper and Kelly, 1984). Long periods of inactivity may be in the nature of the job, therefore job redesign would be necessary to alleviate the problem because 'boredom' and 'lack of challenge' were significant predictors of raised anxiety, depression and reported job dissatisfaction. Lack of stimulation may be potentially more damaging at night when the individual could have difficulty adjusting to the change in sleep pattern, but does not have enough work to keep alert (Poulton, 1978).

Both work overload and underload may also result from irregular flow of work which is not under the control of the worker. This is not restricted to paced assembly lines; many outdoor occupations are paced by climatic conditions. Pace may therefore vary from complete shutdown to very hectic as workers try to keep to contract deadlines. In addition to financial gain, the promise of the 'next' contract may be dependent on successful completion of the current job.

Qualitative overload. There is evidence that qualitative overload as a source of stress is significantly linked to low levels of self-esteem (French *et al.*, 1965), although the evidence is based solely on white-collar occupations. Qualitative overload may be perceived by the blue-collar worker promoted to a supervisory capacity on the grounds of superior work performance, but who has no past experience of supervision of others or work delegation. A good, reliable worker is therefore placed under considerable stress because the skills to do the new job are lacking. The stress situation may be compounded if the individual has to take disciplinary action against a previous co-worker.

Qualitative underload. This may be as damaging as overload, in that an individual is not given the opportunity to use acquired skills, or to develop full potential ability. As with quantitative underload, boredom and 'shifts' or lapses in attention may have serious consequences. Underload due to lack of stimulation leads to low morale and poor motivation to work. The individual feels that s/he is 'not getting anywhere', and is powerless to show perceived and/or actual skills and talent.

Udris (1981, cited ILO, 1986) suggests that qualitative overload is associated with dissatisfaction, tension, low self-esteem, whereas qualitative underload is linked to dissatisfaction, depression, irritation and psychosomatic complaints.

New technology. In a rapidly changing work environment, the skills of workers may become obsolete. Also the need to constantly become familiar with new equipment and systems may pose a threat to the individual. Unless adequate training is provided, potentially stressful situations may develop when new technology is introduced into the workplace, and the individual feels unable to do the given task.

An additional source of stress in a rapidly changing work environment, which is related to 'overload', is having a boss schooled in the 'old way'. The new employee, trained in the latest methods, and perhaps educated to a higher standard in order to compete in a keen jobs market, may experience overload stress if adequacy of supervision is questionable. Confidence and respect in the ability of those responsible for the efficient and safe operation of a system or plant is vital to good interpersonal relationships at work. Introduction of new technology may expose a supervisor to conflict and the experience of qualitative overload, threaten the subordinate with overload because supervision is perceived as inadequate, and ultimately adversely affect the quality of relationships in the workplace.

Working long hours/overtime. The experience of both quantitative and qualitative over-load may result in the need for an individual to work excessive hours. Simply having too much to do in the normal working day or shift leads to overtime working. Also, the worker who struggles to do a job that is too difficult is likely to take more time to finish the task and may need to work extra hours in order to complete the job to a satis-factory standard.

A link between working long hours and stress and ill health has been established. Breslow and Buell (1960) report findings that supports a relationship between the number of hours worked and death from coronary heart disease (CHD). The study of 'light industry' workers in the USA found that subjects of less than 45 years of age, but working more than 48 hours per week, had twice the risk of death from CHD, compared to similar individuals working 40 hours or less a week. Also, a study of 100 young coronary patients showed that 25% of them had been working at two jobs, and an additional 40% had worked for more than 60 hours or more a week (Russek and Zohman, 1958).

However, a recent study of offshore rig workers indicated significantly lower levels of somatic anxiety (i.e., tiredness, exhaustion and general aches and pains) among this group who work continuous 12-hour shifts/7 days per week, than for comparable onshore blue-collar workers, presumably working approximately 40 hours over a 5-day period (Sutherland and Cooper, 1986). The result is surprising in that the issue of "insufficient sleep" offshore was rated as a stressor by 41% of the sample, and disturb-ance in the living accommodation also rated high on the list of stressors. However, the offshore worker does have an opportunity to 'catch up' in the long periods of time off and so overall may experience less tiredness and exhaustion.

The impact of working long hours also has an overall impact. The individual spends less time in social relationships and so the benefits of social support as a buffer in a stressful job are reduced. It must however be acknowledged that some individuals regard work, and working long hours, as a psychological haven and a means of escape from the pressure of home and family and unsatisfactory personal relationships.

The stress associated with workload is complex. French and Caplan (1973) suggest that both quantitative and qualitative load produces many different symptoms in addition to psychological and physical strain; i.e., job dissatisfaction, job tension, lowered self-esteem, threat, embarrassment, high cholesterol levels, increased heart rate, skin resistance and more cigarette smoking. Cooper and Marshall (1978) also remind us that objective work-load should not be viewed in isolation. It is necessary to consider perceived demand and ability in relation to the individuals actual capacity and personality.

Although all reasonable steps should be taken to improve the quality of working life, the stress experienced in a situation, overall job and life satisfaction and the well-being of the individual need to be considered in relation to 'expectation', 'needs' and the level of social support identified. Thus, the blue-collar worker employed on a paced assembly line may report dissatisfaction with the job, but does not display a typical manifestation of response to stress because the job is viewed as purely instrumental to the goals of a satisfactory way of life outside.

REPETIVENESS, MONOTONY AND BOREDOM

New technology and the increasing automation of industry can lead to simplification of work and repetitive jobs that are potentially stressful in terms of work-load.

Although a hectic work-pace is stressful, work that is dull, repetitive and monotonous is equally detrimental to physical and mental well-being (Kornhauser, 1965). For example, Kritsikis *et al.* (1968) observed a high incidence of angina pectoris among industrial workers employed on a conveyer line system. However, recent methodology for unobtrusive monitoring of heart rate and blood pressure demonstrates that the heart rate of medical nurses was 'sensitive' to emotional stress, whereas the response among truck assembly-line workers was a function of the physical work and activity (O'Brien *et al.*, 1979). Also, Salvendy and Knight (1983) used on-line monitoring of blood pressure to demonstrate that industrial workers in machine-paced tasks did not display any greater stress response risk than in self-paced tasks. They state that CHD risk is a complex equation of individual characteristics (age and personality), perceived stress level in the job environment and the interaction between factors.

Use of physiological monitoring may help to discover the extent to which stress is implicated as a cause of these prominent killers in modern society. However, the perception of stress and the psychological response is also critical; e.g., Broadbent and Gath (1979) found an association between reported levels of job dissatisfaction and somatic symptoms among assembly-line workers. Those engaged in paced work tasks reported more anxiety and depression.

Lack of stimulation, under-utilization of skills and boredom characterizes many blue-collar occupations. Benyon and Blackburn (1972) report the feelngs of tension resulting from boredom among workers on a packing-line system. The work provides no sense of achievement or satisfaction. The job stress associated with passive, low skill demands, lack of variety, repetitiveness, and low decision latitude factory work also spills over into leisure time, and so negatively affects life outside of work (Gardell, 1976 cited ILO, 1986). Lack of stimulation may also be dangerous: Cheliout *et al.* (1979-cited ILO, 1986) report a high incidence of deactivation episodes among electronic assemblers (monitored by continuous electro-encephalography, EEC, over the entire day). The theta rhythm observed, referred to as 'micro-sleep', is indicative of the boredom and tedium experienced by the workers, and may be responsible for accident occurrence.

Various programmes of job enlargement, job enrichment, job rotation, increased participation in decision-making and shared ownership may be introduced to alleviate some of these problems; but they also create separate problems and different sources of stress in the work environment; for example, disruption to social relationships, role ambiguity and status incongruence.

EXPOSURE OF RISK AND HAZARD

The risk and hazards associated with certain occupations may be a source of stress. Blue-collar workers in the USA rated 'health and safety hazards' as a highly significant source of job discontent (Wallick, 1972). Various occupational groups are identified as 'high-risk' in terms of physical danger, for example, police officers, mine-workers, soldiers, prison personnel, firefighters and workers on oil and gas exploration and production installations (Davidson and Veno, 1980; Kalimo, 1980; Kasl, 1973; Elliott, 1985).

However, it is not known if the special risks associated with these occupations are perceived as sources of stress by the competent and trained employee. It is, however, possible that a continued emphasis on the need for safety in a hazardous environment is the greater source of stress. Bohemier (1985) suggests that it is human nature to avoid thinking about danger or death in a hazardous or risky environment, and that it is necessary to block out some of the realities which the worker must otherwise continually face. As Cherry (1974) declares in a study of high-building iron workers, ''many workers learn to combine a hard-boiled veneer about job hazards with abiding private anxieties''.

Various studies indicate that some workers do perceive the risk and hazard associated with the job as a source of stress. Casters in the steel industry and crane operators acknowledge the dangers of the job (Kelly and Cooper, 1981; Cooper and Kelly, 1984). Awareness of the dangers and the consequences of making a mistake were significant predictors of depression and anxiety among crane operators. In a Norwegian study, 36% of offshore platform personnel felt unsafe about helicopter transport; 34% felt unsafe about evacuation facilities, and 24% were concerned about the risk of fire and explosion (Hellesøy, 1985). Risk of exposure to certain chemicals is frequently reported as one of the most harmfully perceived stressors among blue-collar workers (ILO, 1986). This includes the inhalation of vapours and dust, and exposure to chemicals that are irritants to the skin. Adequate protective clothing is vital, but training and education is equally important in reducing the stress associated with working in a potentially hazardous environment. The perceived adequacy of medical facilities and the ability to cope with an emergency situation will mitigate the potentially stressful risk situation.

The risk and hazard associated with many occupations cannot be changed, but the employees perception of the risk can be reduced by training and education. Anxious, obsessional and phobic workers are less motivated to work, have low morale and are more vulnerable to accidents; and in the long term may suffer the consequences of stress related illness, including heart disease and ulcers.

Generally, our understanding about the stress associated with the physical demands of blue-collar work is extensive, although less is known about the stress of task demands, particularly 'workload'. The most significant problem for researchers is the way in which the various factors intrinsic to the job interact to form stress chains and how perception of a stressor and/or demand might be meaningfully measured. Task demands of a job are also associated with the role of the individual in the organization. This stress category is discussed next.

The role of the individual in the organization

Within the organization, certain behaviours and demands are associated with the role fulfilled. However, dysfunction may occur at two different levels (Kahn *et al.*, 1964) and be a major source of worker stress: role conflict (i.e., conflicting job demands) and role ambiguity (i.e., lack of clarity about the task). Rizzo *et al.* (1970) suggest that role conflict and role ambiguity are related to job dissatisfaction and inappropriate organizational behaviour. The issue of 'responsibilty' associated with the role of the individual will also be included within this category of potential stressors.

Role conflict

Role conflict exists when an individual is torn by the conflicting demands of other members in the organization; doing tasks that are not perceived to be part of the job; or by being involved with a job that conflicts with personal values or beliefs. Stress is caused by the inability to meet various expectations or demands. Van Sell *et al.* (1981) and Kahn *et al.* (1964) found that men who suffered more role conflict had lower job satisfaction and higher job tension. Role conflict is also related to physiological stress (French and Caplan, 1970); telemetry records of male office workers illustrated that increased heart rate and feelings of tension about the job were strongly related to reported role conflict. Miles and Perreault (1976) identify four different types of role conflict:

1. Person–role conflict. The individual would like to do the task differently from that suggested by the job description.
2. Intrasender conflict. The individual receives an assignment without sufficient personnel to complete the task successfully.
3. Intersender conflict. The individual is asked to behave in such a manner that one person will be pleased with the result, while others will not be.
4. Role overload. The individual is assigned more work than can be effectively handled.

Role overload has already been discussed; although it would seem intuitive that the blue-collar worker would be stressed by the other role conflicts described, very little evidence supports the notion. For example, the data from a large-scale study of Kibbutz members (Shirom *et al.*, 1973) indicates that there are differences between occupational groups. They found that occupations requiring greater physical exertion, e.g., the agricultural workers, did not show the pronounced relationship between role conflict and role ambiguity and abnormal electrocardiographic readings. Also, Kotlarska *et al.* (1956 cited in ILO, 1986) in Poland, found a much higher incidence of hypertension among elementary school teachers and bank clerks exposed to conflicting situations and overload of responsibility, compared to miners and labourers. These findings suggest that some workers, e.g., blue-collar workers (Kasl, 1978), may suffer less from the interpersonal dynamics of the organization, but more from the physical working conditions. However, these studies do not report psychological response to role conflict. Kasl also states that correlations between role conflict, ambiguity and job-dissatisfaction are strong while correlations with mental health measures tend to be weak; and personality traits are an important determinant of response to role conflict.

It is possible that the blue-collar worker may experience stress from intersender conflict: while satisfying the demands of one superior, or department, another may be displeased, e.g., working in a manner to meet production needs could incur reprimand from a safety officer (and vice versa). Role conflict is a more serious problem for the individual working at organizational boundaries (Cooper and Marshall, 1978). Although supervisors or middle managers are more likely to develop ulcers than shopfloor workers (Margolis *et al.*, 1974) because they occupy boundary roles, many blue-collar workers deal with the public, or play a role in a trade union and thus find themselves in a potential stressful boundary role situation.

b) *Role ambiguity*

An additional source of stress may be present in the workplace when an employee does not have adequate information in order to carry out the task; or does not understand or realize the expectations associated with that particular role. Stress arising from unclear goals and/or objectives ultimately leads to job dissatisfaction, lack of self-confidence, feelings of futility, a lowered sense of self-esteem, depression, low motivation to work, increased blood pressure and pulse rate, and intention to leave the job (Kahn *et al.*, 1964; French and Caplan, 1970; Margolis *et al.*, 1974).

Workers may experience ambiguity by moving from one job to another; in times when many jobs are disappearing from manufacturing and heavy industry, this is often of necessity, not by choice for some occupations. Each industry has its own technical language, jargon and colloquialisms, which serve to exclude, confuse and isolate a new employee. Unless training is provided to overcome these problems, the uninitiated, although skilled, employee could be exposed to a stressful situation, vulnerable to error and accident involvement. Training to be in the new environment is needed, not necessarily training to do the task.

c) *Responsibility*

Responsibility is identified as a potential stressor associated with one's role in the organization. Distinction is made between 'responsibility for people' and 'responsibility for things' (budgets, equipment, etc.), with the former acknowledged as significantly more likely to lead to cardiovascular disease (Wardwell *et al.*, 1964; French and Caplan, 1970; Pincherle, 1970). However, it should also be noted that lack of responsibility may also be stressful if the individual perceives this as work underload. For some workers, responsibility for other people's lives and safety is a major source of stress. For example, the crane driver is aware of the consequences of a mistake (Opbroek, 1983; Cooper and Kelly, 1984). The offshore drilling crew also recognize the consequences of making a mistake, the need to work as a team, and 'watch over' the new employee. A mistake by the petroleum engineer on the rig can result in a 'blow-out', or explosion, which could cause large-scale injury or death, including the total loss of the drilling rig itself (Sutherland and Cooper, 1986).

Being responsible for other people's work and performance also demands that more time is spent interacting with others. Doll and Jones (1951) demonstrated that foremen and executives had more than the expected rate of duodenal ulcers, whereas various unskilled and non-supervisory groups had ulcer rates as expected. Various studies support this finding, but it is necessary to consider the informal networks within an organization. 'Responsibility for other people' may be self-imposed, in order to feel safe and secure. As one rig worker declared (about new, young workers) "you feel obliged to 'educate' them...because it might be my neck as well as theirs."

This issue of responsibilty as a source of stress leads to the consideration of relationships at work as potential stressors.

Relationships and interpersonal demands

Relationships at work

Selye (1974) suggests that having to live with other people is one of the most stressful aspects of life. Good relationships between members of a work group are considered a central factor in individual and organizational health (Argyris, 1964; Cooper, 1973).

Poor relationships at work are defined as having 'low trust, low levels of supportiveness, and low interest in problem solving within the organization'. Mistrust is positively related to high role ambiguity, which leads to inadequate interpersonal communications between individuals, and psychological strain in the form of low job satisfaction, decreased well-being, and feelings of being threatened by ones superior and colleagues (Kahn *et al.*, 1964; French and Caplan, 1973).

Supportive social relationships with peers, superiors and subordinates at work is less likely to create the interpersonal pressures associated with rivalry, office politics and competition. Lazarus (1966) and McLean (1979) suggest that social support in the form of group cohesion, interpersonal trust and liking for a supervisor is associated with decreased levels of perceived job stress, and better health. Inconsiderate behaviour on the part of a supervisor appears to contribute significantly to feelings of job pressure (Buck, 1972; McLean, 1979) and close supervision and rigid performance monitoring can also be stressful; work-load and work pressure are perceived to be higher, and the relationship between the supervisor and employee suffers (Smith *et al.*, 1981).

The nature of superior–subordinate interaction was referred to in the discussion on work-load and new technology. It is also necessary to understand that the supervisor, or boss with a technical or scientific background, may regard 'relationships at work' as low priority. Their orientation is towards 'things' not 'people' (Cooper and Marshall, 1978), and so consideration for working relationships is viewed as trivial, mollycoddling, petty, time-consuming and an impediment to doing the job well.

Poor working relationships among co-workers in an organization is a potential source of stress at work. Hellesøy (1985) reports that good health among offshore platform workers in Norway was fairly consistently related to perceived social support on the platform. The finding is important because these individuals must live and work together in close proximity for extended periods of time. However, it is not known to what extent this occupational group may strive harder towards good working relationships *because* they must also live together. As Hellesøy states, "generally social support will protect against the negative effects of unfamiliarity and uncertainty by defining for others what is, or is not potentially threatening, dangerous, challenging, or harmful."

b) *Interpersonal demands*   *There are*

Quick and Quick (1984) identify five specific interpersonal stressors which arise from the demands and pressures of social system relationships at work: status incongruence; social density; abrasive personalities; leadership style; and group pressure. Some of these issues have already been mentioned in the discussion of relationships as it is not possible to look at these factors totally in isolation.

STATUS INCONGRUENCE

Status and social esteem of workers in society varies greatly and is related to skill level, professional and technical competence, educational background and the status and value placed on a particular industry. For example, Shostak (1980) believes that, overall, the general public think little of manual work when measuring its standards against the dimensions used in assessing a job, i.e., money, power, prestige, the nature of work and amount of job prerequisites (e.g., schooling, etc.). Although this may be a potential source of stress for the individual, within each organization status incongruence may also exist by virtue of one's job category, nationality, etc., and when the individual believes, or perceives that status expectations are not met. Incongruence between actual status at work, and what the worker believes it should be, leads to stress and frustration, especially when status is lower than expectations demand. Stress and insecurity will also be experienced by the individual who perceives that the status position assigned to a job is higher than the individual feels rightfully entitled to.

The introduction of participative styles of management and the use of quality circles could expose more employees to stress associated with status incongruence if the systems are not introduced carefully. Increasingly more individuals could also be exposed to perceived status incongruence due to the current trend of using a flexible, 'contract-labour' force. A situation arises where two individuals will work side-by-side, doing exactly the same work, but in no respect equal in terms of status within the organization. A 'them' and 'us' situation develops, where even the permanent staff feel threatened and insecure, and this leads to frustration, job dissatisfaction, reduced well-being and increased vulnerability to accidents.

SOCIAL DENSITY

Evidence suggests that there is an association between 'crowding' and psychological stress, which leads to an increase in both contagious and non-contagious illness (Cox, V. C. *et al.*, 1982). Where individuals do not have adequate workspace, work performance suffers, increased blood pressure is observed, and job dissatisfaction is reported (Evans, 1969).

However, each individual has varying needs for interpersonal space and distance; it may be perceived as too much, or too little. A source of social stimulation to one individual may be perceived as aggravation and annoyance to another. Crane drivers report the isolation of work in the cab (Cooper and Kelly, 1984), and the need for casters in the steel industry to wear ear defenders isolated them from their peers and restricted conversation (Kelly and Cooper, 1981). As Quick and Quick suggest, "a balance in social density is desirable."

Little is known about individual differences and the reaction to violation of personal space and territory, yet this is important where individuals work and live together in close proximity for long periods of time. Although the concept of burn-out (i.e., the stress associated with a high degree of contact with others) is normally applied to professional, occupational groups, there is a need to understand burn-out in terms of the blue-collar worker. The consequences are equally important to all occupational groups. Hartman and Perlman (1982) define three components of being burned out: emotional and/or physical exhaustion; lowered job productivity; and over depersonalization. Behavioural response includes increased absenteeism, high labour turnover and drug abuse.

ABRASIVE PERSONALITIES
Some individuals in the organization may unwittingly cause stress to others because they ignore the interpersonal aspects of feelings and sensibilities in social interaction. Levinson (1978) labels these individuals 'abrasive personalities'. They are usually achievement oriented, hard driving and intelligent, but function less well at an emotional level. The need for perfection and the preoccupation with self, and the condescending, critical style of the abrasive personality induce feelings of inadequacy among other workers.

As Levinson suggests, the abrasive personality as a peer is both difficult and stressful to deal with; but as a superior, the consequences are potentially very damaging to interpersonal relationships, and highly stressful for subordinates in the organization.

LEADERSHIP STYLE
As already mentioned above, leadership style is a potential source of stress at work for employees. Lewin *et al.*, (1939) document the effects of exposure to an authoritarian style of leader. The scientific/technical manager, oriented to 'things' rather than 'people', may also adopt an interactive style that is stressful to subordinates. They are less likely engage in a participative form of leadership or appeciate that feedback on performance and recognition for effort is also beneficial to the superior–subordinate relationship. Good relationships between boss and subordinate lead to increased productivity, lower labour turnover, and improved mental well-being (Coch and French, 1948).

There is a delicate balance between the positive effects of stimulating individuals to growth and development, and creating a negative environment of pressure and hostility. Tensions may be expressed by outward calm, passive, repressive attitudes, which will manifest physiologically as elevated blood pressure; or there might be an overt display of aggression and conflict. This latter behaviour may be better for the individual, but is not tolerated in the workplace, and would be a stressful situation for co-workers.

GROUP PRESSURE
Benefits of the work group are well documented (Smith, J.M. *et al.*, 1982). Individual needs for affiliation are satisfied, and the group offers social support to the worker which is a source of strength. However, both formal and informal groups in the

organization put considerable pressure on an individual to conform to group norms which may concern production rates, status and style of relationships etc.; this may be a source of stress if the values, beliefs and behaviour of the individual are suppressed. Sullivan (1953 cited Quick and Quick, 1984) and Laing (1971) suggest that these inter-personal group pressures cause various psychological and behavioural disorders.

Roelisberger and Dickson (1939) indicated the power of informal group norms in controlling behaviour in the work environment. Social influence can affect product-ivity rates and attitudes to work and safety, which could be detrimental to both the individual and the organization.

Career development

This fourth category of potential stressors includes job insecurity, over-promotion, under-promotion and thwarted ambition. Definition of the concept of 'career' is controversial, and the use of the term in relationship to blue-collar occupations is also questionable. However, it is considered appropriate in this discussion for two main reasons:

1. The definition of blue-collar worker (Shostack, 1980) incorporates a wide variety of occupations at levels of skill ranging from unskilled manual work to highly skilled craftsmen and operatives; thus there is a concept of growth and development to con-sider.

2. Within an industrial climate of rapid technological, economic and social change, the need to consider retraining and total change of career during a working life becomes a reality for an increasingly wider proportion of the population.

Career development is therefore the term applied to all levels of blue-collar workers to refer to job activities pursued over time, which can involve several jobs and various occupations over the course of time (Hall, 1976).

Actual job change can be a potent source of stress, especially if the individual is required to relocate (Lazarus, 1981). Related to this is the stress associated with job in-security.

Job insecurity

Fear of job loss and the threat of redundancy are common features of working life. Jobs in manufacturing and heavy industry are disappearing, and the subsequent rise in the number of jobs in the service sector are more likely to provide employment for women (especially part-time) and school leavers. Job insecurity may also be related to the intro-duction of new technology—automation not only simplifies jobs, machinery does the work of many people. Also added to the threat of unemployment is the stress as-sociated with 'job deskilling'. Cakir et al. (1974) found that when the qualification level of a job was changed after automation, the workers complained of monotony even though the job was not repetitive.

Threat of job loss is a potent source of stress associated with several serious health problems, including ulcers, colitis and alopecia (Cobb and Kasl, 1977), and increased muscular and emotional complaints (Smith, M.J. *et al.* (1981). The morale and motivation of the workforce is effected, with subsequent negative impact on productivity and efficiency.

Indirectly, fear of job loss and insecurity in times of high unemployment adversely affects both the individual and the organization. A keen, competitive job market may threaten the quality of peer relationships at a time when social support is of particular importance. The stress associated with feelings of insecurity may otherwise be reduced by the buffering effect of good supportive relationships at work; and this may be broken down if the workforce perceives that competition is necessary to retain a job. Other individuals may stay in a job that is disliked or unsuitable because no alternative for change exists. Forty-one per cent of offshore rig workers reported stress to be associated with "feeling trapped into offshore work because no suitable onshore work is available" (Sutherland and Cooper, 1986). This leads to job dissatisfaction, reduced well-being and increased vulnerability to accidents.

Finally, the stress associated with the need to change and/or retrain is also likely to manifest at a time of life when the individual is most vulnerable. An individual under the strain of impending job loss realizes that in middle age, learning seems to take longer, energy is more scarce, opportunities are less, and the threat of a keen, younger workforce competing for jobs is a formidable obstacle. Fear of rejection, and rejection itself, is damaging to morale, self-esteem and confidence.

Overall the perception of the stability of the organization and employment affects the well-being of employees. In the times of instability poor conditions are tolerated—exposure to long hours, arduous conditions, poor quality work—all adding to the stress chain (Kelly and Cooper, 1981), and one condition exacerbates another.

Status incongruence of over-promotion and under-promotion

The current economic climate forces budget reviews, and the cutbacks introduced usually incorporate personnel reduction measures. Opportunity for promotion may therefore be more restricted and competitive. Kroes *et al.* (1974) found that the ability to use and develop skills was a significant predictor of self-esteem. Therefore the individual with career aspirations will feel thwarted if these expectations are denied. The chronic frustration of an incongruent state will have deleterious consequences for both the individual and the organization: disruptive behaviour, poor morale and poor quality interpersonal relationships are associated with the stress of perceived disparity between actual status within the organization and that expected. Quale and Godø (1986, cited in Hellesøy, 1985) identified 'limited career opportunity' as a problem creating frustration and reduced motivation among offshore platform workers in Norway: 29% were dissatisfied with promotion opportunities, and a further 33% expressed neither satisfaction nor dissatisfaction, suggesting that perhaps they had no expectations regarding promotion. This is an important observation. Under-promotion will only be a source of stress when expectations are not realized. For example, Arthur and Gunderson (1965) found that promotion lag in a military environment was significantly related to psychiatric illness and job dissatisfaction. In this highly structured hierarchical environment, with clearly defined career paths, a state of incongruence is evoked in these individuals who feel that their career is not matching expectations.

The stress associated with over-promotion has already been mentioned in terms of overload. Low self-esteem is experienced by the overworked individual who has been promoted too soon. Also, conferred status on the basis of ability alone does not protect the individual from feelings of status incongruence; if perceived ability and status does not match conferred status the promoted employee will experience stress. However, it is suggested that too little responsibility can be as damaging as too much. Lack of promotion prospects is a potential source of stress for the individual who has successfully mastered a job, but does not gain recognition in the form of advancement. Lack of stimulation and challenge, and the inability to develop skills will add to the stress of being passed over for promotion. Brook (1973) describes case studies of individuals showing behavioural disorders ranging from minor psychological symptoms and psychosomatic complaints to more serious mental disorders as a result of over- or under-promotion.

The final category of potential organizational stressors 'external' to the individual is defined by Cooper and Marshall (1978) as simply, 'being in the organization', and the threat to freedom, autonomy and identity of the individual that this imposes.

Organizational structure and climate

Landy and Trumbo (1980) suggest that organizational climate consists of four factors: autonomy, structure, reward and consideration orientation. Thus the organization has a 'personality' to the extent that these factors may be seen as the way in which the organization treats its members. How the employees perceive the culture, customs and climate of the organization is important in the understanding of potential sources of stress resulting from being in the organization: satisfaction or dissatisfaction is ultimately related to perception and evaluation of structure and climate. For example, Freidlander and Greenberg (1971) found that perceived organizational supportiveness was the significant predictor of success in the evaluation of a training program. The way in which the program was presented was as important as the content.

Stress factors identified within this category mainly focus on the amount of job involvement or participation on the part of the employee and the concept of social support.

Lack of participation in the decision-making process, lack of effective consultation and communication, unjustified restrictions on behaviour, office politics and no sense of belonging are identified as potential souces of stress. Margolis et al. (1974) and Caplan et al. (1975) found that lack of participation in work activity is associated with negative psychological mood and behavioural response including escapist drinking and heavy smoking. Increased opportunity to participate results in improved performance, lower staff turnover, and improved levels of mental and physical well-being (Margolis et al., 1974). Participation should also extend to worker involvement in the improvement of safety in the workplace; this will help to overcome the apathy among blue-collar workers which is acknowledged as a significant factor in the cause of accidents (Robens et al., 1972).

Karasek (1979) supports these suggestions: a 6-year prospective study demonstrated that job control (i.e., intellectual discretion) and work schedule freedom were significant predictors of risk of coronary heart disease. Restriction of opportunity for participation and autonomy results in increased depression, exhaustion, illness rates and pill consumption. Feelings of being unable to make changes concerning a job and lack of consultation are commonly reported stressors among blue-collar workers in the steel industry (Kelly and Cooper, 1981), among offshore operators and drilling personnel in Norway (Hellesøy, 1985) and by contractor personnel on rigs and platforms in the UK and Dutch sectors of the North Sea (Sutherland and Cooper, 1986).

Participation in the decision-making process increases 'investment' in the organization, helps to create a sense of belonging and improves communication channels. Related to 'participation' and the sense of belonging is the concept of social support, which is acknowledged as a buffer against the impact of stress in the environment. Social support may be classified as interpersonal (based on the individual's relationships) or institutional (from general social and communal systems) (ILO, 1986). The 'personality' of the organization therefore plays a part to the extent that an environment is created in which the employee may or may not perceive a sense of belonging. The feeling of attachment and security which is perceived in a supportive environment is critical to the perception of mastery over situations (Thoits, 1982).

Several schemes exist which attempt to overcome the stress associated with the rigid structure of the organization, lack of autonomy and consideration, and the inequitable reward systems that are so often reported by blue-collar workers. The introduction of autonomous work groups, quality circles, representation on the board, profit share schemes, and share ownership aim to improve organization structure and climate and the quality of working life, but are not without their own problems.

Chapter 2

3. *Extra-organizational demands*

This category of potential stressors, external to the individual, includes all the elements concerning the life of the person which might interact with life and work events within an organization and thereby put pressure on the individual. Personal life events will have an effect upon an individual's performance, efficiency and adjustment at work (Bhagat, 1983), and must be taken into account when assessing sources of occupational stress.

Issues concerning the family (Pahl and Pahl, 1971; Handy, 1978; Hall and Hall, 1980), life crises (Dohrenwend and Dohrenwend, 1974; Cooper and Marshall, 1978), financial difficulties, conflicting personal and company beliefs, and the conflict between company and family demands, may all put a strain on the individual at work, in the same way that stress at work may spill over and have a negative impact on family and personal life.

However, it should be acknowledged that personal life events may mitigate the effects of organizational stressors. Thus, social support acts in the form of a 'buffer' against stress (House, 1981). Conversely, satisfaction at work may help the individual to cope with stressful personal life events by acting either as a buffer, or in a compensatory manner. Various forms of social support operate; an individual derives emotional, instrumental, informational and appraisal support from social relationships at home and from the community. Evidence suggests that blue-collar workers in the USA are generally less happy about their community and country, interpersonal lives, and jobs than they were 20 years ago (Weiss, 1979, cited Shostack 1980), and so the opportunity of support from these sources may be more restricted than in the past.

⌐ The strain of home, family and financial obligations among blue-collar workers is well documented (*see* Shostack, 1980). Supportive wives shield their partners from the full story of the family's economic stringency in order to spare them additional worries, but as Kreitman (1968) observes, one partner's problems may contribute to the mental ill health of the other. Often the blue-collar worker faces the sources of stress associated with the 'professional' dual career couple, because the spouse or partner must also work in order to make a financial contribution to the family income. ⌐

The problems are compounded if the individual needs to remain geographically mobile in order to stay in employment. This may require relocation of the family or working away from the home and family for extended periods of time. Although some individuals thrive and cope with this way of life, for others the experience is stressful and traumatic. If this happens, it becomes a 'lose-lose' situation for all concerned—the individual, the family, the organization and the local community—because close ties are not established or developed (Packard, 1977; Cooper, 1981).

⌐ Some individuals successfully compartmentalize the different aspects of their lives and thereby reduce the stress of 'overspill', but many other workers take the strains of home and personal life into the workplace. Organizational stress cannot be fully understood unless reference is made to these extra-organizational demands. It is therefore important that future studies of psychosocial and occupational stress among blue-collar workers consider a holistic approach by looking at life and events outside the work environment. However, to determine the costs of stress, it is also necessary to accept that certain characteristics of the individual may be modifiers or mediators of the response to stress.

Chapter 3.

4. *Characteristics of the individual*

The contemporary, interactive view of stress is that situations are not inherently stressful (McMichael, 1978). Psychological, physiological and/or behavioural responses to stress are products of the situation and the individual—including specific personality traits and characteristics, and behaviour patterns based on attitudes, needs, values, past experience, life circumstances and ability (i.e., intelligence, education, training, learning).

Thus the impact of a stressor is not invariant; one man's meat is another man's poison (Cassel, 1976). In this discussion individual modifiers, which may either be predisposing or protective in the response to stress, will be considered.

Recent reviews classify individual/internal modifiers in various ways. McMichael (1978) refers to 'personal conditioning' variables; Innes (1981) describes 'mediating factors' of a set of learned responses, which may be construed as fairly stable personality dispositions. These stable, individual differences in coping skills, and the ability to learn them, are acknowledged as making a person more or less susceptible to stress. Modifiers are identified by Beehr and Newman (1978) as 'the personal facet'. This includes any characteristic of the human being that influences an individual's perception of stressful events, and incorporates the physiological and psychological condition of the person, and their life stage characteristics. Internal qualities of the individual are discussed by Schuler (1980) under the categories of needs and values, abilities and experience, and personality characteristics of the person. All are seen as important to the individual's perception of the work environment.

Certain personality characteristics are considered signiffcant modifiers of response to stress. These will be discussed first, together with various traits, behaviour styles and needs and values which may render the person more, or less, susceptible to stress. Secondly, ability and experience as conditioning variables will be reviewed, followed by 'ethnicity'. Potent socialization processes establish and develop culture and customs which may be modifiers of the response to a stress situation. Finally, the variables of 'age' and 'physical condition' are considered as conditioning variables—last, but not least, as a reminder that vulnerability to stress is ever changing. Each life stage brings its own particular problems, and so response to stress is not static, but a dynamic process.

Personality, behavioural style and needs and values

Research into personality characteristics as modifiers of the response to stress focuses mainly on individual differences between high and low stressed individuals. Typically this may examine the relationship between psychometric measures (e.g., the MMPI, Minnesota Multiphasic Personality Inventory; the 16PF, Cattell's 16 Personality Factors scale; or the EPI/EPQ, Eysenck Personality Inventory/Questionnaire) and reponse to stress and/or stress related illness. Some attempt has also been made to look at personality characteristics as modifiers of accident vulnerability. Accident involvement may be both a symptom and outcome of the stress response and will thus be considered in this discussion as a significant cost of stress at work, which is particularly relevant to blue-collar occupations.

Personality and illness

A review of studies using the MMPI (Jenkins, 1971a) indicates that patients with fatal CHD tend to show greater neuroticism and depression than those who incur and survive coronary disease. In a prospective study, Lebovits *et al.* (1967) showed that MMPI scores for hypochondria, depression and hysteria differ between those who remain healthy and those who develop CHD. Manifestation of CHD increases the deviation in scores even further.

The degree of extraversion and/or neuroticism is also suggested as a modifier of response to stress (Eysenck, 1967; Brebner and Cooper, 1978). The extravert is seen as 'geared to respond' and will attempt a response when given the opportunity.

Studies utilizing the 16PF indicate links between emotional instability, high conformity, submissiveness, seriousness, high self-sufficiency and angina pectoris (Baaker, 1967; Finn *et al.*, 1969; Lebovits *et al.*, 1967). However, these studies are mainly retrospective and thus the observed emotional instability, anxiety and introversion may be a reaction to heart disease and not a precursor. One investigation does implicate personality as a significant predictor of fatal CHD: high anxiety and neuroticism scores among students were predictive of fatal CHD, the cause of death indicated on death certificates years later (Paffenbarger, *et al.*, 1966).

Personality and direct response to stress

Kahn *et al.* (1964) found that reaction to role conflict was mediated by personality. Introverts reacted more negatively and suffered greater tension than extraverts. On the dimension of flexibility/rigidity, the 'flexible' personality (who is more open to influences from other people and thus more likely to become overloaded) also experienced high levels of tension in a high conflict situation, whereas the rigidity factor appeared to act as a modifier of response. 'Rigids' were only susceptible to conflict situations when presented with a rush job from superiors. Kahn *et al.* (1964) also found that anxiety-prone individuals perceived high conflict more intensely.

Other personality characteristics, or traits, identified as modifiers of response to stress include introversion–extraversion (Brief, 1981), anxiety (Chan, 1977) and tolerance for ambiguity (Ivancevich and Matteson, 1980). Self-esteem also appears to be an important modifier trait. Mueller (1965) demonstrated that individuals with reported low self-esteem were also more likely to perceive greater work-load. 'Self-esteem' may act as a buffer against adverse stress reaction; for example, CHD risk factors rise as self-esteem declines (Kasl and Cobb, 1970; House, 1972).

Personality and accidents

It is suggested that an individual under stress may be more likely to be involved in an accident at work (Warsaw, 1979). Role ambiguity, poor communications, conflict of expectation and lack of training are related to unsafe behaviours and accident occurrence (ILO, 1980). Accidents are more likely to occur in physically dangerous and hazardous conditions; the acceptance of risk and the recognition of risk may be reduced or impaired among employees who are exposed to additional environmental stress. It is therefore suggested that 'personality' will act as a modifier in the perception and subsequent reaction to a stressor. For example, reaction to noise shows marked individual differences and McKennell and Hunt (1966) suggest that personality may be a mediating factor. Those individuals most at risk in a noisy environment tend to exhibit higher levels of anxiety and habituate more slowly than normals (Lader, 1971). It is also certain that character traits play some part in the ability to adapt to irregular hours and sleep patterns (Carter and Corlett, 1981). The basis of this is biological and psychological. Research also indicates that individuals scoring high on extraversion are more likely to have been involved in a recorded accident or driving violation (Fine, 1963; Mackay *et al.*, 1969). Other investigations have shown a highly significant relationship between industrial accidents and extraversion (Craske, 1968); for example, accident rates among pilots in South Africa were associated with neuroticism and extraversion (cited by McKenna, 1987), higher levels of aggression were observed among taxi drivers with a high frequency of accident involvement (Feldman, 1971), and Type A behaviour pattern (to be discussed later) also appears to be a predictor of accident involvement (Sutherland and Cooper, 1986).

Although the term 'accident prone' still appears to be out of favour because stable, permanent personality traits are not identified (Haddon *et al.*, 1964; Lindsey, 1980), various characteristics/traits have been implicated, e.g., overactivity, aggressiveness and hostility. However, it is suggested that accident involvement is associated with certain temporary states, i.e., fatigue, alcohol use, and where certain hazards or stressors exist in the environment (Hirschfeld and Behan, 1963). The young and inexperienced are also more vulnerable to accidents, and some individuals are considered better than their peers at recognizing hazardous situations at certain times (McKenna, 1987).

These observations beg the questions: Why do some individuals resort to escapist drinking? To what extent does personality develop in adulthood? Why are some individuals *better* at perceiving hazards?

The personality–accident proneness argument seems to revolve around how 'personality' is perceived, and the definition of 'proneness'. If it is accepted that personality characteristics (learned or innate) modify the response to stress, it would seem unacceptable to deny the existence of 'personality' as a factor in vulnerability to accidents. Indeed, Haddon *et al.* (1964) say, "unacceptability of the concept of accident proneness in a technical sense should not, however, be taken to mean that personal factors do not play an important role in accidents."

Not enough is understood about the direct and indirect role of psychosocial factors in the causation of accidents (ILO, 1986) and still less about the role of personality as a mediator of response to stress, especially among blue-collar occupations. The report on shiftwork and accidents (Carter and Corlett, 1981) recommends that focus on the causes of accidents should also include the study of personality characteristics and/or traits of individuals involved in near miss events, *and* those who remain accident-free. The debate and controversy on the concept of personality (i.e., if it exists, and/or is innate or socially learned) should not impede the identification of potentially harmful ways of responding to a stress situation. This also applies to the following 'behavioural styles', i.e., locus of control and the type A/B behaviour pattern, which may also be modifiers of response to stress.

Behavioural styles

LOCUS OF CONTROL

Locus of control as a relatively stable characteristic (Rotter, 1966) is identified as an internal moderator of response to stress. The concept is based on a social learning theory, 'interactionist' view of the person, in that the individual learns from the environment through 'modelling' and past experience. Reinforcement of certain behaviours affect expectancy and so eventually expectancy leads to behaviour. Locus of control refers to the degree of perceived control over a given situation. The 'internal' oriented person believes that personal decisions and actions influence the outcome. Believed control in the personal determination of events is viewed as a factor in the expectation of coping with a stressful situation; and so less threat is experienced by the 'internal' compared to the 'external' oriented individual, who tends to believe in luck or fate. However, 'internals' may display more anxiety in situations perceived to be not within their control.

Style of behaviour in response to a stressor also varies. Internals tend to seek information and engage the problem, whereas externals are more likely to react with helplessness. Lefcourt and Ludwig (1965) and Griffin (1962 cited in Fisher, 1985) report a tendency for association between high externality scores and underprivilege and poverty. This observation might explain "the surprising absence of severe distress in those engaged in repetitive work" (Baldamus, 1961). An externally oriented, unskilled manual worker will not have expectations regarding control over the highly repetitive, paced work environment. The situation is, therefore, not stressful (although other aspects, e.g., physical demands, may be), but according to the theory, would be a significant source of stress for an 'internal'. Although the numbers are small, and the study retrospective, the recent study of offshore rig workers (a highly controlled environment characterized by noise, vibration and constant company) would support this suggestion: the lowest rate of accident involvement was observed on installations where the highest percentage of true 'externals' (a score of 16 or over on Rotter's control measure) and the lowest percentage of true 'internals' (a score of 7 or less) were identified (Sutherland and Cooper, 1986). Only 20% of UK production platform employees reported accident involvement leading to injury, compared to 26% and 29% of Dutch drilling and production platform personnel, respectively.

The degree of perceived control in relationship to noise as a stressor has been extensively studied (Glass and Singer, 1972). The degree of perceived control, and the ability to predict and govern the onset of noise, appears to be crucial in mediating disruption of both mood and performance (Graeven, 1975; Jones, 1983).

Recent research suggests that locus of control is not a unidimensional scale. There may be different domains of control, e.g., 'personal' and socio-political control. Also, internality–externality distinctions are more readily manifest in situations where the outcome is likely to be negative (Lefcourt, 1983). Locus of control is only one, singular expectancy construct, and should not be expected to account for a large share of the variance in a situation; other interacting variables must be taken into account (Lefcourt, 1976).

TYPE A

Type A coronary prone behaviour is also a 'style of behaviour' which acts as a modifier of response to stress (see McMichael, 1978, for a detailed discussion). Many investigations into Type A behaviour as an independent risk factor for CHD have focused on white-collar occupations. However, the evidence that does exist suggests a positive association between Type A behaviour pattern and occupational status (related to socio-economic status, education and income) (Chesney and Rosenman, 1980).

This finding is supported by the Framingham Heart Study (Haynes *et al.*, 1981). At the 10-year follow-up, the association of Type A behaviour with CHD was apparent only among men in white-collar occupations, not among blue-collar employees, including manual, protective, services, clerical and kindred jobs. Also, in a recent British study of almost 6000 men, a strong link was observed between Type A scores (using the Bortner scale) and social class. Significantly higher scores were observed for the non-manual groups. However, in this investigation, over a 6-year period Type A did not predict major ischaemic heart disease events among the random sample of men, aged 40–59 (Johnston *et al.*, 1987).

In the wide range of occupations studied by Caplan *et al.* (1975), the highest Type A scores were recorded for family physicians and administrative professors, although the indices of ill health were greater for the blue-collar groups observed—tool and die makers scored the highest with assemblers on machine-paced lines and continuous flow monitoring the lowest. However, it is necessary to consider that 'self-selection' into jobs entailing a high exposure to stimulation may be in operation, and that more information on blue-collar groups is needed before any conclusions might be made regarding self-selection. It is also necessary to observe whether individuals in particular jobs become more or less Type A with time. If Type A is a behavioural disposition and a potent conditioning variable, the work environment may elicit and reinforce this pattern of responding. Although Type A pattern may not be indicative of increased CHD risk, evidence suggests that Type A behaviour could be a predictor of accident involvement (Sutherland and Cooper, 1986). A study of offshore rig workers showed that 36% of individuals identified as Type A reported accident involvement leading to injury, whereas only 13% of Type B individuals report being involved in such an incident. This difference may reflect only an individual's predisposition to report an occurrence. However, it was also observed that Type As were significantly more dissatisfied with their job, demonstrated a greatly reduced level of mental well-being and were more anxious and depressed than their Type B counterparts.

Increased risk of accident involvement may be a direct consequence of this style of behaviour, i.e., haste, time urgency, aggression and hostility. Thus the relevance and importance of understanding this style of behaviour among blue-collar workers may be in relation to accident vulnerability, rather than risk of heart disease. This should *not* be ignored, bearing in mind the general concern about inceasing morbidity and mortality due to heart disease and circulatory disorders. However, the CHD risk-factor situation is still not clear for blue-collar occupational groups (Kasl, 1978).

Needs and values

Implicit in this discussion is that personality, viewed as either stable, enduring traits or as learned behaviour, results in a predisposition to respond in a certain way, and is therefore an important moderator variable in the response to a stressor in the environment. The presence or absence of a trait or behaviour pattern increases or decreases the likelihood that a particular event or condition will be perceived as stressful (Quick and Quick, 1984). This also applies to the needs and values of an individual which are viewed as "defining the desires of the individual, in helping to determine the perception of opportunity, constraint and demands of the environment, and the relative importance of the outcomes'' (Schuler, 1980). Needs and values identified as mediators in the response to organizational stressors include 'achievement' (Seashore, 1972; McClelland, 1965; Herzberg, 1978), 'self control, certainty and predictability' (Zaleznick *et al.*, 1977), 'feedback' (Corson, 1971), 'fairness and justice' (Adams, 1965), 'interpersonal recognition and acceptance' (Volicer, 1974), 'ethical conduct' (Kahn *et al.*, 1964), 'responsibility and meaningfulness of purpose' (Hackman and Oldham, 1975), 'personal space and ownership' (Sundstrom, 1977), 'stimulation' (Levi, 1967) and 'intrinsic satisfaction' (Harrison, 1975). Knowing an individual's needs and values, whether innate or learned, is necessary in understanding whether the individual will experience stress from his or her perception of the working environment.

Ability and experience

Research on ability and experience as moderators of the response to organizational stress is scarce but they are viewed as potentially important in that they influence perception of opportunity, demand and constraint and, consequently, the choice of strategy to deal with a stressor (Schuler, 1980).

The factor of 'ability' is incorporated in the research on role/work overload (Kahn *et al.*, 1964) in that quantitative overload (French and Caplan, 1973) may be interpreted in terms of the ability of the employee, in addition to the time available to do the job (Beehr and Newman, 1978). An individual with greater ability can accomplish more work in less time than an employee with less ability for the job. In this light, Sales (1970) has shown that objective quantitative overload is negatively related to self-esteem, and positively to tension and heart rate. French and Caplan (1973) support this finding with reported 'subjective' measures of work overload. Qualitative work overload also relates to this moderator variable of 'ability' in that some employees could not complete the work successfully, regardless of the time allowed, because they do not have the skill required to complete the task.

McGrath (1970) suggests that 'experience' in terms of familiarity with a situation, should also be considered as a moderator of response to stressors in the work environment. Past exposure, practice and training to deal with a situation can reduce uncertainty and thereby modify reaction to stress. This may explain why the method of 'role-play' is more successful in attitude/behaviour change in training situations than lectures, posters or discussions alone (Janis and Mann, 1965).

Ethnicity

Membership of a particular racial and/or minority group can affect an individual's response to stress, in addition to being a source of stress itself. Shostack (1980) states that stress is experienced when, ''the common need to be part of the community at work is thwarted by sharp edged divisiveness.'' Racial prejudice may promote feelings of inadequacy, inferiority and/or low self-esteem among employees in an organization and these will indirectly act as modifiers of response to stress; for example, low morale and poor motivation will reduce tolerance to other stressors. Lack of role models in an organization may also create a stress situation, and exacerbate response to other stress, which leads to role conflict and role ambiguity for the racially different or distinct individual occupying a job for the first time, without the support of a sympathetic group.

However, expectations and aspirations (products of the socialization process which is a potent conditioner in the formation and maintenance of culture and custom) also mediate response to stress. The perception of stress associated with opportunity, constraint and/or demands in the organization may be moderated in accordance with the norms and values of a particular ethnic group.

Age and physical condition

'Age' is an important characteristic which modifies response to stress. Each life stage has its own particular vulnerability and coping mechanism (McLean, 1979). The response of older individuals to experimental stressors indicates a stronger activation of the sympathetic nervous system; but in real-life working conditions, individual coping strategies may counter-balance this effect (ILO, 1986). Certain stressors, for example, related to career development, i.e., over- and under-promotion, can only be understood in relation to the stage of life of the individual concerned. As Levinson (1978) states "regardless of occupation and individual differences, there are seasons of a man's life which when documented will point to likely periods of stress and why they occur."

In a study of middle-aged construction workers, Theorell (1976) found the measure of 'discord' among employees to be much higher in the 41–56 age group than in the 56–65 year olds. This suggests that age may perform a moderator role in the perception of job stress, linked to the factors of expectation and aspiration. Buchholz (1978) found that job discontent in the USA was related to age, and was more prominent among younger blue-collar workers. Their expectations and idealistic notions about work soon disappeared, and they felt exploited and disillusioned (Buchholz, 1978 cited in Shostack, 1980).

The impact of stress may be influenced by the age of an individual in two ways: the biological condition of the person will mediate the response—for example, complaints about the physical strain of work, such as difficulties in adapting to shift work increase with age—and age, in relation to past experiences, will effect the way stress is perceived.

As observed, physical condition may be related to the age of the individual. Intuitively it is likely to mediate response to stress in that an unfit or ill (physically or mentally) employee may be less tolerant and more vulnerable to other stressors at work. Hennigan and Wortham (1979) demonstrated that individuals in good physical condition, and who are not cigarette smokers, are able to maintain a low heart rate during the normal stress of the work day, whereas stress is more likely to increase the heart rate of others less physically fit. Low capacity to respond to a situation due to ill health or disease can exacerbate a stress reaction.

Reduced physical or mental well-being becomes a source of stress because the normal coping mechanism is impaired. Wolff (1953) refers to this as the 'Achilles heel' or 'organ inferiority' hypothesis. Individual differences in response are in part due to response stereotypes. Quick and Quick (1984) cite the following examples: a person with stomach ulcers tends to respond to stress with gastric secretion (Wolff, 1953); a diabetes sufferer responds to stress with greater changes in blood glucose than normals (Hinkle and Wolff, 1952); individuals with cardiovascular disease exhibit more variability in heart rate and respiration (Masuda *et al.*, 1972); and hypertensives and non-hypertensives with a family history of hypertension responded to various stressors with a greater rise in blood pressure (Shapiro, 1961).

Many areas of this 'personal facet' that may be modifiers or mediators in the stress response still require investigation, especially among blue-collar occupational groups. Much of the research to date is correlational, and therefore leaves questions of causation unanswered (Beehr and Newman, 1978). However, the need to consider these 'internal' conditioning variables (Selye, 1976) is as important as acknowledging 'external' variables; that is, the climate and social setting of the stress situation.

5. Conclusions

Stress in the workplace is a serious threat to individual well-being and ultimately to organizational survival. Research must continue to highlight the sources of stress, so that we can take remedial action and plan preventative measures, if we are to make work and the workplace the ideal that Studs Terkel highlights in his acclaimed book *Working*, "it is about a search, too, for daily meaning as well as daily bread, for recognition as well as cash, for astonishment rather than torpor; in short, for a sort of life rather than a Monday through Friday sort of dying."

References

Adams, J.S. (1965). Inequity in social exchange. In L. Berkowitz (ed.), *Advances in Experimental Social Psychology*. Vol. 2 (New York: Academic Press).

Akerstedt, T. (1977). Invasion of the sleep-wakefulness pattern: Effects on circadian variation in psychophysiological activation. *Ergonomics*, **20**, 459–474.

Alfredsson, L., Karasek, R., Theorell, T., Schwartz, J. and Pieper, C. (1982). Job, psychosocial factors and coronary heart disease, In H. Denolin (ed.), *Psychological Problems Before and After Myocardial Infarction*, Advanced Cardiology, Vol. 29 (Basle: S. Karger).

Argyris, C. (1964). *Integrating the Individual and the Organization* (New York: John Wiley).

Baaker, C.D. (1967). Psychological factors in angina pectoris. *Psychosomatic Medicine*, **8**, 43–49.

Baldamus, W. (1961). *Efficiency and Effort* (London: Tavistock).

Beehr, T.A. and Newman, J.E. (1978). Job stress, employee health and organizational effectiveness: A facet analysis model and literature review. *Personnel Psychology*, **31**, 665–699.

Benyon, H. and Blackburn, R.M. (1972). *Perceptions of Work: Variations within a Factory* (Cambridge: Cambridge University Press).

Bhagat, R.S. (1983). Effects of stressful life events upon individual performance effectiveness and work adjustment processes within organizational settings: A research model. *Academy of Management Review*, **8**, (4), 660–671.

Bohemier, (1985) Mar-Tech, 1985, Montreal. Reported *Lloyds List*. May 23rd, 1985, p. 1.

Brebner, J. and Cooper, C. (1979). Stimulus or response induced excitation: A comparison of behaviour of introverts and extraverts. *Journal of Research into Personality*, **12**, 306–11.

Breslow, L. and Buell, P. (1960). Mortality from Coronary Heart Disease & Physical Activity of Work in Claifornia. *Journal of Chronic Diseases*, **11**, 615–626.

Brief, A.P., Schuler, R.S. and Van Self, M. (1981). *Managing Job Stress* (Boston: Little, Brown & Co).

Broadbent, D.E. and Little, F.A. (1960). Effects of noise reduction in a work situation. *Occupational Psychology*, **34**, 133–140.

Broadbent, D.E. and Gath, D. (1981). Symptom levels in assembly-line workers. In G. Salvendy and M.J. Smith (eds), *Machine Pacing and Occupational Stress* (London: Taylor & Francis), pp. 243–252.

Buck, V. (1972). *Working Under Pressure* (London: Staples Press).

Cakir, A., Hart, D.J. and Stewart, T.F.M. (1979). *Visual Display Terminals* (New York: John Wiley).

Caplan, R.D., Cobb, S., French, J.R.P., Van Harrison, R. and Pinneau, S.R. (1975). Job Demands and Worker Health: Main Effects and Occupational Differences, *NIOSH Research Report*.

Caplan, R.D. (1983). Person-environment fit: past, present and future. In C.L. Cooper (ed.), *Stress Research, Issues for the Eighties* (Chichester: John Wiley).

Carter, F.A. and Corlett, E.N. (1981). *Shiftwork and Accidents*. Report to the European Foundation for the Improvement of Living and Working Conditions, Ireland.

Cassel, J.C. (1976). The contribution of the social environment to host resistance. *American Journal of Epidemiology*, **104**, 107–123.

Chan, K.B. (1977). Individual differences in reactions to stress and their personality and situational determinants. *Social Science and Medicine*, **11**, 89–103.

Cherry, N. (1978). Stress, anxiety and work: longitudinal study. *Journal of Occupational Psychology*, **51**, 259–270.

Chesney, M.A. and Rosenman, R.H. (1980). Type A behaviour in the work setting. In C.L. Cooper and R. Payne (eds), *Current Concerns in Occupational Stress* (Chichester: John Wiley).

Chissick, S.S. and Derricott, R. (eds). (1981) *Occupational Health and Safety Management* (Chichester: John Wiley).

Cobb, S. and Kasl, S.V. (1977). Termination—The consequences of job loss. *HEW Publication*, 77–224 (Cincinnati, OH: NIOSH).

Coch, L. and French, J.R.P. (1948). Overcoming resistance to change. *Human Relations*, **1**, 512–532.

Cohen, A. (1974). Industrial noise, medical absence and accident record data on exposed workers. In W.D. Ward (ed.), *Proceedings of the International Congress on Noise as a Public Health Problem* (Washington, DC: US Environmental Protection Agency).

Cohen, A. (1976). The influence of a company hearing conservation program on extra-auditory problems in workers. *Journal of Safety Research*, **8**, 146–162.

Cooper, C.L. (1973). *Group Training for Individual and Organizational Development* (Basle: S. Karger).

Cooper, C.L. (1980). Work stress in white and blue collar jobs. *Bulletin of the British Psychological Society*, **33**, 49–51.

Cooper, C.L. (1981a). *The Stress Check* (Englewood Cliffs, NJ: Prentice-Hall).

Cooper, C.L. (1981b). *Executive Families Under Stress* (Englewood Cliffs, NJ: Prentice-Hall).

Cooper, C.L. (1984). What's new in stress. *Personnel Management*, June, 1984.

Cooper, C.L. (1985). The stress of work: an overview. *Aviation, Space and Environmental Medicine*, July, 627–632.

Cooper, C.L. (1986). Job distress: recent research and the emerging role of the clinical occupational psychologist. *Bulletin of the British Psychological Society*, **39**, 325–331.

Cooper, C.L. and Kelly, M. (1984). Stress among crane operators. *Journal of Occupational Medicine*, **26**(8), 575–578.

Cooper, C.L. and Marshall, J. (1978). *Understanding Executive Stress* (London: Macmillan).

Cooper, C.L. and Payne, R. (1978). *Stress at Work* (Chichester: John Wiley).

Cooper, C.L. and Smith, M. (1986). *Job Stress and Blue Collar Work* (Chichester: John Wiley).

Corson, S.A. (1971). The lack of feedback in today's societies—a psychosocial stressor. In L. Levi (ed.), *Society, Stress and Disease*, Vol. 1 (London: Oxford University Press).

Cox, T. (1978). *Stress* (London: Macmillan).

Cox, T. and Mackay, C.J. (1976). A psychological model of occupational stress. A paper presented to the Medical Research Council, London.

Cox, V.C., Paulus, P.B., McCain, G. and Karlovac, M. (1982). The relationship between crowding and health. In A. Baum and J. Singer (eds), *Advances in Experimental Psychology*, Vol. 4 (Hillsdale, NJ: Lawrence Erlbaum).

Craske, S. (1968). A study of the relation between personality and accident history. *British Journal of Medical Psychology*, **41**, 399–404.

Crown, S. and Crisp, A.H. (1979). *Manual of the Crown-Crisp Experimental Index* (London: Hodder & Stoughton).

Davidson, M.J. and Veno, A. (1980). Stress and the policeman. In C.L. Cooper and J. Marshall (eds), *White Collar & Professional Stress* (Chichester: John Wiley).

Dohrenwend, B.S. and Dohrenwend, B.P. (1974). *Stressful Life Events* (New York: John Wiley).

Doll, R. and Jones, A.F. (1951). Occupational factors in the aetiology of gastric and duodenal ulcers. *Medical Research Council Special Report Series*, No. 276 (London: HMSO).

Elliott, D.H. (1985). The offshore worker. *The Practitioner*, **229** (June), 565–571.

Evans, G.W. (1979). Behavioural and psychological consequences of crowding in humans. *Journal of Applied Social Psychology*, **9**, (1), 27–46.

Eysenck, H.J. (1967). *Biological Basis of Personality* (Springfield, IL: Charles C. Thomas).

Feldman, M.P. (1971). *Psychology in the Industrial Environment* (London: Butterworths).

Fine, B.J. (1963). Introversion, extraversion and motor driver behaviour. *Perceptual and Motor Skills*, **16**, 95.

Fink, D.J. (1978). More on cancer. *Business Week*, November 27, 66.

Finn, F.N., Hickey, N. and O'Doherty, E.F. (1969). The psychological profiles of male and female patients with CHD. *Irish Journal of Medical Science*, **2**, 339–341.

Fisher, S. (1985). Control and blue collar work. In C.L. Cooper and M.J. Smith (eds), *Job Stress and Blue Collar Work* (Chichester: John Wiley).

Flamholtz, E. (1971). Should your organization attempt to value its human resources? *California Review*, **5**(1), 82–86.

Frankenhaeuser, M., Nordheden, B., Myrsten, A.-L. and Post, B. (1971). Psychophysiological reactions to understimulation and overstimulation. *Acta Psychologia*, **35**, 298.

Frankenhaeuser, M. and Johansson, G. (1986). Stress at work: psychobiological and psychosocial aspects. *International Review of Applied Psychology*, **35**, 287–299.

French, J.R.P., Tupper, C.J. and Mueller, E.I. (1965). *Workload of University Professors* (Ann Arbor, MI: University of Michigan).

French, J.R.P. and Caplan, R.D. (1970). Psychosocial factors in coronary heart disease. *Industrial Medicine*, **39**, 383–398.

French, J.R.P. (1973). Person–role fit. *Occupational Mental Health*, **3**, 1.

French, J.R.P. and Caplan, R.D. (1973). Organizational stress and individual strain. In Marrow, A.J. (ed.), *The Failure of Success* (New York: Amacon), pp. 30–66.

Friedlander, F. and Greenburg, S. (1971). Effect of job attitudes, training and organisational climate on performance of the hard core unemployed. *Journal of Applied Psychology*, **55**, 287–295.

Friedman, M., Rosenman, R.H. and Carroll, V. (1958). Changes in the serum cholesterol and blood clotting time in men subjected to cyclic variation of occupational stress. *Circulation*, **17**, 852–861.

Gardell, B. (1976). Technology, alienation and mental health. *Acta Sociologica*, **19**, 83–94.

Glass, D.C. and Singer, J.E. (1972). *Urban Stress: Experiments on Noise and Social Stressors* (New York: Academic Press).

Graeven, D.B. (1975). Necessity control and predictability of noise annoyance. *Journal of Social Psychology*, **95**, 85–90.

Hackman, J.R. and Oldham, G.R. (1975). Development of the job diagnostic survey. *Journal of Applied Psychology*, **60**, 159–170.

Haddon, W., Suchman, E. and Klein, D. (1964). *Accident Research: Its Methods and Approaches* (New York: Harper & Row).

Hall, D.T. (1976). *Careers in Organizations* (Santa Monica, CA: Goodyear Publishing).

Hall, D.T. and Hall, F.S. (1980). Stress and the two-career couple. In C.L. Cooper and R. Payne (eds), *Current Concerns in Occupational Stress* (New York: John Wiley), pp. 243–266.

Handy, C. (1978). The family: help or hindrance. In C.L. Cooper and R. Payne (eds), *Stress at Work* (New York: John Wiley), pp. 107–123.

Harrison, R.V. (1975). Job stress and worker health: person-environment misfit. Paper presented to the American Public Health Association Convention, Chicago.

Hartman, E.A. and Pearlman, B. (1982). Burnout: summary and future research. *Human Relations*, **35**,(4), 283–305.

Haynes, S.G., Feinleib, M. and Eaker, E.D. (1981). Type A behaviour and the ten year incidence of coronary heart disease in the Framingham Heart Study. In Rosenman, R.H. (ed.), *Psychosomatic Risk Factors and Coronary Heart Disease: Indication for Specific Preventative Therapy* (Bern: Hans Huber).

Hellesøy, O.H. (1985). *Work Environments. Statfjord Field.* (Bergen: Universitetsforlaget).

Hennigan, J.K. and Wortham, A.W. (1975). Analysis of workday stress on industrial managers using heart rate as a criterion. *Ergonomics*, **18**, 675–681.

Hersey, R.B. (1932). *Workers' Emotions in the Shop and Home: A Study of Individual Workers from the Psychological and Physiological Standpoint.* (Philadelphia, PA: University of Pennsylvania Press).

Herzberg, F. (1978). The Human Need for Work. *Industry Week*, July 24, pp. 49–52.

Herzberg, F., Mausner, B. and Snyderman, B.B. (1959). *The Motivation to Work* (New York: John Wiley).

Hirschfeld, A.H. and Behan, R.C. (1963). The accident process: I. Etiological considerations of industrial injuries. *Journal of the American Medical Association*, **186**, 193–199.

Hirschfeld, A.H. and Behan, R.C. (1966). The accident process. III. Disability: acceptable and unacceptable. *Journal of the American Medical Association*, **197**, 125–129.

Hockey, G.R. (1970). Effect of loud noise on attentional selectivity. *Quarterly Journal of Experimental Psychology*, **22**, 28–36.

House, J.S. (1972). The relationship of intrinsic and extrinsic work motivation to occupational stress and coronary heart disease risk. PhD Dissertation, University of Michigan.

House, J.S. (1981). *Work Stress & Social Support* (Palo Alto, CA: Addison-Wesley).

ILO (1983). *Accident Prevention. A Workers Education Manual* (Geneva: International Labour Office).

ILO (1986). *Psychosocial Factors at Work: Recognition and Control.* Report of the Joint ILO/WHO Committee on Occupational Health, 1984 (Geneva: International Labour Office).

Innes, J.M. (1981). Social psychological approaches to the study of the induction and alleviation of stress: influences upon health and illness. In G.M. Stephenson and J.M. Davies (eds), *Progress in Applied Social Psychology*, Vol. 1. (Chichester: John Wiley).

Ivancevich, J.M. and Matteson, M.T. (1980). *Stress at Work* (Glenview, IL: Scott Foresman).

Janis, I.L. and Mann, L. (1965). Effectiveness of emotional role playing in modifying smoking habits and attitudes. *Journal of Experimental Research in Personality*, **1**, 84–90.

Jenkins, C.D. (1971). Psychological and social precursors of coronary disease. *New England Journal of Medicine*, **284**,(5), 244–255.

Johnston, D.W., Cook, D.G. and Shaper, A.G. (1987). Type A behaviour and ischaemic heart disease in middle-aged British men. Paper presented at the Society of Behavioural Medicine, Washington, DC, March 1987.

Jones, D.M. (1983). Noise. In R. Hockey (ed.), *Stress and Fatigue in Human Performance* (Chichester: John Wiley).

Kahn, R.L., Wolfe, D.M., Quinn, R.P., Snoek, J.D. and Rosenthal, R.A. (1964). *Organisational Stress: Studies in Role Conflict and Ambiguity* (Chichester: John Wiley), p. 41.

Kalimo, R. (1980). Stress in work: Conceptual analysis and a study on prison personnel. *Scandinavian Journal of Work Environment Health*, **6**(3), 148.

Karasek, R.A. (1979). Job demands, job decision latitude and mental strain. Implications for job redesign. *Administrative Science Quarterly*, **24**, 285–306.

Kasl, S.V. and Cobb, S. (1970). Blood pressure changes in men undergoing job loss: a preliminary report. *Psychomatic Medicine*, **32**, 19–38.

Kasl, S.V. (1973). Mental health and work environment. An examination of the evidence. *Journal of Occupational Medicine*, **15**, 506–515.

Kasl, S.V. (1978). Epidemiological contributions to the study of work stress. In C.L. Cooper and R. Payne (eds), *Stress at Work* (Chichester: John Wiley).

Katz, D and Kahn, R.L. (1978). *The Social Psychology of Organizations*, 2nd edition (New York: John Wiley).

Keenan, V. and Kerr, W. (1951). Psychological climate and accidents in an automotive plant. *Journal of Applied Psychology*, **35**(2), 108–111.

Kelly, M. and Cooper, C.L. (1981). Stress among blue collar workers. A case study of the steel industry. *Employee Relations*, **3**(2), 6–9.

Kerr, W.A. (1950). Accident proneness and factory departments. *Journal of Applied Psychology*, **34**, 167–170.

Kirmeyer, S.L. (1985). Coping by police officers: A study of role stress and Type A and Type B behaviour patterns. *Journal of Occupational Behaviour*, **6**, 183–195.

Knauth, R. and Rutenfranz, J. (1982). Development of criteria for the design of shiftwork systems. *Journal of Human Ergology*, **11**, Suppl., 337–367.

Kornhauser, A. (1965). *Mental Health of the Industrial Worker* (New York: John Wiley).

Kreitman, N. (1968). Married couples admitted to mental hospital. *British Journal of Psychiatry*, **114**, 699–718.

Kritsikis, S., Heinemann, A.L. and Eitner, S. (1968). Die Angina Pectoris in Aspeckt Ihrer Korrelation mit Biologischer Disposition, Psychologischen und Soziologischem Emflussfaktoren. *Deutsche Gesundheit*, **23**, 1878–85.

Kroes, W.H., Margolis, B. and Quinn, R. (1974). Job stress: an unlisted occupational hazard. *Journal of Occupational Medicine*, **16**,(10), 659–661.

Kummer, R. (1983). Noise in oil and gas extractive industries. In *Safety and Health in the Oil and Gas Industries* (London: Graham and Trotman).

Lader, M.H. (1971). Response to repetitive stimulation. In L. Levi (ed.), *Society, Stress and Disease*, Vol. 1 (London: Oxford University Press).

Laing, R.D. (1971). *The Politics of the Family and Other Essays* (New York: Pantheon).

Landy, F.J. and Trumbo, D.A. (1980). *Psychology of Work Behaviour* (Homewood, IL: Dorsey Press).

Lawler, E.E. (1971). *Pay and Organizational Effectiveness* (New York: McGraw-Hill).

Lazarus, R.S. (1966). *Psychological Stress and the Coping Process* (New York: McGraw-Hill).

Lazarus, R.S. (1981). Little hassles can be hazardous to health. *Psychology Today*, July, 58–62.

Lebovits, B.Z., Shekelle, R.B. and Ostfeld, A.M. (1967). Prospective and retrospective studies of CHD. *Psychosomatic Medicine*, **19**, 265–272.

Lefcourt, H.M. (1976). *Locus of Control* (Chichester: John Wiley).

Lefcourt, H.M. (1983). *Research with the Locus of Control Construct. Vol. 2. Developments and Social Problems* (London: Academic Press).

Levi, L. (1967). *Stress: Sources, Management and Prevention; Medical and Psychological Aspects of the Stress of Everyday Life* (New York: Liveright).

Levi. L. (1971). Society, stress and disease. In *The psychosocial environment and psychosomatic diseases*, Vol. 1 (London: Oxford University Press).

Levinson, D.J. (1978). *The Seasons of a Man's Life* (New York: Alfred A. Knopf).

Levinson, H. (1978). The abrasive personality. *The Harvard Business Review*, **56**, May/June, 86–94.

Lewin, K., Lippitt, R. and White, R.K. (1939). Patterns of aggressive behaviour in experimentally created social climates. *Journal of Social Psychology*, **10**, 271–299.

Lindsey, F. (1980). Accident proneness—does it exist? *Occupational Safety & Health*, 10 Feb, 8–9.

Mackay, G.M., De Foneka, C.P., Blair, I. and Clayton, A.B. (1969). *Causes and Effects of road accidents*. Dept of Transportation, University of Birmingham, UK.

Margolis, B., Kroes, W. and Quinn, R. (1974). Job stress an unlisted occupational hazard. *Journal of Occupational Medicine*, **1**(16), 659–661.

McClelland, D.C.N. (1965). Achievement and entrepreneurship: A longitudinal study. *Journal of Personality and Social Psychology*, **1**, 389–392.

McGrath, J.E. (1970). A conceptual formulation for research on stress. In J.E. McGrath (ed.), *Social and Psychological Factors on Stress* (New York: Holt, Rinehart & Winston) pp. 10–21.

McKennell, A.C. and Hunt, E.A. (1966). *Noise Annoyance in Central London* (London: HMSO).

McLean, A.A. (1979). *Work Stress* (Palo Alto, CA: Addison-Wesley).

McKenna, E.F. (1987). *Psychology in Business: Theory and Applications* (London: Lawrence Erlbaum).

McMichael, A.J. (1978). Personality, behavioural and situational modifiers of work stressors. In C.L. Cooper and R. Payne, (eds), *Stress at Work* (Chichester: John Wiley).

Miles, R.H. and Perreault, W.D. (1976). Organisational role conflicts: its antecedants and consequences. *Organisational Behaviour and Human Performance*, **17**, 19–44.

Monk, T.H. and Folkard, S. (1983). Circadian rhythms and shiftwork. In R. Hockey (ed.), *Stress and Fatigue in Human Performance* (Chichester: John Wiley).

Monk, T.M. and Tepas, D.I. (1985). Shift work. In C.L. Cooper and M.J. Smith (eds), *Job Stress and Blue Collar Work* (Chichester: John Wiley).

Mueller, E.F. (1965). Psychological and physiological correlates of work overload among university professors, PhD dissertation, University of Michigan, Ann Arbor.

Murchinsky, P.M. (1977). Employee absenteeism: A review of the literature. *Journal of Vocational Behaviour*, **10**, 316–340.

NOISH (1984). *Occupational Risk Factors in Psychological Disorder: An Overview* (Cincinnati, OH: National Institute for Occupational Safety & Health).

O'Brien, C., Smith, W.S., Goldsmith, R., Fordham, M. and Tan, G.L. (1979). A study of the strains associated with medical nursing and vehicle assembly. In C. Mackay and T. Cox (eds), *Response to Stress: Occupational Aspects* (London. IPC Science and Technology Press).

Ojesjo, L. (1980). The relationship to alcoholism of occupation, class, and employment. *Journal of Occupational Medicine*, **22**, 657–666.

Opbrock, H.A. (1983). *Men and materials handling in offshore operations*. In Safety and Health in the Oil and Gas Industries (London: Graham and Trotman).

Packard, V. (1972). *A Nation of Strangers* (New York: McKay).

Paffenbarger, R.S., Wolf, P.A. and Notkin, J. (1966). Chronic disease in former college students. *American Journal of Epidemiology*, **83**, 314–328.

Pahl, J.M. and Pahl, R.E. (1971). *Managers and their Wives* (London: Allen Lane).

Pincherle, G. (1972). Fitness for work. *Proceedings of the Royal Society of Medicine*, **65**,(4), 321–324.

Porter, L.W. and Steers. R.M. (1973). Organisational, work, and personal factors in employee turnover and absenteeism. *Psychological Bulletin*, **80**, 151–176.

Poulton, E.C. (1978). Blue collar stressors. In C.L. Cooper and R. Payne (eds), *Stress at Work* (Chichester: John Wiley).

Quick, J.C. and Quick, J.D. (1984). *Organizational Stress and Preventive Management* (New York: McGraw-Hill).

Ramsey, J.D. (1983). Heat and Cold. In R. Hockey (ed.), *Stress and Fatigue in Human Performance* (Chichester: John Wiley).

Rizzo, J., House, R.E. and Lirtzman, J. (1970). Role conflict and ambiguity in complex organisations. *Administrative Science Quarterly*, **15**, 150–163.

Robens, Lord *et al.* (1972). *Safety and Health at Work*, The Robens Report (London: HMSO).

Roethlisberger, F. and Dickson, J.J. (1939). *Management and the Worker* (Cambridge, MA: Harvard University Press).

Rotter, J.B. (1966). Generalized expectancies for internal versus external control of reinforcement. *Psychological Monographs*, **80**,(1), No. 609, 28 pp.

Russek, H.I. and Zohman, B.L. (1958). Relative significance of heredity, diet and occupational stress in CHD of young adults. *American Journal of Medical Sciences*, **235**, 266–275.

Russek, H. (1965). Stress, tobacco, and coronary heart disease in North American professional groups. *Journal of the American Medical Association*, **192**, 189–194.

Rutenfranz, J., Colquhoun, W., Knauth, P. and Ghata, J. (1974). Biomedical and psychosocial aspects of shift work. *Scandinavian Journal of Work Environment and Health*, **3**, 165–182.

Sales, S.M. (1970). Some effects of role overload and role underload. *Organizational Behaviour and Human Performance*, **5**, 592–608.

Schuler, R.S. (1980). Definition and conceptualization of stress in organizations. *Organizational Behaviour and Human Performance*, **25**, 184–215.

Seashore, S.E. (1972). A survey of working conditions in the United States. *Studies in Personnel Psychology*, **4**, 7–19.

Selye, H. (1956). *The Stress of Life* (New York: McGraw-Hill).

Selye, H. (1976). *Stress in Health and Disease* (London: Butterworths).

Shirom, A. Eden, D., Silberwasser, S. and Kellerman, J.J. (1973). Job stress and risk factors in coronary heart disease among occupational categories in Kibbutzim. *Social Science and Medicine*, **7**, 875–892.

Shostak, A.B. (1980). *Blue-Collar Stress* (Palo Alto, CA: Addison-Wesley).

Singer, G. (1985). New approaches to social factors in shiftwork. In M. Wallace (ed.), *Shiftwork and Health* (Bundoora, Australia: Brain Behaviour Research Institute).

Smith, J.M., Beck, J., Cooper, C.L., Cox, C., Ottaway, D. and Talbot, R. (1982). *Introducing Organizational Behaviour* (London: Macmillan).

Smith, M.J., Cohen, H.H., Cleveland, R. and Cohen, A. (1978). Characteristics of successful safety programs. *Journal of Safety Research*, **10**, 5–15.

Smith, M.J., Cohen, R.G., Stammerjohn, L.W. and Happ, A. (1981). An investigation of health complaints and job stress in video display operations. *Human Factors*, **23**, 389–400.

Smith, M.J., Colligan, M.J. and Tasto, D.L. (1982). Health and safety consequences of shift work in the food processing industry. *Ergonomics*, **25**, 133–144.

Steers, R.M. and Rhodes, S.R. (1978). Major influences on employee attendance: A process model. *Journal of Applied Psychology*, **63**, 391–407.

Sundstrom, E. (1977). Interpersonal behaviour and the physical environment. In L. Wrightsman (ed,), *Social Psychology* (Monterey, CA: Brooks Cole).

Surry, J. (1968). *Industrial Accident Research: A Human Engineering Appraisal* (Toronto: Ontario Department of Labour).

Sutherland, V.J. and Cooper, C.L. (1986). *Man and Accidents Offshore: the Costs of Stress among Workers on Oil and Gas Rigs* (London: Lloyd's List/Dietsmann (International) NV).

Tepas, D.L. and Colligan, M.J. (1978). Health consequences of shift work. *Stanford Research Institute Technical Report*, Project URU–4426, Menlo Park, CA.

Theorell, T. (1976). Selected illness and somatic factors in relation to two psychosocial stress indices—a prospective study on middle aged construction building workers. *Journal of Psychosomatic Research*, **20**, 7–20.

Thoits, P.A. (1982). Conceptual, methodological and theoretical problems in studying social support as a buffer against life stress. *Journal of Health and Social Behaviour*, **23**, 145–149.

Van Sell, M., Brief, A.P. and Schuler, R.S. (1981). Role conflict and role ambiguity: Integration of the literature and directions for future research. *Human Relations*, **34**,(1). 43–71.

Volicer, B.J. (1974). Patients perceptions of stressful events associated with hospitalization. *Nursing Research*, **23**, 235–238.

Wallick, F. (1972). *The American Worker: An Endangered Species* (New York: Ballantine).

Wardwell, W.I., Hyman, M. and Bahnson, C.B. (1964). Stress and coronary disease in three field studies. *Journal of Chronic Diseases*, **17**, 73–84.

Warsaw, L.J. (1979). *Managing Stress* (Reading, MA: Addison Wesley).

Wolff, H.G. (1953). *Stress and Disease* (Springfield, IL: Charles C. Thomas).

Womack, R. (1985). An appreciative investment. *Scottish Business Insider*, **2**, March.

Whitlock, F.A., Stoll, J.R. and Rekhdahl, R.J. (1977). Crises, life events and accidents. *Australian and New Zealand Journal of Psychiatry*, **11**, 127.

WHO (1984). *Psychosocial Factors and Health: Monitoring the Psychosocial Work Environment and Workers' Health* (Geneva: World Health Organization).

Yerkes, R.M. and Dodson, J.D. (1908). The relation to the strength of the stimulus to the
    rapidity of habit formation. *Journal of Comparative Neurology and Psychology*, **18**,
    459–482.

Zaleznik, A., Kets de Vries, M.F.R. and Howard, J. (1977). Stress reactions in organisations:
    syndromes, causes and consequences. *Behavioural Science*, **22**, 151–161.

2

Differentiating between Daily Events, Acute and Chronic Stressors: A Framework and its Implications

Laurie I. Pratt and Julian Barling

1. Introduction

There has been a tremendous increase in research on work stress in the 1980s. This is apparent in the increasing focus on stress in the areas of social, cognitive and clinical psychology (Staw, 1984). Paralleling this focus is an emphasis on the prevention (Levi, 1981) and treatment (Mancuso, 1983) of stress in organizations, and the appearance of a new journal devoted solely to stress in the workplace (*Work and Stress*). However, despite considerable research efforts on work stress, there remains little agreement about what stress is.

The first aim of this chapter is to address the confusion regarding the basic constructs used in the stress literature. Secondly, a conceptual framework which provides guide-lines by which to distinguish between different types of stressors will be advanced. Some implications of this framework (i.e., the nature and timing of outcomes, the role of coping resources, and methodological issues such as the use of different designs and measurement techniques) will be discussed. Without a specific prior conceptualization of the nature of a construct, any investigation involving that construct remains questionable (Cook and Campbell, 1979).

The term 'stress' has been conceptualized in several fundamentally different ways (Cooper, 1983; Duckworth, 1985):

1. As an organism's *response* to a demand or to events that challenge it (Selye, 1976).
2. As an *event* external to the individual that places demands on him/her (Kahn *et al.*, 1964).
3. As a *characteristic of the environment* that poses a threat to the individual (Caplan *et al.*, 1975).
4. As a state which results from a *misfit* between a person's skills and the demands placed upon him/her (person–environment fit) (French *et al.*, 1974; McGrath, 1976).

Another criticism of the definition of stress is that it is too broad a construct (Duckworth, 1985). As an example of this criticism, stress has been defined as a condition in which an individual is confronted with an opportunity, a constraint, or demand to be/have/do what is desirable where the successful resolution is uncertain yet highly valued by the individual (Schuler, 1980).

Certainly, 'stress' is a term beset with conceptual confusion (Winnubst, 1984), which is partly due to this lack of definitional and operational agreement (Beehr and Newman, 1978; Chesney and Rosenman, 1983; Glowinkowsi and Cooper, 1985). If we do not know exactly what is meant by the term 'stress', resulting problems with construct validity will both hinder the construction of measures of stress, and weaken the validity of conclusions drawn in studies employing such measures. Under such conditions, it is questionable whether the understanding, prediction and/or control of 'stress' in its consequences is possible.

✕ Several theories propose factors that are 'stressful'. One theory suggests that lack of control, unpredictability and/or uncertainty lead to stress (Spacapan and Cohen, 1983; Thoits, 1983). Another theory suggests that change results in stress (Jackson *et al.*, 1983; Werbel, 1983). Beehr and Newman (1978) believe that stress results when environmental factors interact with a person such that the person is forced to deviate from normal functioning. Others state that stress results if the individual cognitively appraises or defines the situation as stressful (Redfield and Stone, 1979; Cooper, 1983; Fleming *et al.*, 1984). Yet none of the factors that supposedly lead to stress can be determined until there is a precisely defined, uniform conceptualization of what stress is.

2. Stress, stressor, strain

Stress, stressor and strain are three terms commonly used in the stress literature. These terms are both theoretically and practically useful. However, there is a great deal of confusion and overlap in the meaning of these three concepts.

For our purposes here, the definitions presented by Kahn *et al.* (1964), and followed by Eden (1982), will be employed, as they clearly differentiate between the three concepts in question. The term 'stressor' refers to 'objective stress', those objective characteristics of the environment that impinge on the perceptual and cognitive processes of normal individuals, " . . . these events are verifiable independently of the individual's consciousness and experience" (Eden, 1982, p. 313). 'Stress' is defined as "those properties of the environment as they are experienced by the person and represented in his consciousness" (Eden, 1982, p. 313). 'Strain' is "an individual's maladjustive psychological and physiological response to stress" (Eden, 1982, p. 313). In sum, stressors are objective environmental events, stress is the subjective experience of the event, and strain is the person's psychological and/or physiological response to stress (the outcome).

There is frequent confusion in the literature concerning the meaning of these three constructs. For example, in a study of depression and coping. Billings and Moos (1984) concluded that role *strains* and life *events* were associated with dysfunction in depressed individuals; strains supposedly leading to the outcome (dysfunction). In other studies strain is believed to be the outcome (Eden, 1982; Cooke and Rousseau, 1983). Hendrix *et al.* (1985) imply that *stress* is both the antecedent of the outcome itself. Also, psychological reactions 58 months after the Three Mile Island accident have been called 'chronic *stress*' (Davidson and Baum, 1986) instead of psychological strain, while Loo (1986) talks of *stress* reactions as the outcome of acute work events.

The same stressor (environmental event) may affect different people in different ways and to varying degrees (Redfield and Stone, 1979; Selye, 1983), as the potential impact of a stressor is dependent upon how it is perceived and appraised by the individual (Duckworth, 1985). Therefore, it is as important to understand how an individual perceives and responds to an event, as it is to understand the qualities of the events themselves (Redfield and Stone, 1979). Although the appraisal of a stressor, and any outcome thereof, is important, it is not an issue that will be discussed further here. We shall focus on a more precise conceptualization of stressors only. Stress and strain, although as important, are dependent on prior stressors. Consequently, an adequate basis for the understanding of stress and strain remains dependent on a clearer conceptualization of stressors.

3. Differentiating between psychological stressors

This chapter attempts to differentiate between types of stressors mentioned in the literature, including acute and chronic stressors, daily events, minor life events and disasters. Distinguishing between these types of stressors is important as they may result in different outcomes (Payne *et al*, 1982; Keenan and Newton, 1985; Caspi *et al*., 1986), necessitate different coping strategies (Payne *et al*., 1982), and require diffferent methodologies for their investigation (Eden, 1982; Werbel, 1983).

Some researchers do distinguish between different types of stressors (Eckenrode, 1984; Payne *et al*. 1982, Werbel, 1983), but they are not the majority (Cooper, 1983), A decade review (January 1976 – December 1985) of all articles on work stress in four journals* showed that, with few exceptions, little or no mention is made about the specific nature of the stressor under investigation. Even when a specific type of stressor is investigated, there are few definitions of the type of stressor measured. For example, Keenan and Newton (1985) state that they measured acute stressful work events rather than chronic work stress, but at no point is a definition of acute or chronic stressors offered. Also, Payne *et al*. (1982) point to the importance of distinguishing between the terms 'acute' and 'chronic', but do not offer any definition or explanation of what they mean by these terms. Eckenrode (1984) studied the relative effects of minor life events, chronic and acute stressors on mood. Again, no definitions of chronic or acute stressors are provided.

Even when different types of stressors are distinctly defined, clear conceptual differences between the types are not always provided. For example, by definition, daily hassles are conceptually distinct from other types of stressors, yet have been equated with chronic stressors (Fleming *et al*., 1984), and with minor life events (Stone and Neale, 1982; Monroe, 1983).

Also, there is much overlap in the examples provided of the different types of stressors. For example, across different studies, role conflict, role overload and role

---

*All articles on work stress in *Journal of Applied Psychology*, 13 articles, *Journal of Personality and Social Psychology*, 15 articles, *Journal of Occupational Psychology*, 17 articles, and *Organizational Behavior and Human Performance*, 7 articles, covering the period January 1976 – December 1985 were examined.

ambiguity have sometimes been described as chronic stressors (Werbel, 1983; Billings and Moos, 1984) and elsewhere as acute stressors (Keenan and Newton, 1985). Similarly, uncertainty, crowding and noise have been classified as both chronic stressors and daily hassles (Fleming *et al.*, 1984).

The above examples portray the current confusion in definition and usage of acute and chronic stressors.** Not only is a precise conceptual and operational distinction between chronic and acute stressors and daily events needed (Eden, 1982; Payne *et al.*, 1982), but also further conceptualization of the differences and similarities between all types of stressors is required. Recognition of this need is not new (Eden, 1982; Payne *et al.*, 1982; Eckenrode, 1984) yet a distinct conceptualization of types of stressors remains elusive in the literature.

4. Current definitions of the different types of stressors

Although the following definitions are currently used in the stress literature, they are often not precise enough to be useful in differentiating between the different types of stressors. In the stress literature it is implied that acute stressors are most readily distinguishable from the others. The term 'acute' is defined as "severe but of short duration" (Guralnik, 1984, p. 15). Acute stressors are said to involve change (Werbel, 1983) and are frequently equated with life events (Fleming *et al.*, 1984). Acute stressors have a more clearly defined time onset (Eckenrode, 1984) and their intensity decreases over time (Werbel, 1983).

'Chronic' is defined as "lasting a long time or recurring often" (Guralnik, 1984, p. 254). Chronic stressors are those "aspects of the environment that are demanding on an ongoing and relatively unchanging basis" (Eckenrode, 1984, p. 911). They have a less clearly defined time onset (Eckenrode, 1984) and their intensity remains constant over time (Werbel, 1983).

Daily hassles are defined as "irritating, frustrating, distressing demands that to some degree characterize everyday transactions with the environment" (Kanner *et al.*, 1981, p. 3). Daily hassles are "experiences and conditions of daily living that are appraised as salient and harmful/threatening" (Ivancevich, 1986, p. 40). Their counterpart, daily uplifts, are defined as positive experiences that are appraised as favourable to a person's well-being (Kanner *et al.*, 1981).

Minor life events are more mundane, less severe life events (Stone and Neale, 1982). Minor life events (Stone and Neale, 1984a) and daily hassles and uplifts (Kanner *et al.*, 1981) are different terms offered by different researchers to represent the same idea. There is agreement that minor life events are conceptually equivalent to a combination of daily events. Here we will use these terms interchangeably.

Work-related disasters (Chisholm *et al.*, 1983) and crises (Hoiberg and McCaughey,

---

**In selecting studies on a non-random basis throughout this chapter to illustrate what we believe are critical issues, we do so fully aware of the fact that there are many other studies that make the same, or similar, errors of omission or commission. Our point is not to suggest that some individuals have an exclusive right to these problems, but rather to illustrate their pervasive nature.

1984) should also be mentioned. Most researchers assume that disasters or crises are the most intense stressor possible, and are also time-bound in nature.

Based on a literature review, a more precise conceptualization of the different types of stressors can be presented. Stressors can be differentiated depending on how they vary in four orthogonal dimensions: specificity of time-onset; duration frequency or repetitiveness; and severity. → *dainfall les .*

Acute stressors always have a specific time onset, are of short-term duration, occur very infrequently, and are of high intensity. Examples include getting fired or laid off (Stone and Neale, 1982), a strike (Barling and Milligan, 1987), job transfer (Sarason and Johnson, 1979), and involvement in a shooting, for example, for police officers (Loo, 1986).

Chronic stressors have no specific time onset, are repeated frequently, may be of short or long duration, and may be of high or low intensity. It is usually difficult to determine the time of onset of a chronic stressor. Examples of long-term, chronic stressors are role conflict and ambiguity, job insecurity and noise in a manufacturing plant.

Minor life events or daily events have specific time onset, are of short-term duration, occur infrequently, and are of low intensity. Examples of daily events are a disappointment, getting caught up in traffic (Stone and Neale, 1982), experiencing difficulties with a client, losing or misplacing things (Kanner *et al.*, 1981). Although the same daily events may occur again in the future, they do not occur repeatedly at the same point in time such as constant noise in the workplace (a chronic stressor). (Whether a daily event represents an uplift or a hassle depends on the subjective appraisal of that event and is beyond the scope of this chapter.)

Disasters have a specific time onset, are of either a short- or long-term duration, occur extremely infrequently, and are of high intensity. Unlike acute and chronic stressors and minor life events, disasters have also been classified along other dimensions, namely the threat to life, prolonged suffering, the scope of the impact, and also the way in which the event influences an entire community (Green *et al.*, 1983).

As mentioned previously, these four dimensions, viz., specificity of time onset, duration, frequency and intensity) vary independently of each other. If a stressor occurs frequently, this does not imply that the stressor is more intense or severe; a high frequency stressor is not to be equated with a high intensity stressor. For example, the accumulation of different acute events is sometimes equated with a chronic stressor. Holmes and Rahe (1967) mathematically combine *different* life events (acute stressors) and conclude that together they are equivalent to a chronic stressor. However, an acute stressor, by definition, is a single event of high intensity that occurs very infrequently, whereas a chronic stressor is a single event of high or low intensity that occurs repeatedly. An accumulation of *different* acute events that occur infrequently over time should not be equated with chronic stressors (*similar* stressors that occur repeatedly). Their intensities may be comparable, but chronic and acute stressors still differ according to the specificity of time onset and frequency of occurrence.

A similar misunderstanding surrounds daily events. It is assumed that when *different* minor life or daily events are summated they have a higher intensity, and therefore, may be equated with chronic stressors (Kanner *et al.*, 1981; Eckenrode, 1984). The intensity of summated daily hassles may reach the intensity level of chronic stressors, but daily hassles and chronic stressors still differ on the specificity of timing of onset and frequency (the same daily hassle occurs very infrequently, whereas a chronic stressor is one that occurs repeatedly).

5. Implications of poor construct validity

Previous failure to distinguish between the different types of stressors has resulted in poor construct validity and affected the development of reliable and valid instruments measuring work and/or life stressors. Several difficulties with many scales used to measure stressors can be identified. Such difficulties include confounding the measurement of the stressor with either the outcome (symptoms of psychological strain) or with other types of stressors; failure to measure responses of those individuals who experience stressors yet do not suffer any strain; and the averaging of scores over a certain time period and assuming the averaged scores represent a different *type* of stressor than the initial instrument was designed to measure.

Measuring minor life events

The Hassles Scales and the ADE

It is difficult to justify the use of many of the items included in either the Hassles Scale or the Assessment of Daily Experiences (ADE; Stone and Neale, 1982), which share many similar or identical items (e.g., sickness/health of a family member; general housework/home maintenance; fired, quit, resigned or laid off from work or out of a job; emotional interactions with co-workers/employees). Both scales confound daily hassles (Kanner et al., 1980) or daily events (Stone and Neale, 1982) with major life events (Monroe, 1983). Major life events that make up some of the items of the scales (i.e., laid off from work, health of a family member) may increase the risk of experiencing a greater frequency of daily hassles (i.e., misplacing or losing things, social obligations), but do not represent daily hassles in and of themselves. In addition, neither scale is able to measure responses of individuals who experience 'daily events' but are not bothered by them (Dohrenwend and Shrout, 1985; Cohen, 1986; Flannery, 1986). The event cannot be recorded as a hassle using the Hassles Scale, thereby confounding stressors with stress. Many of the items of the Hassles Scale reflect chronic stressors rather than daily hassles (i.e., not enough money for housing, health of family members, thoughts about death, concerns about job security, the meaning of life, debts). It has also been suggested that the Hassles Scale in particular confounds daily hassles with psychological disorder. Many items appear to be more directly related to psychological problems (i.e., trouble relaxing, not getting enough sleep) than to minor everday difficulties (i.e., planning meals, home maintenance) (Monroe, 1983; Dohrenwend and Shrout, 1985; Depue and Monroe, 1986).

As with the Daily Hassles Scale, checklist scores of the ADE are summed and averaged over several days, the exact number of days being dependent on the particular study. For example, on one study responses were recorded daily but aggregated at the end of a 1-week period (Stone, 1981). The aggregated occurrence of events was then used in calculating the correlation between daily events and mood (Stone, 1981). This is very similar to the Holmes and Rahe (1967) procedure where events are summed over a specific time period and their cumulative impact on different indices of well-being is assessed. Conceptually, as mentioned previously, the occurence of different events summed over a time period does not result in the same type of stressor as the occurrence of the same events summated over a specific time period. The summation of the same events would constitute a measure of chronic stressors, whereas a summation of different events would simply represent an aggregate of daily hassles.

The Industrial Relations Event Scale

Bluen and Barling (in press) developed the Industrial Relations Event Scale (IRES) to assess acute stressors involved in the industrial relations process. Respondents indicate events that occurred during the previous 12 months, and rate their positive or negative impact. The items are supposed to represent acute industrial relations stressors, yet items such as 'job insecurity' and 'injustice and inequality' may be better indicators of chronic stressors. Other items of the IRES may be more representative of daily hassles than acute stressors: 'being disciplined', 'representing others', 'problems with accommodation, transport, school, etc.'

The Organizational Change Inventory

This measure is designed to assess changes in the work situation (Sarason and Johnson, 1979). Respondents indicate which events thay have experienced and rate their impact on a scale from -3 to $+3$. The summed positive and negative ratings are used to indicate the extent of the desirable or undesirable change required within a specific work environment. The items comprising this scale (e.g., promotion, transfer, new supervisor, reduction in pay, strike) seem to measure what the authors devised the instrument to measure. The items measure acute work events and do not confuse these events with chronic stressors or daily hassles.

In general, current scales purporting to assess psychological stressors all require more precise stipulations as to what type of stressor they are intended to measure. Until this requirement is met, their continued usefulness may be limited. As there is reason to question exactly what the above scales measure, any results obtained using these instruments remain questionable.

6. Some implications of refining work stressors

Achieving greater differentiation between types of stressors would allow the examination of several new issues. These include the possibility that different types of stressors are associated with different outcomes, that different methodologies are required to study different types of stressors, that the time lag in the stress/outcome relationship depends on the nature of the stressor, and that different coping mechanisms are required for different stressors.

Methodology unique to the type of stressor

The idea that longitudinal analysis is mandatory for a comprehensive understanding of stress and its consequences is not new (Cooper and Marshall, 1976; Schuler 1980; Payne *et al.*, 1982; Stone and Neale, 1984b; Barling and Rosenbaum, 1986). For example, effects of stressors not found cross-sectionally may still be manifest longitudinally (cf. Helmreich *et al.*, 1986). Nonetheless, longitudinal analyses of stress/outcome relationships remain extremely rare (Beehr and Newman, 1978). Along with the need for longitudinal designs, there may also be a need for more idiographic and specific analyses, such as a time series analysis (Eden, 1982) or a facet approach (Beehr and Newman, 1978; Shirom, 1982), with the type of analysis dependent on the type of stressor involved.

Measuring daily experiences may demand a small sample size. On the other hand, studying chronic stressors may require a larger sample. The effects of daily events might be better measured once a day over a period of a couple of weeks. Acute stressors may be better understood with a before-after or during-after type design, where effects are investigated in both the presence and the absence of the stressor. Practical considerations often hinder such an approach, however, Often, the onset of an acute stressor (e.g., a strike) or disaster (e.g., an explosion, Barling *et al.*, in press) is unknown, so no pre-event measure is available. On the other hand, chronic stressors may require fewer testing periods, with larger samples, when 'typical' events are recorded.

Differential outcomes

The duration of the stressor may be an essential factor in determining its outcome (Beehr and Newman, 1978; Payne *et al.*, 1985). For example, Keenan and Newton (1986) suggest that the most common reponse to an acute stressor may be anger, whereas the most common response to a chronic stressor may be anxiety. Also, chronic stressors may incur more negative and costly effects than acute stressors (Fleming *et al.*, 1984).

Researchers investigating the effects of stressors on mood sometimes discover stressor-specific effects. For example, severe daily events (Stone and Neale, 1984a) and daily hassles (Eckenrode, 1984) affect same-day mood (Stone and Neale, 1984b), but acute stressors do not (Eckenrode, 1984).

When psychological symptomatology is the criterion, differential effects dependent on the type of stressor emerge. Kanner *et al.* (1981) concluded that aggregated daily hassles were a significant predictor of psychological symptom level, but acute stressors (as measured by life events) were not (Kanner *et al.*, 1981; Ivancevich, 1986). In a prospective study by Monroe (1983), minor life events (also labelled as 'hassles' by Monroe) were better predictors of subsequent psychological symptoms than were major life events. Clearly then, a precise specification of the nature of the stressor is crucial as studies seem to indicate that acute stressors may have fewer long term consequences than chronic stressors or daily hassles (Loo, 1986).

The short-term effects of disasters or crises usually become apparent soon after the occurrence of the event (post-traumatic stress disorder), while long term consequences are not as fully understood (Hoiberg and McCaughey, 1984). Where the crisis persists, people can be affected for up to two years (Chodoff, 1963; Lifton, 1963; Chisholm *et al.*, 1982), and possibly even six years after the event (Davidson and Baum, 1986). In a study of employees at the Three Mile Island Nuclear Plant, Kasl *et al.* (1981) concluded that the crisis experienced by workers there had both a major and a long-lasting impact on their psychological well-being. The long-lasting strain on workers at TMI has been attributed to the underlying chronic stressors (long-term uncertainty as to whether there has been any exposure to radiation) resulting from the disaster (Chisholm *et al.*, 1983). Thus, the duration and/or the intensity of the *strain* may be a result of the type of stressor.

Timing of outcome

The issue of the time lag between causally related variables remains one of the frequently neglected topics in industrial/organizational research (Campbell *et al.*, 1982). Also, the question of when the consequences of a stressor will become apparent, or whether different stressors exert their effects at different time periods, remains unanswered. The timing of consequences of stressors may be contingent on the type of stressor present. Data suggest that minor life events and daily hassles have immediate, same-day effects on mood, but do not affect mood of the following day (Eckenrode, 1984; Stone and Neale, 1984b; Caspi *et al.*, 1986). Chronic stressors may have more long-term effects, whereas acute stressors may have effects lasting only as long as the stressors themselves. In a study of police officers following a shooting incident, Loo (1986) showed that most of the consequences of acute stressors are manifest very soon after the event (in this case, within three days). After that, the strain became dissipated. Thus, a knowledge of the specific nature of the stressor enables a more precise prediction not only of the nature of the outcome, but also its duration. From this, better prevention and intervention strategies could be designed.

Different coping strategies for different stressors

Coping techniques may also be dependent on the type of stressor involved. Eckenrode (1984) suggests that one of the major differences between chronic and acute stressors is that acute stressors tend to result in a more specific set of time limited coping responses.

Personality hardiness (Kobasa, 1979) and social support (House, 1981; Cohen and Wills, 1985) are two coping resources that are frequently discussed in the literature. In the event of an acute stressor, personality hardiness may be essential for adequate coping. An acute stressor has a sudden impact, is of high intensity and occurs infrequently. As such, it requires imediate coping. Because hardiness is a personality resource that is stable over time (Kobasa, 1979), it may be present precisely when it is required to influence how one copes with the sudden impact of an acute stressor. Social support is a social resource whose availability and accessability may require time. Thus, social support may be more helpful in coping with chronic stressors which, by definition, occur repeatedly. In a study of Israeli women whose husbands were called up for active duty at very short notice, personality resources, in the form of personal mastery, buffered negative emotional reactions (Hobfall and London, 1986). Social support exerted no immediate effect on those trying to cope with the acute stressor presented in this situation. Because of the central role that coping strategies fulfil in ensuring that stressors do not inevitably result in psychological strain, the issue of whether the benefits derived from coping mechanisms are stressor specific should be investigated further.

7. Conclusions

To advance the understanding of work stressors, we must first take a step backwards. This chapter argues for such a step. Before we can understand issues such as the nature and timing of the consequences of psychological stressors, or the coping mechanisms necessary to avoid any negative effects (i.e., strain) arising from such stressors, a clearer perspective of the specific methodologies required to measure the different types of stressors is needed. The specific methodologies required will result only when the different types of stressors are clearly defined and delineated from one another. The implementaion of intervention strategies aimed at combatting stressors will be made possible only after all the above issues are clarified.

Acknowledgements

Financial support from the Social Sciences and Humanities Research Council of Canada (Grant No. 410–85–1139) and Imperial Oil to the second author is gratefully acknowledged. The authors express their appreciation to S.D. Bleun, M. Laliberte and K.E. MacEwen for their constructive comments on earlier versions of this manuscript.

References

Barling, J., Bleun, S.D. and Fain, R. (in press). Psychological functioning following an acute disaster. *Journal of Applied Psychology.*

Barling, J. and Milligan, J. (1987). Some psychological consequences of striking: a six month, longitudinal study. *Journal of Occupational Behaviour.*

Barling, J. and Rosenbaum, A. (1986). Work stressors and wife abuse. *Journal of Applied Psychology*, **71**, 346–348.

Beehr, T.A. and Newman, J.E. (1978). Job stress, employee health, and organizational effectiveness: a facet analysis, model, and literature review. *Personnel Psychology*, **31**, 665–699.

Billings, A.G. and Moos, R.H. (1984). Coping, stress, and social resources among adults with unipolar depression. *Journal of Personality and Social Psychology*, **46**, 877–891.

Bluen, S.D. and Barling, J. (in press). Stress and the industrial relations process: Development of the industrial relations event scale. *South African Journal of Psychology*.

Campbell, J.P., Daft, R.L. and Hulin, L.L. (1982). *What to Study: Generating and Developing Research Questions* (Palo Alto, CA: Sage).

Caplan, R.D., Co, S., French, J.R.P., Jr, Van Harrison, R. and Pinneau, S.R., Jr. (1975). *Job Demands and Worker Health*. (Washington, DC: US Department of Health, Education and Welfare (NIOSH).

Caspi, A., Bolger, N. and Eckenrode, J. (1987). Linking person and context in the daily stress process. *Journal of Personality and Social Psychology*, **52**, 184–195.

Chesney, M.A. and Rosenman, R.H. (1983). Specificity in stress models: Examples drawn from Type A behaviour. In C.L. Cooper (ed.), *Stress Research, Issues for the Eighties* (New York: John Wiley). pp. 21–34.

Chisholm, R.F., Kasl, S.V. and Eskenazi, B. (1983). The nature and predictors of job related tension in a crisis situation: reactions of nuclear workers to the Three Mile Island accident. *Academy of Management Journal*, **26**, 385–405.

Chodoff, P. (1963). Late effects of the concentration camp syndrome. *Archives of General Psychiatry*, **8**, 232–333.

Cohen, S. (1986). Contrasting the Hassle Scale and the Perceived Stress Scale: who's really measuring appraised stress? *American Psychologist*, **41**, 716–718.

Cohen, S. and Wills, T.A. (1985). Stress, social support and the buffering hypothesis. *Psychological Bulletin*, **98**, 310–357.

Cook, T.D. and Campbell, D.T. (1979). *Quasi-experimentation: Design and Analysis Issues for Field Settings*. (Chicago, IL: Houghton-Mifflin).

Cooke, R.A. and Rousseau, D.M. (1983). Relationship of life events and personal orientations to symptoms of strain. *Journal of Applied Psychology*, **68**, 446–458.

Cooper, C.L. (1983). *Stress Research: Issues for the Eighties* (New York: John Wiley).

Cooper, C.L. and Marshall, J. (1976). Occupational sources of stress: a review of the literature relating to coronary heart disease and mental ill health. *Journal of Occupational Psychology*, **49**, 11–29.

Davidson, L.M. and Baum, A. (1986). Chronic stress and post-traumatic stress disorders. *Journal of Clinical and Consulting Psychology*, **54**, 303–308.

Depue, R.A. and Monroe, S.M. (1986). Conceptualization and measurement of human disorder in life stress research: the problem of chronic disturbance. *Psychological Bulletin*, **99**, 36–51.

Dohrenwend, B.P. and Shrout, P.E. (1985). Hassles in the conceptualization and measurement of life stress variables. *American Psychologist*, **40**, 780–785.

Duckworth, D.H. (1985). Is the 'organizational stress' construct a red herring? A reply to Glowinkowski and Cooper. *Bulletin of the British Psychological Society*, **38**, 401–404.

Eckenrode, J. (1984). Impact of chronic and acute stressors on daily reports of mood. *Journal of Personality and Social Psychology*, **46**, 907–918.

Eden, D. (1982). Critical job events, acute stress, and strain: a multiple interrupted time series. *Organizational Behaviour and Human Peformance*, **30**, 312–329.

Fleming, R., Baum, A. and Singer, J.E. (1984). Toward an integrative approach to the study of stress. *Journal of Personality and Social Psychology*, **46**, 939–949.

French, J.R.P., Jr, Rogers, W.L. and Cobb, S. (1974). Adjustment as person-environment fit. In G. Coelho, D. Hamburg and J. Adams (eds), *Coping and Adaptation* (New York: Basic Books).

Glowinkowski, S.P. and Cooper, C.L. (1985). Current issues in organizational stress research. *Bulletin of The British Psychological Society*, **38**, 212–216.

Green, B.L., Grace, M.C., Lindy, J.D., Titchener and Lindy, J.G. (1983). Levels of functional impairment following a civilian disaster: the Beverly Hills Supper Club Fire. *Journal of Consulting and Clinical Psychology*, **51**, 573–580.

Guralnik, D.B. (ed.) (1984). *Webster's New World Dictionary* (New York: Simon and Schuster).

Helmreich, R.L., Sawin, L.I. and Carsrud, A.L. (1986). The honeymoon effect in job peformance: Temporal increases in the predictive power of achievement motivation. *Journal of Applied Psychology*, **71**, 185–188.

Hendrix, W.H., Ovalle, W.K. and Troxler, R.G. (1985). Behavioural and physiological consequences of stress and its antecedent factors. *Journal of Applied Psychology*, **70**, 188–210.

Hobfall, S.E. and London, P. (1986). The relationship of self concept and social support to emotional distress among women during war. *Journal of Social and Clinical Psychology*, **2**, 189–203.

Hoiberg, A. and McCaughey, B.G. (1984). The traumatic after-effects of collision at sea. *American Journal of Psychiatry*, **141**, 70–73.

Holmes, T.H. and Rahe, R.H. (1967). The social readjustment rating scale. *Journal of Psychosomatic Research*, **11**, 213–218.

House, J.S. (1981). *Work Stress and Social Support*. (Reading, MA: Addison-Wesley).

Ivancevich, J.M. (1986). Life events and hassles as predictors of health symptoms, job performance, and absenteeism. *Journal of Occupational Behaviour*, **7**, 39–51.

Jackson, P.R., Stafford, E.M., Banks, M.H. and Warr, P.B. (1983). Unemployment and psychological distress in young people: the moderating role of employment commitment. *Journal of Applied Psychology*, **68**, 525–535.

Kahn, R.L., Wolfe, D.M., Quinn, R.P., Snoek, J.D. and Rosenthal, R.A. (1964). *Role Stress: Studies in Role Conflict and Ambiguity* (New York: John Wiley).

Kanner, A.D., Coyne, J.C., Shaefer, C. and Lazarus, R.S. (1981). Comparisons of two modes of stress measurement: daily hassles and uplifts versus major life events. *Journal of Behavioural Medicine*, **4**, 1–39.

Kasl, S.V., Chisholm, R.F. and Eskenazi, B. (1981). The impact of the accident at the Three Mile Island on the behavior and well-being of nuclear workers: Part I: Perceptions and evaluations, behavioral responses, and work-related attitudes and feelings. *American Journal of Public Health*, **71**, 472–483.

Keenan, A. and Newton, T.J. (1985). Stressful events, stressors, and psychological strains in young professional engineers. *Journal of Occupational Behaviour*, **6**, 151–156.

Kobasa, S.C. (1979). Stressful life events, personality, and health: An inquiry into hardiness. *Journal of Personality and Social Psychology*, **37**, 1–11.

Levi, L. (1981). *Preventing Work Stress* (Reading, MA: Addison-Wesley).

Lifton, R.J. (1963). Psychological effects of the atomic bomb in Hiroshima. *Daedalus*, **92**, 462–497.

Loo, R. (1986). Post-shooting stress reactions among police officers. *Journal of Human Stress*, **12**, 27–31.

Mancuso, J.S.J. (ed.) (1983). *Occupational Clinical Psychology* (New York: Praeger).

McGrath, J.E. (1976). Stress and behaviour in organizations. In M.D. Dunnette (ed.), *Handbook of Industrial and Organizational Psychology* (New York: John Wiley), pp. 1351–1395.

Monroe, S.M. (1983). Major and minor life events as predictors of psychological distress: Further issues and findings. *Journal of Behavioural Medicine*, **6**, 189–205.

Payne, R., Jick, T.D. and Burke, R.J. (1982). Whither stress research?: an agenda for the 1980s. *Journal of Occupational Behaviour*, **3**, 131–145.

Redfield, J. and Stone, A; (1979). Individual viewpoints of stressful life events. *Journal of Consulting and Clinical Psychology*, **47**, 147–154.

Sarason, I.G. and Johnson, J.H. (1979). Life stress and job satisfaction. *Psychological Reports*, **44**, 75–79.

Schuler, R.S. (1980). Definition and conceptualization of stress in organizations. *Organizational Behaviour and Human Performance*, **25**, 184–215.

Selye, H. (1976). *The Stress of Life* (New York: McGraw-Hill).

Selye, H. (1980). The stress concept today. In I.L. Kutash and L.B. Schlesinger (eds). *Handbook on stress and anxiety* (CA: Jussey Bass) pp. 127–143.

Selye, H. (1983). The stress concept: past, present, and future. In C.L. Cooper (ed.). *Stress Research* (New York: John Wiley), pp. 1–20.

Shirom, A. (1982). What is organizational stress? A facet analytic conceptualization. *Journal of Occupational Behaviour*, **3**, 21–37.

Spacapan, S. and Cohen, S. (1983). Effects and after-effects of stressor expectations. *Journal of Personality and Social Psychology*, **45**, 1243–1254.

Staw, B.M. (1984). Organizational behaviour: a review and reformulation of the field's outcome variables. *Annual Review of Psychology*, **35**, 627–666.

Stone, A.A. (1981). The association between perceptions of daily experiences and self- and spouse-rated mood. *Journal of Research in Personality*, **15**, 510–522.

Stone, A.A. and Neale, J.M. (1982). Development of a methodology for assessing daily experiences. In A. Baum and J.E. Singer (eds). *Advances in Environmental Psychology—Environmental and Health* (Englewood Cliffs, NJ: Lawrence Erlbaum), pp. 49–83.

Stone, A.A. and Neale, J.M. (1984a). Effects of severe daily events on mood. *Journal of Personality and Social Psychology*, **46**, 137–144.

Stone, A.A. and Neale, J.M. (1984b). New measure of daily coping: development and preliminary results. *Journal of Personality and Social Psychology*, **46**, 892–906.

Thoits, P. (1983). Dimensions of life events that influence psychological distress: An evaluation and synthesis of the literature. In H.B. Kaplan (ed.), *Psychosocial stress: Trends in Theory and Research* (New York: Academic Press), pp. 33–103.

Werbel, J.D. (1983). Job change: a study of an acute stressor. *Journal of Vocational Behaviour*, **23**, 242—250.

Winnubst, J.A.M. (1984). Stress in organizations. In P.J.D. Drenth, H. Thierry, P.J. Willems and C.J. de Wolff (eds), *Handbook of Work and Organizational Psychology* (New York: John Wiley).

3

Psychometric Measurement of Occupational Stress: Current Concerns and Future Directions

Richard S. DeFrank

1. Introduction

In order to explore future directions for the psychometric measurement of occupational stress, it is necessary to investigate where we are now and what techniques are currently in use. It is hoped that this approach will highlight some of the problems with existing procedures and point the way to improved measurement techniques. This chapter attempts to accomplish this, though not by detailing a list of specific measures. The author was involved in writing a recent report for NIOSH (Jenkins *et al.*, 1984) which used that approach in surveying psychometric measures of job stress and job satisfaction, with the general conclusion that the available scales tend to have adequate reliability, uncertain validity and heterogeneity in measurement styles. In addition, they tend to focus on professional groups, with some targeting specific populations such as teachers, nurses and physicians.

For the present purposes, however, that approach (using an annotated review of each scale) seems unlikely to establish systematically the measurement features exemplified in these various instruments. We need to take a step back and look at these measures as a group and try to determine their commonalities and differences, and to suggest some of the ways in which these characteristics may influence the responses of subjects. Thus, this paper will outline some important features of scales on job stress, note examples of these features and suggest some implications of these approaches for the adequate assessment of occupational stress. Emphasis here will be less on the specific content of scales than on the impact of scale format on subjects' responses. Additional directions for future work will also be suggested that may help clarify the importance of job stress in the life experiences of employed populations.

2. Focus: situations or feelings

One way of categorizing occupational stress scales is whether their items focus on situations that occur on the job or on feelings that are experienced while at work. These two approaches presuppose somewhat different conceptualizations of stress at the

54

workplace. The former targets the situations or stressors that may exist in the work setting and determines their occurrence and general impact, while the latter focuses on specific feelings and emotions that may be generated by work experiences. Thus the situation emphasis is directed at an earlier point in the stressor–response linkage than the feeling emphasis.

Some examples may help to clarify this divergence of perspective. The Teacher Stress Inventory (TSI; Fimian, 1984) focuses more than half of its items on situations that may occur in school, including such categories as personal/professional stressors, professional distress, discipline and motivation. The Nursing Stress Scale (NSS; Gray-Toft and Anderson, 1981) addresses itself even more specifically to work events, and includes factors relating to death and dying, conflict with physicians, inadequate preparation, lack of support, conflict with other nurses, work-load and uncertainty regarding treatment. A third example of this type of scale is the measure of teacher stress proposed by Pettegrew and Wolf (1982). These items deal with issues surrounding role problems, school and task stress, management style and other aspects of a teacher's occupational experience. Note that for many scales the situation/feeling dichotomy really reflects a preponderance of one or the other type of item, as the TSI has a significant number of feeling or reaction items, while the NSS and Pettegrew and Wolf scales have relatively less.

A number of measures focus more directly on the feeling/emotion area, good examples being the group of scales assessing burnout. The most commonly used index of this group in the Maslach Burnout Inventory (MBI; Maslach and Jackson, 1981), which addresses feelings of emotional exhaustion, depersonalization and personal accomplishment, all in relation to one's job. Other measures assess similar constructs, such as the Tedium Scale (Pines *et al.*, 1981), which evaluates physical, emotional and mental exhaustion, and the Emener–Luck Burnout Scale (ELBOS; Emener *et al.*, 1982), which surveys feelings regarding work tasks and interactions. Somewhat similar to these scales is the modification of the State–Trait Anxiety Inventory (STAI; Spielberger *et al.*, 1970) by Schriesheim and Murphy (1976), which asks subjects to report 'how they usually feel on the job' in terms of emotions related to anxiety and calmness. A different perspective was taken by Kahn *et al.*, (1964) and Indik *et al.*, (1964), who proposed the Job-Related Tension (JRT) and Job-Related Strain (JRS) scales, respectively. These measures, virtually identical 15-item questionnaires, do not focus on exhaustion or anxiety but rather on how much subjects are bothered by negative feelings related to role difficulties on the job.

In sum, occupational stress measures tend to have items which reflect an orientation to assess either the situations that occur while on the job or the feelings and emotions that are generated in work-related settings. Also, some scales tend to have one or the other type of item, while others include representations of each. What needs to be pointed out is that the difference between these kinds of items is not just a matter of style but rather is an indication of the investigators' conceptualization of stress as an environmental occurrence or a psychological and/or behavioural response. This is a fundamental issue that has been debated over the years, and it is not likely to be resolved in this chapter. It is an issue that requires the attention of anyone interested in the adequate measurement of job stress, however, because conceptualization of that construct will help to dictate the item format of such a scale. Which of these formats is 'better' is a question that is not easily answered, as each provides different information that may be of assistance in addressing various hypotheses. Whether they can be included appropriately in the same measure is also unclear, as they assess different levels of experience, and simple addition of items together as is done in the JRT/JRS may lose valuable information. A more efficient approach may be that of Fimian (1984), whose TSI contains separate subscales for sources and manifestations of stress, which then can be analysed separately. This technique can be useful in obtaining as clear a data set as possible, but does not absolve researchers of the requirement to consider more carefully which type of approach will be most relevant for the hypotheses under study.

Another factor that should be of concern to occupational stress researchers is whether the selection of item content, especially situations, is appropriate for the population being considered. It may be true that there are common stressors in the work experiences of carpenters and bank executives, but it is also likely that many aspects of their jobs that are troublesome are not shared. Given this, scales that are general in nature and not job-specific may at best be only somewhat inappropriate and at worst completely at odds with what is typically experienced on the job. A number of measures have focused specifically on particular jobs (such as the TSI and NSS mentioned above), and Crump *et al.* (1980) have suggested that the Repertory Grid technique may be used to generate the specific sources and manifestations of stress in the various occupations under study. Totally idiosyncratic scales for every job, however, would make attempts at inter-occupation comparisons quite difficult. Therefore, it would be helpful to have scales developed that contain items on issues potentially relevant to most jobs (e.g., work overload, role ambiguity) and job-specific items that address the unique stressors in an occupation. This would produce a richer base of knowledge regarding the stress experienced in a variety of employment situations along with the capability to do some evaluations of the relative degrees of stress perceived in a range of jobs. Of course, this approach will require some consensus as to what factors are common across occupations, an agreement that could be established by a review if available data and preliminary investigations among a number of samples utilizing existing *ad hoc* scales. These dual features, commonality and specificity, of adequately developed into useful assessment tools, will be extremely important in developing a corpus of research on occupational stress rather than a collection of unconnected studies.

3. Item valence

Another topic of importance in the design of occupational stress scales is the valence or positive/negative slant of the items. In surveying the available measures, a large proportion were found to have items phrased negatively, listing emotions and/or situations which generally appear to be undesirable. For example, the Stress Diagnostic Survey (SDS), developed by Ivancevich and Matteson (1984), consists of 60 items which detail various conditions and occurrences on the job. All of these descriptions are negative (e.g., ''Employees have no influence over how to do their jobs'') and subjects are asked to rate how often these situations are sources of stress. The NSS (Gray-Toft and Anderson, 1981) divides its 34 items into seven factors, each of which, as noted earlier, relate to negative aspects of nursing such as conflict and lack of support. In addition, the Teacher Occupational Stress Factor Questionnaire (TOSFQ; Clark, 1980), the Role Conflict (RC) scale by Rizzo *et al.* (1970) and the JRS and JRT (Indik *et al.*, 1964; Kahn *et al.*, 1964) all couch their items in terms of undesirable events. Only one scale—the Role Ambiguity (RA) measure by Rizzo *et al.* (1970)—was constructed with all positive or neutral items. Several tests, such as the Administrative Stress Index (ASI; Koch *et al.*, 1982), the Rahim Organizational Conflict Inventory-I (ROCI-I; Rahim, 1983) and measures of burnout like the ELBOS (Emener *et al.*, 1982) and the MBI (Maslach and Jackson, 1981) have a mixture of negative and positive or neutral items. An example of a positive item is "My skills are fully utilized on the job" (ROCI-I), and a more neutral item might be "Writing memos, letters, and other communications" (ASI).

Given that a number of these scales contain solely or mostly negative items, why is this important for the measurement of job stress? While little research has been done on the impact of this feature of scale format, several effects may be reasonably hypothesized. One is that the presentation to subjects of a consistently negative set of items may exacerbate the existence of response sets such as 'yea-saying'. If some respondents are likely to agree with whatever is asked of them, the presence of items all worded in one direction would serve to bias the results in the direction of higher levels of perceived stress. This possibility can be guarded against by having similar items worded in different directions allowing an assessment of the reliability of subjects' reports. This is difficult to accomplish, however, if all items are worded from the same perspective.

A second effect of this limitation is that it gives us an incomplete picture of what situations may be stressful for certain people under certain circumstances. Following Lazarus (1966), the cognitive appraisal of a situation is a crucial factor in determining its stressfulness, and thus some events which ordinarily appear to be positive or neutral may often assume a more negative aspect. If we focus briefly on the item from the ASI noted earlier, "writing memos, letters, and other communications", we can easily generate a number of circumstances under which this activity would be perceived as stressful. For example, one person may be unused to expressing him/herself on paper, and may find the task of writing a memo quite onerous. Another person may have a job that includes writing letters to inform people of the repossession of their homes or other bad news, which is perceived as a very distressing task. It is likely, then, that the inclusion of items that are more neutral in tone would uncover some job characteristics that are stress producers for certain worker groups.

A third drawback of negatively-couched scales is that they not only give an incomplete picture of the sources of stress for a worker, but they also give a somewhat distorted image of the job itself. It is difficult to infer from a scale what is positive about a job when subjects are asked only to indicate the presence or absence of negative features. Using this type of undirectional approach, we have no way of estimating whether the good aspects of the job outweigh the bad, and what are the relative weights of the positive and negative perceptions. It could be argued that much of this information can be gained from examination of the existing negative items. It seems unlikely, however, that rating an item such as "my job lacks any variety—it is the same old thing over and over" as never stressful (SDS) is the same thing as feeling that one's job is interesting and involving; or that rating as not stressful "feeling that poor communications exist among teachers in my school" (TOSFQ) is isomorphic with the perception that one can freely talk with one's co-workers. While it is true that the focus of the scales under review here is on job stress, we should not loose sight of the broader occupational context in which each of these events occurs, and that a greater emphasis on the interrelationships among positive and negative job elements may improve our ability to predict the impact of work experiences on work-, health- and psychologically-related outcomes.

4. Response modes

Thus far we have seen that job stress scales may consider either or both feelings and situations, and may differ on the positivity/negativity of the items presented. The ways in which subjects are asked to respond to these items also show a wide variation, and these response modes may impact significantly on how subjects perceive the questions being asked and the relevance of the response for the hypotheses of interest. Generally, four types of responses are utilized by the measures reveiwed here. One mode is to determine whether various situations or feelings exist on the job, with the total score of a scale being the summated presence of these stress-related factors. This determination has been done in a number of ways, however. Several scales use a yes/no or true/false format, such as the Interaction Strain measure of Parry and Warr (1980) and the anxiety–stress questionnaire of House and Rizzo (1972). But most measures using this mode ask subjects to rate on 4–7 point scales whether the item does or doesn't apply (Revicki and May, 1983; Parker and DeCotiis, 1983), is very false or very true (Rizzo et al., 1970; Ford et al., 1983), exists not at all or very much so (Schriesheim and Murphy, 1976), or whether the subject agrees with the statements (Pettegrew and Wolf, 1982).

Another approach is to assess the frequency with which situations and feelings occur. Some measures give subjects a response scale from 'never' to 'often' (e.g., Quinn and Shepard, 1974; Keenan and McBain, 1979; Sutton and Rousseau, 1979), while other authors use scales ranging from 'never' to 'always' or 'all the time" (e.g., Pines et al., 1981; Emener et al., 1982). This distinction may seem to be quite trivial, but assumes greater significance than expected, as will be seen below. A third response mode focuses on the perception by subjects that their experiences are stressful. One set of scales, based on the JRS/JRT, ask how frequently respondents are 'bothered' by the listed situations (Indik et al., 1964; Kahn et al., 1964; Lyons, 1971; Koch et al., 1982). Another two scales require the assessment of how often the situations are stressful (Gray-Toft and Anderson, 1981) or a source of stress (Ivancevich and Matteson, 1984). In addition, two measures ask how stressful each of the events listed is (Clark, 1980; Johnson et al., 1982). Finally, three scales assess both the intensity or strength of the feeling or situation and the frequency of the item as well, the latter measured from 'never', 'almost never' or 'a few times a year' to 'almost always' or 'every day' (Maslach and Jackson, 1981; Parasuraman and Alutto, 1981; Fimian, 1984).

While the range of response modes utilized in these scales is fairly wide, a close examination of what these alternatives really mean reveals an even broader set of implications. For example, consider the item "I work on unnecessary things" from Rizzo *et al*.'s (1970) measure of role conflict. Since potential responses may range from very false to very true, we can imagine a subject marking 'somewhat true' to this item. But what does this mean? It is not clear how often this situation occurs to this subject, or whether it has any negative impacts on him/her. The item "My administrative head gives me full information about the things which directly involve my work" from Pettegrew and Wolf (1982) requires response on a scale from strong agreement to strong disagreement. Given a subject for whom this situation occasionally occurs, agree and disagree responses could both be construed as correct, creating problems both for subjects completing the scale and for researchers interpreting the resultant data. Thus response modes targeting agreement with the item or presence of the item may be ambiguous in their wording and not provide other important data such as the frequency of the event.

Measures utilizing frequency have their own problems, however. One concern is the importance of frequent events. An item from the Emener *et al*. (1982) ELBOS burnout measure is "My boss gives me negative feedback about my work and what I do", which is to be rated on a nine-point scale of whether it occurs none of the time to all of the time. If we assume that for a particular individual this event happens all the time, we still are unsure as to the meaning of this occurrence for the subject's adaptation. It may be that the boss talks that way to everyone and can generally be ignored. On the other hand, it might be that the subject is in serious trouble on the job and under continuous supervisory pressure. Knowing solely the extent to which an event occurs does not allow us to make confident predictions of its impact, and a combination of frequency and intensity measures as used by Maslach and Jackson (1981), Parasuraman and Alutto (1981), Fimian (1984) and Numerof and Abrams (1984) seems to be helpful in estimating the effects.

A perhaps more basic issue is whether we really know how often events occur even when subjects do make frequency estimates such as the ones cited. Do people interpret these five-, seven- and nine-point scales in a similar manner? It appears unlikely that they do. Pepper (1981) cites research indicating that the typical meaning reported by subjects of 'sometimes' ranges across studies from 20% to 46% of the time, and that 'seldom' varies from 9% to 22% of the time. Even a term such as 'always' has evidenced variability among studies between 99 and 100%, and 'never' between 1 and 0%. Pepper cited a number of potential reasons for these discrepancies, one major one being the context of the question. She cites some of her own work to show that the term 'very often', when not embedded in the context of an event, was rated by subjects as meaning (on average) 86·45% of the time. However, given the context of "a single earthquake in California", the phrase 'very often' dropped to 39·12%. Similarly, 'almost never', without a context, was judged to refer to 4·18% of the time. When embedded in the context of "shooting in Hollywood westerns", however, this figure increased to 10·30%. Clearly the expected occurrence of an event will influence a sample's perceptions of the meaning of frequency estimates for that event. Applying this perspective to the measurement of job stress, we might suggest that much of the 'noise' in self-report data may result from differing within-sample conceptions of the meaning of frequency estimates and disparate perceptions of the relative occurrence of stress-related situations and feelings. As Pepper (1981) suggests: "In view of the observed variability in the numerical meanings of frequency expressions, it would be unwise to assume that the frequency terms used by respondents convey precise inform-ation about the actual rates with which events occur . . . Even such apparently precise terms as 'always' and 'never' cannot be assumed to provide exact information about the occurrence of behaviors or events. Thus, one obvious and very important implic-ation of the existing research is that frequency expressions should not be taken literally" (p. 37). Frequency is still an important type of data to obtain in relation to occupational stress, however, and a recommendation will be made below to address some of these measurement difficulties.

Similar problems of attributed meaning are evident with the measures that employ such terms as 'stressful' or 'bothered' in their responses. How do naive subjects define 'stress' or 'bothered', and how likely is it that there will be considerable variability in these conceptions? The knowledge that there may be widely disparate perceptions of situations among respondents has apparently not filtered down to the developers of job stress scales, as few offer any guidance to subjects as to what reactions these terms re-present. One exception is the SDS by Ivancevich and Matteson (1984), which defines stress as "existing whenever you experience feelings of *pressure, strain,* or *emotional upset* at work". Note, however, that even this definition allows considerable latitude in response, particularly since the scale does not require a rating to be made on the intensity of these feelings. A second concern is the use of the term 'bothered' in a number of these scales. Is this the same to subjects as 'stressed', and if not, how does it differ? We can imagine a job on which one might feel 'bothered by' "being unclear on what opportunities for promotion and advancement exist for me" (Indik *et al.*, 1964), but is this the same as feeling 'stressed' over this situation? Further reasearch on the comparability of these terms would be extremely helpful in determining subjects' per-ceptions of job stress measures and in turn their responses to them. A final point on this type of measure is that several of these scales ask how stressful an event is, without est-ablishing at the same time whether or not the event actually occurs. This highlights the need for *both* frequency and intensity information to obtain a clearer picture of the extent of occupational stress in a subject's work experience.

The response modes surveyed have generally addressed whether an event or a feeling occur or are applicable, how often they occur, and how intense these situations and emotions are perceived to be. Two other approaches suggest themselves that were not used by the reviewed measures. One technique would be to assess the duration of impact of the event or feeling. That is, "conflict with a supervisor" (NSS, Gray-Toft and Anderson, 1981) may be rated as occurring only occasionally but might last for hours or days when it does happen. On the other hand, "criticism from a physician" (from the same scale) may occur frequently but be of significantly shorter duration. Deriving an esti-mate of the length of the occurrence, coupled with information on frequency and inten-sity, should further sharpen our estimates of the extent of stress in the occupational setting.

A second focus would be to address the manifestation of the impact of stress; that is, to assess how people respond to their stress-related work experiences. The various burnout measures discussed earlier tend to do this but target a somewhat narrow range of reactions, and the suggestion made here is to broaden the range of potential responses that could be selected. An attempt at this type of analysis was done by Payne *et al.* (1982), in which they developed the Job Reaction Questionnaire (JRQ). This measure consists of twenty different situations on the job (e.g., "using a telephone", "going for a promotion interview", "telling off subordinates", "being late for an important meeting", and so on). Subjects rate the extent to which they experience eight different responses in each of these 20 situations. These response modes include "my heart seems to beat faster", "my emotions interfere with what I'm doing", "I want to get out of the situation", "I perspire a lot more than usual", "I find I need to go to the toilet frequently", "my mouth gets dry", "I get a queasy feeling in my stomach" and "I feel very tense". This technique has the advantage of specifying exactly what kind of response is to be reported and removes much of the interpretation of what the term 'stressed' means from the subjects.

One concern with this approach is the lack of frequency information to determine the actual prevalence of these stress-related responses. A second concern is the restricted range of responses, which focuses primarily on psychophysiological indices. It would be of interest to extend the alternatives to include emotional, behavioural (including work activities) and interpersonal reactions. Thirdly, however, as a number of responses increases, the number of items given to subjects rises dramatically. Payne *et al.* (1982) had 20 times 8 or 160 items, and significant expansion of the list of situations and/or responses would quickly lead to an unmanageable load for subjects. Using this technique, then, requires some *a priori* consideration of the types of situations and reactions of most interest, and a winnowing down of items to avoid overloading respondents. This practice, of course, is of value before proceeding with any research project, but is of special significance when the type of measurement technique used requires more attention to be paid to constraints of time and subject fatigue and cooperation.

A final note on this topic is that while the focus and valence of items and response modes have been addressed as independent entities, they are utilized in a wide variety of combinations in the reviewed scales, and it has not yet been determined whether a degree of dependence occurs among these factors. That is, are some response modes more appropriate to use with feelings than with situations? What is the effect, if any, of having a preponderance of negative feelings in a measure versus a majority of negative situations? These issues may be difficult to explore empirically, but consideration of them by scale constructors and users may produce some creative thought as to the most effective permutations of measure components.

5. Recommendations for scale development

In view of the above discussion, a number of suggestions can be made that might be employed in developing measures of job stress and in evaluation of existing scales.

1. More emphasis needs to be placed on obtaining information on both work situations and the reactions to those situations by the subjects. As noted earlier, some selectivity should be used in choosing examples of each, and as much thought and breadth of selection should be given to choice of reactions as to situations.

2. Attempts should be made to include items that are relevant for most jobs as well as items that are specific to the particular occupation under study. This latter point applies to feelings as well as situations, since reactions such as fear of physical stressors and dangers may be more prevalent in some occupations (e.g., building trades) than in other job categories.

3. The items presented should have a balance of positive, neutral and negative formats to avoid the problem of response sets and to allow for the possibility of assessing subject consistency, if desired.

4. Response alternatives should incorporate estimates of frequency, intensity and duration of situations and responses. Frequency and duration alternatives should utilize concrete time references wherever possible.

6. Further directions for job stress measurement

A number of issues and trends exist that may have a significant effect on the development of the occupational stress field in the next decade and which have direct implications for psychometric measurement approaches. One concern is whether occupational stress reflects state or trait aspects of the individual and/or the work environment. How constant subjects and their settings are with regard to their stress-related characteristics and responses is a topic that is wide open for research and has serious implications for job stress measurement. Not only should test–retest reliability of available scales be under closer scrutiny, but also changes in the sources of stress will have to be reflected in the scales used. These changes are less at the micro level—changing a supervisor in an office should be reflected on current instruments, for example—than at the macro scale, with trends that effect large segments of the working population, such as the impact of new technologies, the effect of mergers on job security, worker and manager interactions and satisfaction with pay and benefits. Investigators will have to be sensitive to such changes in order to adequately address their impact on the stress experienced by their target populations.

Increasing pressure will develop to evaluate the validity of job stress measures. This is due in part to increasing numbers of stress-related worker's compensation lawsuits (especially in the USA) and the concurrent and growing necessity for companies to document the effectiveness of stress management interventions (Ivancevich et al., 1985), requiring measures with well-established validity. In this effort it will be important to draw supportive data from a variety of areas, as a single source of validational information is unlikely to provide conclusive evidence. For example, perceptions of situations by outside observers, as employed in a study of job characteristics by Dean and Brass (1985), can be important in establishing the veracity of self-reports, along with data from key informants and existing measures of stress-related outcomes (e.g., absenteeism rates, utilization of employee assistance programs, etc.). Of course, investigators must be able to recognize the appropriate data necessary to establish validity. Johnson *et al.* (1982) indicated that they demonstrated the 'validity' of their teacher stress scale by correlating scores on it from a pilot survey of teachers with scores on the same instrument from a sample of education professionals. Since the correlation was significant ($r = 0.75$), these authors reported that the validity of the scale was confirmed. Aside from the concerns regarding how scores from two unrelated samples can actually be 'correlated', it is unclear how this type of analysis satisfies the requirements of content, construct or criterion-related validity (Carmines and Zeller, 1979). These results confirm a commonly held set of perceptions of school situations, but hardly establish that stress is indeed the variable that is being measured. Greater attention must be paid to the specific types of evidence required for validity assessment if this field is to continue to progress.

Another use to which valid measures may be put is to focus on employees at risk. As is being done with cardiovascular and other chronic diseases, it may be possible to screen a population of workers and make some predictions as to which individuals may be most liable to suffer stress-related physical and psychological difficulties. These workers could then be targeted for interventions designed to deal with both personal coping styles and environmental stressors. Even assuming the existence of valid, reliable measures, a number of giant steps need to be taken before this point is reached, however. One is that the same care in developing measures to assess stress in individuals must be given to developing a taxonomy and evaluation technique for stressful situations. That is, it would be extremely helpful to be able to categorize situations on the basis of their stress-related characteristics, much as an individual is classified as Type A or Type B. And like the structured interview assessment of Type A, we may find ourselves relying on a combination of objective characteristics and subjective perceptions. This approach will enable us to better estimate the person–environment fit (Harrison, 1985) that exists in any particular setting. An additional step is to encourage large-scale longitudinal studies which can track the concurrent development of stress and disease over an extended period. While funding for such work may be scarce from government sources, companies which have concerns about stress (e.g., legal, altruistic) and upwardly spiralling health care costs may become interested in this type of research. This analysis also needs to be extended to the populations that have rarely been the focus of job stress research, namely blue-collar, female and minority workers. Greater awareness of the types of positions held by these employees, their familiarity with questionnaire completion and their potentially different responses to work stress will not only improve the applicability of our measurement techniques but will also open new directions for hypothesis construction and risk assessment.

Finally, mention should be made of the interaction of outside sources of stress with the stress that occurs on the job. It seems likely that pressures of family and community life may occasionally influence one's perceptions of, attitudes towards and behaviours on the job, and that these influences should be evaluated in occupational stress research. Conversely, stress on the job clearly can have a significant impact on outside life concerns such as family interaction and community involvement. Recent work by Kandel *et al.* (1985) and Bhagat *et al.* (1985) emphasizes the value of examining both work stress and life stress factors in order to understand the physical and psychological well-being of employees. This dual approach will require even more energy to be put into establishing valid and reliable measures that address both work and non-work issues. While this makes the task of investigating stress more difficult, the recognition that employees' lives do not begin at 8:00 a.m. and end at 5:00 p.m. will move us in this direction to a greater and greater degree in the future.

References

Bhagat, R.S., McQuaid, S.J., Lindholm, H. and Segovis, J. (1985). Total life stress: a multi-method validation of the construct and its effects on organizationally valued outcomes and withdrawal behaviors. *Journal of Applied Psychology*, **70**, 202–214.

Carmines, E.G. and Zeller, R.A. (1979). *Reliability and Validity Assessment*. (Beverly Hills, CA: Sage).

Clark, E.H. (1980). An analysis of occupational stress factors as perceived by public school teachers. Unpublished doctoral dissertation, Auburn University, Alabama.

Crump, J.H., Cooper, C.L. and Smith, M. (1980). Investigating occupational stress: a methodological approach. *Journal of Occupational Behaviour*, **1**, 191–204.

Dean, J.W. and Brass, D.J. (1985). Social interaction and the perception of job characteristics in an organization.. *Human Relations*, **38**, 571–582.

Emener, W.G., Luck, R.S. and Gohs, F.X. (1982). A theoretical investigation of the construct burnout. *Journal of Rehabilitation Administration*, **6**, 188–196.

Fimian, M.J. (1984). The development of an instrument to measure occupational stress in teachers: the Teacher Stress Inventory. *Journal of Occupational Psychology*, **57**, 277–293.

Ford, D.L., Murphy, C.J. and Edwards, K.L. (1983). Exploratory development and validation of a perceptual job burnout inventory: Comparison of corporate sector and human services professionals. *Psychological Reports*, **52**, 995–1006.

Gray-Toft, P. and Anderson, J.G. (1981). The Nursing Stress Scale: development of an instrument. *Journal of Behavioral Assessment*, **3**, 11–23.

Harrison, R.V. (1985). The person–environment fit model and the study of job stress. In T.A. Beehr and R.S. Bhagat (eds), *Human Stress and Cognition in Organizations: An Integrated Perspective* (New York: John Wiley).

House, R.J. and Rizzo, J.R. (1972). Role conflict and ambiguity as critical variables in a model of organizational behavior. *Organizational Behavior and Human Performance*, **7**, 467–505.

Indik, B., Seashore, S.E. and Slesinger, J. (1964). Demographic correlates of psychological strain. *Journal of Abnormal and Social Psychology*, **69**, 26–38.

Ivancevich, J.M. and Matteson, M.T. (1984). Stress Diagnostic Survey (SDS): comments and psychometric properties of a multi-dimensional self-report inventory. Unpublished manuscript, University of Houston, Texas.

Ivancevich, J.M. Matteson, M.T. and Richards, E.P. (1985). Who's liable for stress on the job. *Harvard Business Review*, **63**, 60–62, 66, 70, 72.

Jenkins, C.D., DeFrank, R.S. and Speers, M.A. (1984). *Evaluation of Psychometric Methodologies Used to Assess Occupational Stress and Strain*. National Institute for Occupational Safety and Health-Applied Psychology and Ergonomics Branch Report No. 84–2756.

Johnson, A.B., Gold, V. and Vickers, L.L. (1982). Stress and teachers of the learning disabled, behavior disordered, and educable mentally retarded. *Psychology in the Schools*, **19**, 552–557.

Kahn, R.L. Wolfe, D.M. Quinn, R.P., Snoek, J.D. and Rosenthal, R.A. (1964). *Organizational Stress: Studies in Role Conflict and Ambiguity.* (New York: John Wiley).

Kandel, D.B. Davies, M. and Raveis, V.H. (1985). The stressfulness of daily social roles for women: marital, occupational and household roles. *Journal of Health and Social Behavior,* **26**, 64–78.

Keenan, A. and McBain, G.D.M. (1979). Effects of Type A behaviour, intolerance of ambiguity, and locus of control on the relationship between role stress and work-related outcomes. *Journal of Occupational Psychology,* **52**, 277–285.

Koch, J.L., Tung, R., Gmelch, W. and Swent, B. (1982). Job stress among school administrators: factorial dimensions and differential effects. *Journal of Applied Psychology,* **67**, 493–499.

Lazarus, R.S. (1966). *Psychological Stress and the Coping Process* (New York: McGraw-Hill).

Lyons, T.F. (1971). Role clarity, need for clarity, satisfaction, tension, and withdrawal. *Organizational Behavior and Human Performance,* **6**, 99–110.

Maslach, C. and Jackson, S.E. (1981). *Maslach Burnout Inventory Manual* (Palo Alto, CA: Consulting Psychologists Press).

Numerof, R.E. and Abrams, M.N. (1984). Sources of stress among nurses: an empirical investigation. *Journal of Human Stress,* **10**, 88–100.

Parasuraman, S. and Alutto, J.A. (1981). An examination of the organizational antecedents of stressors at work. *Academy of Management Journal,* **24**, 48–67.

Parker, D.F. and DeCotiis, T.A. (1983). Organizational determinants of job stress. *Organizational Behavior and Human Performance,* **32**, 160–177.

Parry, G. and Warr, P.B. (1980). The measurement of mothers' work attitudes. *Journal of Occupational Psychology,* **53**, 245–252.

Payne, R.L., Fineman, S. and Jackson, P.R. (1982). An interactionist approach to measuring anxiety at work. *Journal of Occupational Psychology,* **55**, 13–25.

Pepper, S. (1981). Problems in the quantification of frequency expressions. In D. Fiske (ed.), *New Directions for Methodology of Social and Behavioral Science, Problems with Language Imprecision,* no. 9 (San Francisco, CA: Jossey-Bass).

Pettegrew, L.S. and Wolf, G.E. (1982). Validating measures of teacher stress. *American Educational Research Journal,* **19**, 373–396.

Pines, A.M., Aronson, E. and Kafry, D. (1981). *Burnout: from Tedium to Personal Growth* (New York: Free Press).

Quinn, R.P. and Shepard, L.T. (1974). *The 1972–73 Quality of Employment Survey* (Ann Arbor, MI: Institute for Social Research, University of Michigan).

Rahim, M.A. (1983). Measurement of organizational conflict. *The Journal of General Psychology,* **109**, 189–199.

Revicki, D.A. and May, H.J. (1983). Development and validation of the Physician Stress Inventory. *Family Practice Research Journal,* **2**, 1–10.

Rizzo, J.R., House, R.J. and Lirtzman, S.I. (1970). Role conflict and ambiguity in complex organizations. *Administrative Science Quarterly,* **15**, 150–163.

Schriesheim, C.A. and Murphy, C.J. (1976). Relationship between leader behavior and subordinate satisfaction and performance: a test of some situational moderators. *Journal of Applied Psychology,* **61**, 634–641.

Spielberger, C.D., Gorsuch, R.L. and Lushene, R.E. (1970). *Manual for the State-Trait Anxiety Inventory* (Palo Alto, CA: Consulting Psychologists Press).

Sutton, R.I. and Rousseau, D.M. (1979). Structure, technology, and dependence on a parent organization: Organizational and environmental correlates of individual responses. *Journal of Applied Psychology,* **64**, 675–687.

4

Situationally Anchored Stress Scales for the Measurement of Work-related Stress

Arie Shirom

1. Introduction

Despite the large and growing body of research on stress, researchers differ widely about its basic definition. Stress has been defined as a stimulus, a response, and a hypothetical state (Flemming, 1984; Sarason, 1984). These articles focused on psychosocial stress at work, to the total exclusion of physical and/or physiological stress (like exposure to intense levels of noise or heat, or to high levels of toxic substances). Even so, there were several alternative conceptualizations of stress to choose from, including those formulated by the followers of the person–environment fit theory (Caplan, 1983), the one proposed by McGrath (1976), and the one developed by Schuler (1980). Those conceptualizations by and large accepted the core definition of stress originated by Lazarus (1966; Lazarus and Delongis, 1983), but elaborated, extended and otherwise modified it to include additional environmental, situational or personality components. It is thus apparent that the Lazarus definition of stress was widely accepted among researchers (Hogan and Hogan, 1982); therefore, it constitutes this chapter's conceptual point of departure. The objective is to present and justify the assessment of work-related stress in organizations by stress measurement scales based on the methodology of behaviourally anchored rating scales (Smith and Kendall, 1963).

According to Lazarus (e.g., Lazarus and Launier, 1978) stress occurs when a person appraises a given relationship with his/her environment as taxing or exceeding the person's resources and thus endangering his/her well-being.

From this conceptual definition of stress, it follows that stress measures should include two perceptual components. They are (*a*) the external demand, and (*b*) the cognition that this external demand depletes or exceeds specific adaptive resources of the individual. The lesson to stress researchers is clear. They should investigate the relation between the external demand that they study and their respondent's specific adaptive resources as perceived by her/him. The relational basis of stress conceptuation, as described above, means that stress is not a property of the person or the environment, nor is it a stimulus (e.g., exam) or a reponse (e.g., anxiety). Rather it is a particular relationship between the person and the environment (*see* Shirom, 1982).

There is an additional important implication that follows from the two perceptual components of the relational view of stress. Both must be relevant and meaningful to one's subjects or respondents. To illustrate this, it is probably irrelevant to measure inter- or intra-sender role conflict among job holders whose work can hardly be supervised, like teachers. This means that the questionnaire items used to measure stress describe demands likely to be actually experienced by the respondents as impinging upon specific resources of those respondents. Thus relevant measures of stress should reflect the dynamic relationship between the external demand and a person's resources, yet another characteristic of the cognitive view of stress (Folkman, 1984).

2. Current measures of stress

Are the currently used measures of psychosocial stress consonant with the relational view of stress, i.e., an external demand exceeding or taxing an employee's resources? Many isolated attempts to develop measures of stress for specific occupational categories such as nursing (e.g., Gray-Tofts and Anderson, 1981) or teaching (e.g., Tellenback *et al.*, 1983) are excluded from this brief review of the prevailing operationalizations of stress at work.

Three major methodological approaches toward the measurement of work-related psychosocial stress exist in the literature: the critical-event-based measurement of stress; the measurement of stress as an ongoing, chronic process; and the operationalization of stress as hassles.

Critical-event-based measurement of stress

Critical-event-based measures of stress at work have been reviewed by Eden (1982). As he noted, studies using them tapped primarily acute stress or critical job events, like examinations for students, or the impending shut-down of a university computer for its users (Eden, 1982). With the exception of Weiss *et al.* (1982), no attempt to systematically measure stressful events at work for any occupational category in a manner analogous to the Holmes and Rahe (1967) Schedule of Recent Experiences was identified. This may be due to the theoretical shortcomings of this approach to stress management, such as the over-emphasis on change, the failure to consider the individual significance of events and the lack of regard of a person's adaptational resources (Lazarus, 1984). Another reason may be the unresolved methodological and statistical problems inherent in this approach to the measurement of stress, reviewed and discussed by Tausig (1982). Yet another major problem with this approach to stress measurement is that it may not be the event itself, but rather the series of stressful episodes that succeed and precede it, which are the real culprits in the causal chain leading to maladaptive responses and disease states (Coyne *et al.*, 1981). Overall, this approach has no affinity to the relational view of stress.

The measurement of stress as an ongoing, continuous process

The study of ongoing or chronic organizational stress has been guided by measurement tools derived from role theory by Kahn and his colleagues (Kahn *et al.*, 1964), further developed and extended by the followers of the person–environment fit theory (Van Harrison, 1978) and used as a survey research instrument by Rizzo *et al.* (1970). While the role conflict and role ambiguity scales developed by Rizzo *et al.* (1970) have been criticized on both theoretical (e.g., Fineman and Payne, 1981) and methodological (e.g., Tracy and Johnson, 1983) grounds, they still constitute the predominantly used measures of ongoing or chronic stress in the literature (Jackson and Schuler, 1985). Therefore, it is appropriate to examine the extent to which they accord with the relational view of stress.

Some of the problems inherent in this approach to stress measurement may be exemplified by considering two representative items, taken from the role conflict scale developed by Rizzo *et al.* (1970): "I receive incompatible requests from two or more people"; and "I have to do things that should de done differently". The difficulties with this approach are many.

First, only the demand component of the relational view of stress is tapped.

Second, the demand is formulated in a format tapping a global disposition, and thus is bound to be quite remote from the actual work experiences of a typical respondent. It follows that this approach is prone to reponse biases such as the tendency of individuals to provide socially desirable responses, or to maintain a public posture of toughness or machismo in the face of very general questions, such as the above. Thus a major objection to the chronic stress measures, as currently used, is that rather than tapping the actual experience of stress on the job by a respondent, they refer her/him to general characteristics of the job environment which may or may not be of immediate pertinence to the individual.

Third, these stress measures were derived from role theory and relate to but few of the chronic stresses which might be associated with employees' roles in organizations. They do not increase our understanding of recurring stressful interactions associated with job-related tasks, technology or work processes. To illustrate, in the job of air traffic controllers, what others (like peers or supervisors) expect them to do may constitute environmental demands of lesser intensity than the demands posed by intra-task or work process problems. Moreover, as Jackson and Schuler (1985) observed, even within the limited confines of role theory, the many followers of this approach towards stress measurement seldom applied readily available conceptual distinctions like intra-sender role conflict in their research. More generally, those researchers paid little attention to the different array of roles that a typical employee plays in his/her work organization. To illustrate, a teacher may play different roles vis-à-vis his/her students, peers, principal, students' parents, local union and community organizations.

The assessment of daily stresses

The third approach to the measurement of stress, which first appeared rather recently, focuses on the assessment of daily stresses, referred to as hassles and uplifts (Kanner *et al.*, 1981). It is based on the theoretical position that the meaning of an event, rather than its simple occurrence, is the determinant of its impact on health and well-being. It claims that daily events provide a more powerful predictor of health and well-being than the traditional critical life or organizational events methodology (Lazarus, 1984).

Within the confines of this novel approach, however, little attention has been paid to the identification and measurement of patterned person–environment interactions appraised by the individual as taxing or exceeding his/her adaptive resources. In this respect, the hassles approach complements the former 'chronic stress' approach. The operationalization of hassles by the followers of this approach emphasizes environmental events or conditions, that is, the demands made on a person's resources, and only implicitly deals with the resources being threatened (Kanner *et al.*, 1981). Lazarus (1984) discussed several other conceptual and methodological difficulties challenging the group of hassles researchers, such as the inclusion of items tapping emotional reactions to stressful experiences in the measurement instruments. To paraphrase Lazarus (1984), it thus appears that the 'paradigm shift' on the conceptual level towards the relational view of stress requires a different, fourth approach to stress measurement, one that takes into account the external demand and the cognitive activity of evaluating the significance of the demand in terms of a person's resources.

3. Constructing situationally anchored stress scales

It is apparent that the reviewed operational definitions of stress reflect one component of the stress interaction, namely the environmental demand impinging upon the individual. The appraisal of the meaning of the demand for the individual's adaptive resources has hardly been pursued by stress researchers.

As pointed out by Ekehammer (1974), adequate description of person–situation interactions is basic to any undestanding of most psychological phenomena. Therefore, the development of a measurement technique which will enable researchers to identify, describe and assess the stressful person-situation interactions holds high priority.

Situationally Anchored Stress Scales (SASS) represent an attempt to remedy these weaknesses by applying to the measurement of stress the methodology of the Behaviourally Anchored Rating Scale (BARS). BARS was first developed by Smith and Kendall (1963) and has been confined to the area of performance evaluation (Jacobs *et al.*, 1980). This application of BARS to construct SASS was guided by an adaptation of the short cut methods for deriving BARS proposed by Green *et al.* (1981). The major steps in the construction of SASS are summarized in Table 4.1.

Step 1 calls for the selection of a set of fairly similar jobs, referred to as a job family, and for the identification of the major interactional subsystems of role occupants in the job family. For example, an elementary school teacher interacts with individual pupils, his/her classes, the principal, co-workers, paperwork, instructional techniques, etc.

Step 2 entails collecting items, describing experienced stress on the job from a sample of employees in the job family considered (Sample A). The items gathered, preferably in a response to an open-ended questionnaire, should be carefully edited to eliminate duplicate and irrelevant items and, insofar as possible, to reflect a relation between a specific external demand and a domain of depleted or exceeded resources. In a study of stressful person–situation interactions among undergraduate students (Shirom, 1985), it was found that when such an open-ended approach to the elicitation of typical stresses was applied in research, the examples provided by the respondents did reflect a

Table 4.1. *Steps and procedure in the construction of situationally anchored stress scales.*

Step No.	Step Title	Procedure
1	Identifying the subsystems of the jobs to be assessed	Select a job family. Analyse the major interactional subsystems which characterize role incumbents. Use job descriptions, participant observation, and the like.
2	Collecting examples of stressful situations (= stress items)	Ask respondents in a representative sample (Sample A) of the job family assessed to provide detailed examples of recently experienced on-the-job stresses. Edit the examples.
3	Classifying the collected stress items into Step 1's subsystems	Using expert judges (Sample B), determine, for each stress item, the interactional subsystem of the job family which it best represents.
4	Assessing the relevancy of the stress items	Ask a third sample of judges (Sample C) to evaluate each stress item resulting from Step 3 on the twin criteria of (1) its frequency of appearance and (2) the amount of stress it generates.
5	Constructing an SASS, administering the SASS to the job family under consideration	Applying psychometric considerations, select the more relevant stress items on the basis of Step 4's data, and construct an SASS. Administer the SASS to a fairly representative sample of the population whose stress is being assessed.

relation between an environmental demand and a domain of depleted or taxed resources.

Step 3 involves the use of a few expert judges (Sample B), preferably the employees' superiors, who are requested to assign each of the items resulting from Step 2 to one of the interactional subsystems identified in Step 1. The purpose of this step is to enable the researcher to group and label the stress items and thus to inspire respondent's trust in the instrument and increase their willingness to co-operate with future data collection efforts. Items retained after this step should have sufficient interjudge realiability.

Step 4 again entails the use of a sample of expert judges, preferably employees from the job family being considered (Sample C). Sample C judges should be asked to place a scale value on each item (in terms of a 5- or 7-point scale) on two adjacent scales: one assessing the item's frequency of appearance, and the other the amount of stress experienced, or the intensity of the stress perception for that item. The former scale presumably assesses more a situational feature, namely exposure to stress, while the latter probably provides an appraisal of individual stress vulnerability, as an individual characteristic (see Barone *et al.*, 1985).

It is suggested that for each item thus scaled, 'relevancy as a stress item' be defined as a multiplicative function of the amount of stress experienced and its frequency of appearance, summed up and averaged across the judges. Psychometric considerations applied to select items for BARS forms (Jacob *et al.*, 1980) should guide a researcher's decision on the final selection of items for SASS.

In *Step 5*, SASS is finally constructed and administered to a representative sample of the employees involved. Note that participants in any of the above samples used for the construction of SASS should be excluded from any subsequent participation in its construction process or administration. For each of the interactional subsystems covered by the thus constructed SASS, it might be possible to build several indices:

1. An index which reflects individual differences in exposure to stressful situations, by summing responses to the frequency scale.

2. An index which reflects individual differences in vulnerability, by summing responses to the intensity scale.

3. An index of individual differences in experienced work-related stress, which results from summing up, for each respondent, frequency times intensity over all items in the interactional domain under consideration.

Theoretical considerations would suggest that the last index should be used in future attempts to test the predictive and concurrent validity of SASS, such as in explaining either individual level or organizational level outcomes by experienced stress.

4. Discussion

What are some of the major advantages and disadvantages of the proposed SASS? Among the advantages, the resultant scales reflect real, actually experienced stressful situations, assessed by informed judges to appear quite frequently and intensively. There is some evidence suggesting that items thus solicited from respondents will reflect a relationship between demands and resources (Magnusson and Stattin, 1981; Shirom, 1985). This SASS appears to adequately reflect the major components of the conceptualization of stress advocated by Lazarus (1976; Lazarus and Cohen, 1977), as presented above. Whereas the predominantly used measures of role conflict and role ambiguity provide a very selective and partial view of chronic stresses in work organization, SASS, by virtue of its elaborate process of construction, has the potential to provide a systematic and comprehensive appraisal of all relevant work-related stresses, be they 'chronic' or event types of stresses.

As proposed, SASS appears to be akin to stress scales constructed for a specific occupational categories of employees, such as those constructed to assess stress among teachers (Kyriacou and Sutcliffe, 1978) or nurses (Gray-Tofts and Anderson, 1981). However, most occupation-specific stress scales do not follow the relational view of stress and do not apply scale construction procedures likely to result in a representative sample of stress items in the relevant employees' real world. In addition, the scale construction procedure of SASS has several other positive spin-offs (*see* Blood, 1974). Items tend to tap employees' slang and culture and are devoid of psychological jargon. Thus the items in SASS are easily understood and meaningful to a respondent in the occupational category being studied. In itself, this tends to increase response rates to an anonymous questionnaire. The involvement of a substantial number of employees in the occupational category being studied, and their superiors in constructing the SASS, increases employee willingness to co-operate with the actual administration of SASS, enhances the acceptability of SASS results, and promotes management's motivation to implement remedial action following SASS results.

SASS, however, does possess certain shortcomings. The construction process is costly in terms of man-hours, including demands made on the time of senior managers. For some steps in the process, expert advice of statisticians and computer time are indispensible. These disadvantages make SASS more affordable to employers of a large workforce. Yet another caveat is that the construction process tends to build up expectations that something will be done to alleviate current organizational stress. That is, there must be a firm commitment of the top organizational echelons not only to collect stress data, but to initiate corrective actions as a result of SASS administration. Researchers may object to the phenomenological nature of SASS, making this instrument less useful for cross-organizational or cross-occupational studies. This criticism has often been voiced against idiographic measures. In response, it might be noted that BARS users have constructed scales applicable to fairly large occupational categories such as nurses, the police and sales clerks (Jacobs *et al.*, 1980), thus allowing intra-occupational comparisons. Inter-occupational comparisons within an organization, e.g., physicians, nurses, administrators, etc., within a hospital, may also be carried out to the extent that there are commonalities among different SASS instruments. Such commonalities, in turn, may provide important clues to organizational characteristics anteceding stress perceptions of different groups of employees.

The last comment leads directly to the identification of an important application of SASS: as a tailor-made diagnostic tool which validly identifies troublesome stressful situations. Corrective actions can be focused on certain demands or targetted on replenishing specific depleted resources. Consequently, stress management efforts become potentially much more effective in comparison with those following the administration of often-used stress scales such as the Rizzo *et al.* (1970) role conflict–ambiguity scales. Following the administration of SASS to the population being considered, the results may be used to determine responsibility for specific stress management efforts: the organization, individuals in the job family, or both, may undertake such a responsibility. Moreover, training activities designed to increase coping skills of a specific kind can be made available for those categories of employees with an expressed need for them (e.g., time management workshops held to enable overloaded employees to structure their time better).

Acknowledgements

The author wishes to thank Dov Eden, Yeacov Ezrahi, Zur Shapira and Ahron Tziner for their helpful comments on an earlier draft of this article.

References

Barone, D.F., Caddy, G.R. Katell, A.D. and Roselione, F. (1985). The work stress inventory: reliability and concurrent validity. A paper presented at the annual meeting of the American Psychological Association, Los Angeles, August 1985.

Blood, M.R. (1974). Spin-offs from behavioral expectation scale procedures. *Journal of Applied Psychology*, **59**, 513–515.

Caplan, R.D (1983). Person environment fit: past, present and future. In C.L. Cooper (ed.) *Stress Research* (New York, John Wiley), pp. 35–78.

Coyne, J.L., Aldwin, C. and Lazarus, R.S. (1981). Depression and coping in stressful episodes. *Journal of Abnormal Psychology*, **90**, 439–447.

Eden, D. (1982). Critical job events, acute stress and strain: a multiple interrupted time series. *Organizational Behavior and Human Performance*, **30**, 312–329.

Ekehammer, B. (1974). Interactionism in personality from a historical perspective. *Psychological Bulletin*, **81**, 1026–1058.

Fineman, S. and Payne, R. (1981). Role stress—a methodological trap? *Journal of Occupational Behaviour*, **2**, 51–64.

Fleming, R. (1984). Toward an integrative approach to the study of stress. *Journal of Personality and Social Psychology*, **46**, 939–949.

Folkman, S. (1984). Personal control and coping process: a theoretical analysis. *Journal of Personality and Social Psychology*, **46**, 839–852.

Gray-Tofts, P. and Anderson, J.G. (1981). The nursing stress scale: development of an instrument. *Journal of Behavioral Assessment*, **3**, 11–23.

Green, S.B., Sauser, W.I., Jr, Fagg, T.N. and Champion, C.H. (1981). Shortcut methods for deriving behaviorally anchored rating scales. *Educational and Psychological Measurement*, **41**, 761–775.

Hogan, R. and Hogan, J.C. (1982). Subjective correlates of stress and human performance. In E. A. Alluisi and E. A. Fleishman (eds), *Human Performance and Productivity*, Volume 3 (Hillsdale, NJ: Lawrence Erlbaum).

Holmes, T.H. and Rahe, R.H. (1967). The social readjustment rating scale. *Journal of Psychosomatic Research*, **11**, 213–218.

Jackson, S.E. and Schuler, R.S. (1985). A meta-analysis and conceptual critique of research on role ambiguity and role conflict in work settings. *Organizational Behavior and Human Performance*, **36**, 16–78.

Jacobs, R., Kafry, D. and Zedeck, S. (1980). Expectations of behaviorally anchored rating scales. *Personnel Psychology*, **33**, 595–640.

Kahn, R.L., Wolfe, D.M., Quinn, R.P., Snoek, J.D. and Rosenthal, R.A. (1964). *Organizational Stress: Studies in Role Conflict and Ambiguity* (New York: John Wiley).

Kanner, A.D., Coyne, J.C., Schaefer, C. and Lazarus, R.S (1981). Comparison of two modes of stress measurement: daily hassles and uplifts versus major life events. *Journal of Behavioral Medicine*, **7**, 1–35.

Kyriacou, C. and Sutcliffe, J. (1978). Teacher stress: prevalence sources, and symptoms. *British Journal of Educational Psychology*, **48**, 159–167.

Lazarus, R.S. (1966). *Psychological Stress and the Coping Process* (New York: McGraw-Hill).

Lazarus, R.S. (1984). Puzzles in the study of daily hassles. *Journals of Behavioral Medicine*, **7**, 375–383.

Lazarus, R.S. and Cohen J.B. (1977). Environmental stress. In I. Altman and J.F. Wohlwill (eds), *Human Behavior and the Environment: Current Theory and Research* Volume 2 (New York: Plenum Press), pp. 89–127.

Lazarus, R.S. and Delongis, A. (1983). Psychological stress and coping in aging. *American Psychologist*, **38**, 245–254.

Lazarus, R.S. and Launier, R. (1978). Stress-related transactions between person and environment. In W.A. Pervin and M. Lewis (eds), *Perspectives in Interactional Psychology* (New York: Plenum Press), pp. 287–327.

Magnusson, D. and Stattin. H. (1981). Methods for studying stressful situations. In H.W. Krohne and L. Laux (eds), *Achievement, Stress and Anxiety* (Washington, DC: Hemisphere Publications).

McGrath, J.G. (1976). Stress and behavior in organizations. In M.D. Dunnette (ed.), *Handbook of Industrial and Organizational Psychology* (Chicago: Rand-McNally), pp. 1351–1395.

Rizzo, J.R., House, R.J. and Lirtzman, S.I. (1970). Role conflict and ambiguity in complex organizations. *Administrative Science Quarterly*, **15**, 150–163.

Sarason, I.G. (1984). Stress, anxiety, and cognitive interference: reactions to tests. *Journal of Personality and Social Psychology*, **46**, 929–938.

Schuler, R.J. (1980). Definition and conceptualization of stress in organizations. *Organizational Behavior and Human Performance*, **25**, 184–215.

Shirom, A. (1982). What is organizational stress? a facet analytic conceptualization. *Journal of Occupational Behavior*, **3**, 21–37.

Shirom, A. (1985). Student's stress. Unpublished manuscript, Graduate School of Management, UCLA, Los Angeles.

Smith, P.C. and Kendall, L.M. (1963). Retranslation of expectations: an approach to the construction of unambiguous anchors for rating scales. *Journal of Applied Psychology*, **47**, 149–155.

Tausig, M. (1982). Measuring life events. *Journal of Health and Social Behavior*, **23**, 52–64.

Tellenback, S., Brenner, S.D. and Lofgren, H. (1983). Teacher stress: exploratory model building. *Journal of Occupational Psychology*, **56**, 19–33.

Tracy, L. and Johnson, T.W. (1983). Measurement of role stress: dimensionality of scale items. *Social Behavior and Personality*, **11**, 1–17.

Van Harrison, R. (1978). Person–environment fit and job stress. In C.L. Cooper and P. Payne, (eds), *Stress at Work* (New York: John Wiley), pp. 175–209.

Weiss, H.M., Ilgen, D.R. and Sharbaugh, M.E. (1982). Effects of life and job stress on information search behaviors of organizational members. *Journal of Applied Psychology*, **67**, 60–66.

5

Methodological Factors in the Investigation of Stress and Health at Work: the Development of the Epidemiological Problem Analysis Approach

Shirley Fisher

1. Introduction

Within the last decade there has been a plethora of research articles, reviews and books on stress at work. The topic is of both practical and theoretical interest. The practical interest arises because stressful work environments are likely to create mental states not conducive to efficient work and because absenteeism through unhappiness or ill health is both expensive and counterproductive.

The study of stress at work provides a microcosm of the methodological difficulties of investigating stress in general life contexts. In addition however, there are special difficulties due to the constrained circumstances which are encountered in work environments and due to the nature of the populations who 'visit' these environments on a daily basis. Perhaps one useful way of looking at it is by analogy with a group of animals who have stopped being free ranging hunter-gatherers and whose means of staying alive is to go to one of a variety of existing specialized locations to encounter particular psychological environments. There they join a tribe of similarly disposed individuals and perform activities of a predetermined kind for about 8 hours of every day, for about 5 days a week, in order to acquire tokens with which to purchase the means for survival. The rules and restrictions, which are part-determined by the nature of the product and part-determined by the 'tribe' who work on the product, act as a set of constraints on the individual's life. Similarly, the pressures created by the need to be productive and competitive create demands.

The work environment can be defined by physical environmental factors (noise, heat, dirt, pollution, vibration, etc). It can also be specified by location and accomodation factors: there may be open-plan or closed-room systems; different room arrangements, etc. There will be a number of psychosocial factors directly determined by acommodation constraints and by organizational structure (*see* Moos, 1988).

The total effect of the work on the individual also includes consideration of the nature of the task. In the case of physical activity, energy expenditure expresses the number of physical actions, but the total demand includes the time period during which these actions must be performed. Thus factors such as cycle time have been found to be factor in work stress for blue-collar workers (see Frankenhaeuser and Gardell, 1976).

Information load may be similarly expressed as a function of the ratio of the number of decisions over time. Thus deadlines, however imposed, act as pacers which force a greater density of mental activity in a period of time and this may directly influence work stress. Friedman *et al.* (1958) demonstrated that cholesterol levels in tax accountants in the USA, increase towards the end of the tax year and are associated with perceived work-load.

It may not just be the task characteristics which determine directly the stress levels in operation. First, the total situation must be taken into account. This includes work posture, frequency of required repetitive movements and other ergonomic considerations. The worker who experiences discomfort due to postural position whilst engaged in processing the product may become irritable and experience raised stress levels (see Frankenhaeuser and Gardell, 1976).

Secondly, the modulating qualities of the total task may vary. The task may involve constant interruptions, as in office work where telephones, computer messages and unexpected visits create distracting working environments. Laboratory based research by Mandler (1975) provides a basis for hypothesizing that interruptive events are likely to be associated with raised arousal which may in some cases translate into anxiety.

The simultaneous occupation of different 'roles' at work may increase the risk of such interruptive conditions. The individual who acts as a secretary and as a typist may find two daily streams of demand imposed. Not only does proficiency at one often imply delays or errors in the other, but there may be a constant interruption, due to the demands of one, on performance of the other and vice versa.

Individuals may also occupy simultaneous roles in life. The work role may need to be integrated with the domestic role. Equally work may create domestic problems, as in situations where the individual works anti-social hours or where the organizational structure does not allow the individual time or planning for domestic matters. Similarly, domestic problems may create an attentional focus at work and may be work-created.

Above all these considerations is the issue of how work functions in the life of the individual. It provides a reason for life; a target for structuring daily routines; a means of judging personal esteem; a means for wealth and influence in society; a source of social relationships. The effect of job loss has been testament to those complex needs that work fulfils in the lives of individuals (e.g. *see* Jahoda, 1979).

Thus the effects of work on the individual may reflect many levels of influence. There are direct work-environment effects, task effects, task setting and accommodation effects, psychosocial effects and effects which can only be understood in terms of how the task functions for the individual in the total context of his or her life.

Life stress research has increasingly emphasized the importance of personal meanings determined by experimental and situational factors (e.g., *see* Fisher, 1984, 1986, 1988). Thus, the reactions which result from different work environments must be understood in terms of *contexts*. Externally paced assembly work may be associated with raised anxiety but is less likely to be associated with anxiety if it is paid on a piece-work basis (*see* Broadbent, 1982). One explanation is that if the individual is receiving money for pacing, this offsets the direct effects of the uncontrolled paced demand levels by creating a re-interpretation of prevailing discomforts.

The problem for the scientist wishing to study stress at work is how to represent the complex interplay of factors. If work conditions are to be improved then it may be essential to try to identify regular recurring elements of situations where there is evidence of job strain. The search for common denominators responsible for main effects has revealed interesting factors such as role overload, poor person–environment fit, adverse demand and control levels. Yet the methodology of investigations in stress at work is frequently so different from that of other scientific contexts, that clear conclusions are difficult. This is partly because of the constraints that operate on stress at work studies and partly because of the intrinsic difficulties of setting up experimental paradigms or conducting comparative studies.

The aim of this chapter is to provide an opportunity to discuss and identify some of the methodological problems in investigations of stress at work. The general focus is not on attacking individual research efforts but rather on building the beginnings of a research methodology. At the very least, identifying some of the problems in advance should help the potential investigator.

2. Problems with the investigation of stress in life situations

A pre-requisite for the study of stress in any situation is that there is an acceptable definition of the term. In fact this is not easily met as a requirement in many stress investigations. Fisher (1986) argued that stress remains a complex umbrella term with varying focuses on the environment, the individual and sometimes the response pattern. Thus stress might be considered to be 'out there'—an 'intense level of every day life'—or an interactional concept depending on personal factors. In the former sense, stress is a condition of the environment which creates disequilibrium— the individual becomes too hot, too cold, or there is too much noise, etc. In the latter case the individual personally creates the ingredients of the perceived stress, because of high ambitions relative to capacity. Thus 'one man's stress can be another man's challenge'. The novice parachute jumper, relative to an experienced counterpart, would be expected to report more stress prior to the jump because of the uncertainty associated with the outcome of the jump and because of the lack of cognitive information concerning likely capability. The executive may differ from the shop-floor worker in coping with a problem at work because of greater facility for influencing or controlling the situation. Irrespective of whether 'control' is an important feature for its own sake, it provides the means of coping with problems.

Threats which are sometimes prevalent in work stress involve status and prestige. These threats need to be understood in terms of the underlying ambitions that drive them. Fear of public humiliation or of being left behind in the promotion stakes, may be driven by the prevalence of powerful ambitions to be successful. The motive may be success in its own right and the personal esteem which may result, or it may relate to the instrumentality of success in gaining monetary rewards, power over life and hence long-term gains in terms of comforts and self-esteem.

Mills (1973) investigated the raised incidence of suicide and anorexia nervosa in adolescents and argued that the pressures of a modern capitalist economy could be responsible for creating aims that could not always be fulfilled. Thus, the individual accepts non-achievable aims as fundamental. This would suggest that the sources of threat are created for the individual by the larger context in which he or she lives.

Even so, Atkinson and Feather (1966) provided an indication of a possible additional influence of personality factors. They identified 'need achievers' who enjoyed tasks of moderate difficulty but would not persist with simple tasks where success would be inevitable, nor with complex tasks where success was impossible. By contrast 'fear of failure' individuals prefer tasks in which success is seen as inevitable or complex tasks where failure is inevitable and therefore where there is protection against the consequence of failure.

Work environments may provide theatres for these kinds of pressures to be operative. However, generally, investigations emphasize common denominators of the *stimulus qualities* of work environments. The change towards emphasis on personal meanings implies some analysis of work environments in terms of the problems experienced by individuals.

3. The changing factors in stress at work

One important implication for the study of stress in work environments is that work conditions are changing rapidly as a result of the impact of economic and technological factors. Thus, there is not a stable environment with which to examine sources of threat; the sources will change across time. One aspect of new technology is the speeding up of the rate of change.

Before the advent of machines, work on a product implied direct use of energy and skill. The advent of machines reduced the effects of physical fatigue and replaced it with machine-related stresses: environments became noisy, hot, dirty, etc. Study of these stresses and their effects on the performance of tasks and the health and safety of the operators become a major topic in psychological research, with obvious applications for design and selection. These stresses initially affected blue-collar workers. However, the advent of World War II, with the need for men to manoeuvre submarines or fly fighter aircraft in difficult environmental conditions whilst under attack, gave further impetus to studies of man–machine interaction in stressful conditions (see Davis, 1948).

The introduction of automation distanced the worker from the product and changed the environment in which he or she operated in such a way as to reduce many environmental stresses. An immediate impact of automation was, however, to create new stresses. Automated environments frequently require fault detection, involving the monitoring of machines for occasional signs of failure. The capital-intensive environment created is frequently boring, characterized by low density information with emphasis on immediate detection of the occasional event.

The monitor of machines in automated environments also has low control over the processing of the product but perhaps high control over how he or she spends time, provided the criterion is met that no faults are missed. Thus technological advances in industry change many factors intrinsic to the work environment simultaneously.

The introduction of computer technology and fast communication systems has produced another step-function change in the work environment. First, there is the possibility of information overload because of the reduced time factor and the increased capacity for multi-channel storage facility. Second, there is the new mechanics of keyboard tasks. The operator of a keyboard system may become a 'mental assembly line' worker, keying in information all day. In Australia, repetitive strain injury produced by such tasks is a legitimate condition for seeking industrial compensation (see Wallace and Buckle, 1987). Equally, the continuous demand of data-input tasks may create raised stress levels which persist after work hours. (See Frankenhaeuser and Johansson, 1982).

The introduction of computer tasks has also created new sources of problems. First, those who are employed as programmers may encounter daily frustrations and interruptions when systems crash or programs do not run effectively (*see* Nishiyama *et al.*, 1984). Second, an office computer package may seem threatening to those who have to use it but lack the knowledge for its correct use.

The use of word-processing systems may not have freed the operator from raised demand. In all probability the time saved on editing does not create rest breaks; demand expands to meet the savings. Also, changes in jurisdiction may occur, and these are likely to be complex. There is the possibility that the skilled operator perceives raised personal control. Files and file names are personally created and the operator has increased jurisdiction over the use of the material stored. However, the 'mental assembly line' operator may be paced by events and have less control over how time is spent at work.

The introduction of computer technology and fast communication systems could be argued to have produced a further step function change in features of the work environment. First, there is the increased possibility of high demand leading to overload. Computer use involves fast inputting, fast storage and often parallel activity. Research has identified periods of post-work stress characterized by high catecholamine levels (*see* Frankenhaeuser and Johansson, 1982). In addition, reports of eye strain, tension headaches and repetitive strain injury (RSI) are commonly associated with high levels of computer use (e.g., Nishiyama *et al.*, 1984).

The introduction of computerized technology also creates new sources of problems. Those who are employed as programmers may encounter daily frustrations and interruptions when software bugs occur or systems crash. As the focus of office work orientates increasingly around computerized systems, there is increased pressure on the personnel involved to maintain systems or create output on time. Half of the computer operators in the study of 437 VDT operators by Nishiyama *et al.* (1984) reported stress such as long writing times, crashes and errors and adverse effects of repetitive work.

Finally, relatively little is known about the impact of 'robotization', where robotic technology frees the worker from many more aspects of the task at work. The worker may be increasingly shifted to the position of the 'unemployed wealthy', needing to

leisure which can replace the functions of the workplace in providing purpose.
Perhaps understanding the possible threats of robotization will require greater understanding of why we all 'love to hate work'.

4. Methodological difficulties in studies on stress and health at work

Against a background of the rapidly changing demands of work, there are changed
requirements for the researcher. Some of the special problems which occupational
stress research presents to the prospective investigator are considered against the background described above. Whilst some of these problems are particularly pertinent to
occupational settings, some of the problems are true of all studies involving stress in
natural or artificial psychological environments. Again, the intention is not to attack
particular research projects but rather to provide some general guide-lines as to main
methodological difficulties and possible solutions.

The difficulties with conducting comparative studies

Most scientific endeavours involve comparative data. The experimental group is
compared with a control group. Only on some occasions is this possible in occupational seetings. Generally, a comparison group even within the same job setting is
likely to differ in a number of ways and may involve self-selection or promotion
factors. Many studies simply report the characteristics of a single group of individuals
in a particular environment or involve between-task comparisons within the same
group.

Very often the lack of an adequate comparison group constrains the interpretation of
findings. For example, if in a hypothetical case 60% of police officers on patrol
reported job stress, this might imply a negative effect. However, if 90% of police in
office work report job stress, this would create the impression that patrol work is better
in this respect. If we also knew that 98% of the general working population reported
job stress then police work appears as a relatively *less* stressed job.

A very good beginning to any work study is therefore the obtaining of normative
data for comparison with the population to be studied. Epidemiological data which
indicates, for example, high suicide rates, absenteeism, illness levels or cardiovascular
disease levels, would provide a very good starting position for a study of stress at work,
especially where comparisons with population norms can be made.

Self-selection processes

Two processes are involved in job selection. First, the employer attempts to attract
prospective applications most likely to fulfil job requirements. Since the employer can
choose between applicants, one factor which will determine features of the workers in
a particular group concerns the employer's concept of what is desirable.

In an unpublished study conducted for a selection agency concerned with employees for banking, Fisher designed a set of questions which best represented what employers looked for in employees. The data on which this was based was obtained from score patterns of executive bankers and bank managers in local branches. It was expected that the predominant feature would be intelligence and business acumen. In fact the dominant (most frequently produced) item was 'a good personal appearance'. This was ranked first on the ordering of attributes by the majority of employers. 'Conversational style and personal skill' was ranked second. Thus, unexpectedly, bank employers were selecting according to appearance and personality. In turn this would mean that the appearance factor was the primary filter which produced the population of workers in that particular environment. The underlying rationale was that people who appear well-dressed and have personal skills will be able to cope with the public who are intimately concerned with financial transactions on which ultimately much bank profit depends.

By contrast, in the police, ability to cope with criminals and offenders dictates the importance of height and strength. A comparable study showed that the height of the prospective policeman was important and that second to this was fitness. The rationale of not having lean muscular, criminals being confronted by short, fat policemen should be obvious to most people!

However, employer choice creates a problem for between-group comparison. Suppose the police who happened to be in office work were compared with equivalent banking clerics. The investigators might in fact be comparing tall, muscular individuals with well-dresssed, personable individuals. What remains unknown is the sorts of personal characteristics which are associated with these differences.

Secondly, employee selection operates. The individual applying for a job is perhaps responding to advertisements which characterize the features of the job: more extraverted personalities might for example be attached to the armed services and the police. The possibility remains that stress-creation or stress-sensitivity are also part of the employee selection process. Thus Carruthers (1974) reported a high noradrenaline based 'arousal jag' in racing car drivers and argued that it was self-selected and that individuals who did not win races might indulge in risk behaviour to achieve raised arousal levels.

One implication therefore, is that we are studying the kinds of individuals who actively gravitate to a particular work environment. The values which are held by the person will feature in the attraction process. It would follow that 'job drift' is likely too. Less competent or less adequate individuals may gravitate to less attractive work environments and may be misfits in terms of not necessarily finding a work environment which is congenial. Identifying 'job drift' as compared with desirable and actively selected components of work, may be more critical for studies involving less attractive and less well-paid grades of work.

Because of these problems, between-job comparisons are difficult and might be replaced by cultural comparisons of the same job (e.g., compare North American, British and European teachers or police). Perhaps better, is to use longitudinal studies or repeated measures designed to look at the changing pattern of responses in work conditions. This could be done with, for example, studies of the stresses imposed by new technology, where periods before and after change can be established for comparison.

The semantic issues and self-report data

The dependent variables in studies of stress at work are the same as in most stress investigations but for many practical reasons involve heavy emphasis on self-report. The self-report data is obtained by means of scales, dichotic (yes/no) decisions or by endorsement of items on pre-established analogue scales. An important assumption is that respondents know what the question means or have an understanding of the concept involved. In particular, a person might be asked about the 'job strain', 'burnout', 'demand', 'overload', 'control', 'workload', 'autonomy', 'discretionality' or 'participation'. A key aspect is whether one individual is using these terms in the same way as another individual. Even more important is that an individual who reports a particular state or source of stress (e.g., overload) should not differ in the use and understanding of the term from an individual who does not report it.

In a recent set of studies of 'homesickness' in boarding school children and students, it was necessary to divide the subjects according to whether or not they had experienced it. This raised the issue of whether there would be high concordance on meaning between 'sufferers' and 'non-sufferers'. It was intuitively plausible that sufferers would have a more detailed knowledge of the experience.

Written definitions were obtained as a pre-requisite to the study and component elements were classified and agreed by all three investigators. Some definitions were long with many component phrases: "it means missing home and your mother and father and wishing you had never come here"; others were short, "depressed because of leaving home". The most frequently reported elements occurred first: "missing home", "missing family" or "missing friends". A plethora of other symptoms, from crying to eating problems and dizziness, was produced with less concordance and low frequency. Fortunately, the correlation between frequency of reported items for homesick and non-homesick groups were high— $+0.7- +0.8$—and there was no foundation for the assumption that the two groups differed in the conceptual understanding of the term. Such semantic checks are necessary in the context of job stress investigations.

Self-report data may also reflect the underlying methodology. As part of the study of homesickness, Fisher *et al.* (1984) provided a diary for the recording of daily problems. When the term homesickness was not actually provided for endorsement, only 18% of a population spontaneously reported it. However, in a later study using the same diary format but with the term provided for endorsement, over 70% of subjects indicated the experience. With one exception, 60–70% incidence has been consistently found in all studies (*see* Fisher, 1988). This is a remarkable difference dictated by the presence or absence of the critical term.

Interpreting the evidence

'Effort after meaning'

Many studies of job stress involve recall of factors in the workplace. Recall is influenced by mood state (e.g., *see* Lloyd and Lishmen, 1975), but the relationship between what is recalled and mood state is complex. Recall of properties of the surrounding environment at work as a function of mood state now needs careful investigation in a work setting. It is possible that self-confirming loops are set up such that negative encounters at home or at work create *selectivity* in recall of the properties of aspects of the work environment. Thus the person already depressed finds negative aspects of the work environment to report.

'Effort after meaning' is a phrase familiar to researchers on life events in coronary heart disease and provides a basis for major problems in attempts to link illness such as cardiovascular disease to provoking and precipitating factors. Patients who are ill may try to justify their illness by over-reporting for example, stressful life events in the immediately preceding months. It is not inconceivable that adverse aspects of work environments might be reported in this way by those already upset. Thus, perhaps a domestic problem creates a precondition for selectivity in reporting adverse effects of stress at work.

Correlational data

A major problem recognized by most researchers is that correlations do not imply causation. Because more car drivers wearing car seat belts are likely to have car accidents than drivers not wearing seat belts, this should not be taken to imply that wearing a seat belt causes a car accident.

Even if a causal link can be hypothesized, the direction of the link remains unknown: perhaps A causes B; B causes A or there is some third factor C which affects both A and B. Therefore an established relationship between work conditions and disorder needs an experimental manipulation for confirmation. If workers in isolated environments are more depressed, it is possible that depression creates isolation (lack of motivation to find ways of socializing), that the effect of isolation is to increase depression, or that a third factor operates. One solution is to try to vary the isolating condition which causes depression in an experimental design. At least the alternative explanations should be stated in research reports.

Frequently, experimental manipulations are difficult in work environments for practical reasons. The researcher may need to find evidence in the laboratory to support the observation in the work setting. Frankenhaeuser and colleagues frequently use techniques such as this. Even so, the hypothesis of causal association, although strengthened, is weakened to the extent of validity problems. A better technique is to seek comparative data where possible.

'Time-locking' of stress and ill health

One of the greatest problems which occurs in all fields of stress and health investigation, is time-locking the occurrence of the stressful condition to the occurrence of the disorder. If, for example, a person is passed over for promotion and later develops heart disease, cancer or an ulcer, the temptation is to make the intuitively plausible causal link. However, the developing illness may proceed and even may have *caused* the conditions that led to, for example, incompetence resulting in lack of promotion. Some estimates now suggest that cancer cells may be in existence up to 20 years before a lump or symptom is noticed. The precondition for coronary heart disease may have been initiated long before the precipitant occurred. Bradley (1988) indicates the possible occurrence of diabetic disorder long before the symptoms are noticed.

A strong case for proposing a causal relationship is when a number of people in a particular kind of working environment show signs of similar disorder or illness. It could be assumed then that the probability of them all developing the disorder spontaneously and creating the stressful condition at work is low. Nevertheless, spontaneous groupings of ailments in locations are known in epidemiological studies and it remains possible that some physical, geographical and psychological factor outside the workplace is responsible, or that personal communication between and within working communities sets up expectations which precipitate the problem.

5. The approach of Epidemiological Problem Analysis

A prevailing tendency has been to investigate 'common denominators' of sources of strain in work environments. Thus investigators may examine overload in executives, autonomy in blue-collar workers, etc. This approach pre-judges what the problems are likely to be and introduces the labelling problem (discussed earlier), namely that individuals may attribute the cause of a strain to a readily available label.

A different approach taken in this laboratory has been what might be described as 'Epidemiological Problem Analysis' (EPA). It is assumed that work environments create daily stresses or hassles which vary in magnitude or persistence. The profile of hassles provides a description of job strain which characterizes a particular job. It is then possible to link indices of strain to the nature of the key problems being reported.

The basic approach is to obtain, by way of weekly problem diaries (illustrated in Figure 5.1), an account of daily problems, together with an indication of periods spent worrying about a problem. Classification of problems provides a crude index of major sources of strain. A fundamental distinction can be made between 'work' and 'domestic' problems and the balance can be assessed for different work environments. A pilot study of sources of stress in the police has for example shown that those on shiftwork report a high proportion of domestic problems (Fisher, to be published). Equally, a comparable diary study with secondary school teachers has shown that approximately 30% of the problems reported by school teachers are domestic in origin.

Further distinctions can then be made in terms of the *sources* of work and domestic strain. For teachers, classroom discipline, preparation time and overload are major sources. For the police, sources include overload, antisocial hours and organization within the force (not dangers associated with crime). Different jobs may have different profiles but also have common sources which can be linked to job strain.

A further development has been the analysis of the problem/worry ratios for different categories of problem. Worry levels are assessed from the reported worry periods for each problem (see Figure 5.1) and the resulting ratio of problems/worries for a particular problem category (e.g., overload) provides an assessment of how intense the effect is in terms of creating mental pre-occupation.

DAY Tuesday   TIME 11 am.   MONTH March   YEAR 1987

Write a description of each problem you can remember for this day. Up to three possible problems may be recorded. Each day will probably vary. Put an 'X' in the cell against the time scale when you remember worrying about the problem. The number of times you remember worrying will vary from day to day (an example is provided so you can check that you understand the instructions).

	A	B	C
Midnight			
1 am			
2 am			
3 am			
4 am			
5 am		X	
6 am		X	X
7 am		X	X
8 am		X	X
9 am			X
10 am			
11 am			
12 am			
1 pm			
2 pm	X		
3 pm			
4 pm			
5 pm			
6 pm			
7 pm			X
8 pm			X
9 pm	X		X
10 pm	X	X	X
11 pm	X	X	X
12 pm	X	X	X

Describe problem here ....   A   Work overload high
Too much marking and no preparation time
....   B   Marking is dreadful, no
time left for family life   Feeling depressed
....   C   Health – feel run down and
ill. Feel very depressed. Hate this job

Figure 5.1. Illustration of the problems and worries reported by a secondary school teacher in one day in a diary format.

alysis of the response of children to the first two weeks of a new boarding
Fisher *et al.* (1984) found this approach to be useful in that although the
children reported more 'school' problems than 'home' problems, the problem/worry
ratios showed that more pre-occupation occurred for 'home' problems (low pro-
blem/worry ratios). Therefore, the pupils were shown to face a plethora of school
stresses, but home difficulties were more intense and persistent in their effects. At least
one explanation is that 'home' problems are less easily controlled because of the
distance factor (*see* Fisher, 1988).

In an analysis of the sources of work stress, demand and control have been identified
as interactive variables likely to influence the risk of strain and ill health (Karasek,
1979), especially cardiovascular disease (Karasek, 1987). High demand and low control
are more likely to be associated with increased risk of cardiovascular disease. However,
control and demand may have different connotations in different job contexts. For an
executive it might mean being able to convince the board that a certain procedure is
desirable. For a blue-collar worker it might mean being able to switch off the assembly
line or decide when processing the product is to occur.

An answer is to define demand and control with respect to the *features of problems
presented by particular groups*. The diary respondents themselves decide how much
demand a particular problem creates and how much control there is over the problem.
Demand is defined by the characteristics of a daily problem. The ability to cope with
and limit the problem defines *control*. Thus, the person whose computer breaks down
may, if he or she is powerful, purchase a new one. The person who is not powerful
struggles for days with the consequences of the problem (work does not meet deadlines, time wasted contacting manufacturer, etc). The low control–high demand
problem should (*a*) recur in the diary; (*b*) be associated with low problem/worry ratios
(i.e., high number of worry periods per problem).

The development of this approach has just begun but the results of some pilot studies with the police, students and teachers at secondary schools have shown the following.

1. The anticipated source of stress on a person in a particular work environment is
often not the one most reported by that person.
2. Domestic problems (sometimes work-created) occupy a significant proportion of
total problems reported at work.
3. Recurring problems are generally associated with high demand and low control.
4. Low value problem/worry ratios (including high mental pre-occupation) are associated with high demand and low control problem assessments.
5. There are high negative correlations between demand and problem/worry ratios
and high positive correlations between control and problem worry ratios.

The possible link with ill health is that certain work problems, especially those associated with high demand and low control, are associated with excessive worrying
(often during work hours). The direct effects are raised levels of stress hormones with
increased risk of structural damage or immunosuppression.

Thus this approach based on the epidemiology and microstructure of reported daily
problems does not pre-judge the sources of stress, provides a realistic basis of assessment
of stress in work environments and reflects job and person characteristics. It prevents

some of the main problems identified with research on stress at work as reported above. This may be an approach which could be developed and linked with other dependent variables such as mood and motivational state and physical health.

References

Atkinson, J.W. and Feather, N.T. (eds) (1966). *A Theory of Achievement Motivation* (New York: John Wiley).

Bradley, C. (1988). Stress and diabetic disorder. In S. Fisher and J. Reason (eds), *The Handbook of Life Stress Cognition and Health* (Chichester: John Wiley).

Broadbent, D.E. (1982). Some relations between clinical and occupational psychology. Paper delivered at the *20th International Congress of Applied Psychology*, Edinburgh, 25–31 July.

Carruthers, M. (1974). *The Western Way of Death* (London: Davis Poynter).

Davis, D.R. (1948). *Pilot Error*, Air Publication No. 3139a (London: HMSO).

Fisher, S. (1984). *Stress and the Perception of Control* (London: Lawrence Erlbaum).

Fisher, S. (1986). *Stress and Strategy* (London: Lawrence Erlbaum).

Fisher, S. (1988). Stress, control strategies and the risk of disease: a psychobiological model. In S. Fisher and J. Reason (eds), *The Handbook of Life Stress Cognition and Health* (Chichester: John Wiley).

Fisher, S., Frazer, N. and Murray, K. (1984). The transition from home to boarding school: A diary study of spontaneously reported problems and worries in boarding school children. *Journal of Environmental Psychology*, **4**, 211–221.

Frankenhaeuser, M. and Gardell, B. (1976). Underload and overload in working life: outline of a multidisciplinary approach. *Journal of Human Stress*, **2**, 35–46.

Frankenhaeuser, M. and Johansson, J. (1982). Stress at work: psychobiological and psychosocial aspects. Paper presented at the *20th International Congress of Applied Psychology*, Edinburgh, 25–31 July.

Friedman, M., Rosenman, R. and Carroll, V. (1958). Changes in the serum cholesterol and blood clotting time in men subjected to cyclic variation of occupational stress. *Circulation*, **17**, 852–861.

Jahoda, M. (1979). The impact of unemployment in the 1930's and 1970's. *Bulletin of the British Psychological Society*, **32**, 309–314.

Karasek, R.A. (1979). Job demands, job decision latitude, and mental strain; implication for job redesign. *Administrative Science Quarterly*, **24**, 285–309.

Karasek, R.A. (1987). Control in the workplace and its health-related impacts. In S.L. Sauter and J.J. Hurrell, Jr. (eds). *Proceedings of NIOSH Sponsored Workshop on Worker Control and Job Stress* (Cincinnati: NIOSH).

Lloyd, G.C. and Lishman, W.A. (1975). Effect of depression on the speed of recall of pleasant and unpleasant experiences. *Psychological Medicine*, **1975**(5), 173–180.

Mandler. G. (1975). *Mind and Emotion* (New York: John Wiley).

Mills, I.H. (1973). Biological factors in international relations. In *The Year Book of World Affairs*, Volume 27 (London: The London Institute of World Affairs; Stevens and Sons).

Moos, R. (1988). Work as a human context. In S. Fisher and J. Reason (eds), *The Handbook of Life Stress, Cognition and Health* (Chichester: John Wiley).

Nishiyama, K., Nataseko, M. and Uehata, T. (1984). Health aspects of VDT operators in the newspaper industry. In E. Grandjean (ed.), *Ergonomics and Health in Modern Offices* (London: Taylor & Francis), pp. 113–118.

Wallace, M. and Buckle, P.W. (1987). Ergonomic aspects of neck and upper limb disorders. *International Reviews of Ergonomics*, **1**, 173–200.

6

Improving Measures of Worker Control in Occupational Stress Research

Daniel C. Ganster

1. Introduction

This chapter addresses several issues pertinent to the concept of control and its potential role in the occupational stress experience. While the notion of control has by no means been ignored in the work stress literature, I do not think that its conceptualization and operationalization have been adequately specified. In the next few pages I will sketch out a general model of control and some research questions that might be addressed.

2. Defining control

Control can be broadly defined as the ability to exert some influence over one's environment, presumably so that the environment becomes more rewarding or less threatening. More specifically, we can define control as the *belief* that one can influence the environment. Researchers have been concerned with the effects of perceived control over important outcomes for a long time (e.g., White, 1959; Rotter, 1966). While theorists such as White (1959) have suggested that there may be an intrinsic need to control the environment, others (Rodin *et al.*, 1980) have argued that the evidence suggests that the motivation for control stems from the belief that it ensures positive outcomes. Whichever is the case, there is rather compelling evidence that, in general, control is associated with myriad positive outcomes, and lack of control with various forms of ill health (see Miller, 1979; Thompson, 1981, for reviews). Furthermore, the evidence suggests that just the belief that one can exercise control may be sufficient to reduce stress when exposed to uncontrollable events (Gatchel, 1980).

Much of the evidence attesting to the importance of control in determining reactions to stressful events was generated from experimental research involving subhuman species, although more recent work has focused on humans ranging from children (Gunnar, 1980) to the elderly (Rodin and Langer, 1980). The implication of much of this literature for occupational stress is that control, or perception of control, may be a variable of central importance.

3. Control in the workplace

Some form of the control construct has been studied in a number of different areas of organizational research including participation in decision-making (Locke and Schweiger, 1979), job redesign (Hackman and Oldham, 1976), goal-setting (Latham and Yukl, 1976), and machine pacing (Hurrell, 1981). Perhaps the most explicit statement of the role of control in occupational stress, however, is Karasek's model of job demands and job decision latitude (Karasek, 1979). Given the centrality of the control construct in this work, Karasek's model merits some review.

Karasek (1979) postulated that stress results from the joint effects of job demands and the level of job decision latitude experienced by the worker. Specifically, job stress, or strain, occurs when the job demands are high and decision latitude is low. The model makes two predictions. First, stress increases as job demands are high and decision latitude is low. Second, incremental increases in competency are predicted to occur when the challenge of the situation (job demands) is matched with the individual's control in dealing with the challenge (decision latitude). Thus, when job demands and decision latitude are high, Karasek defines the job as 'active'. An active job is hypothesized to lead to the "development of new behaviour patterns both on and off the job" (Karasek, 1979, p. 288).

More recently, Karasek *et al.*, (1981) extended the model to the prediction of cardiovascular disease. Specifically, they hypothesized that regenerative processes occur in situations where a match exists between organizational demands and individual control. Thus, pathological consequences are predicted to occur only when high demands are accompanied by low control. Under conditions of high control, high job demands may be conducive to regeneration or the development of the individual's adaptability to environmental demands. From secondary analyses of national survey data from the USA and Sweden, Karasek and his colleagues concluded that strain, in fact, is a function of the interaction of job demands and job decision latitude (Karasek, 1979; Karasek *et al.*, 1981). The implication, of course, is that strain can be reduced by providing workers with more control, even though job demands remain high.

However, before we conclude that control actually buffers the stressful effects of high job demands, we need to make a closer inspection of Karasek's operationalization of control. Karasek defined job decision latitude as "the working individual's potential control over his tasks and his conduct during the working day" (Karasek, 1979, pp. 289–90). This construct has two factors: decision latitude and decision authority. The following items were used to operationalize decision authority in the US data (Quinn *et al.*, 1975):

1. Freedom of how to work.
2. Allows a lot of decisions.
3. Assist in one's own decisions.
4. Have a say over what happens.

These items combined seem to be representative of some general control at work. However, the measure is somewhat restrictive in that the items tap few different areas of personal control in the workplace. These items, moreover, are combined with the following ones to produce the measure of decision latitude:

1. High skill level required.
2. Required to learn new things.
3. Non-repetitive work.
4. Creativity required.

In the Swedish data, the operationalization of decision latitude is even more restrictive, consisting of the following items:

1. Skill level (in years of training/education) required.
2. Repetitive or monotonous work.
3. Expert rating of skill level required.

As an operationalization of the construct of control over one's environment at work, Karasek's job decision latitude measures appear to be flawed. As noted above, the items representing decision authority from the US data would seem to be relevant to a conception of control as the ability to influence one's environment, although they provide a rather limited assessment of this control. In the Swedish data, however, "expert rating of skill level required" hardly seems an adequate representation of personal control. And in both data sets the skill discretion items appear to measure a construct more akin to skill variety (Hackman and Oldham, 1976), general job complexity, or perhaps qualitative workload. One would expect higher level, more complex jobs to be characterized as having more decision authority (or control), and indeed Karasek found these two dimensions to be correlated; but skill level or complexity is not the same construct as personal control.

Given the very questionable measurement of control in Karasek's job decision latitude research, I doubt whether these findings tell us very much about the effects of control in the workplace. In sum, while there is a well developed body of basic experimental research which addresses the effects of control on stress-related outcomes, research in the organizational arena is poorly developed. Moreover, the basic literature suggests a number of questions which merit exploration in the occupational stress context.

Models of control

In this section I would like to discuss some possible causal pathways by which control might affect occupational stress. Figure 6.1 displays a general schematic model for control.

In this model control is seen as affecting job-related strain in three possible ways. Path A hypothesizes a direct effect of control on strain. This hypothesis essentially represents the "intrinsic motivation for control" theory (White, 1959), in which personal control over events enhances the individual's sense of personal competence and self-esteem. It is also possible that control has some direct effect on job demands (path C). If workers perceive that they have some control over events in their job, and if these perceptions are veridical, it is plausible to hypothesize that they will exercise

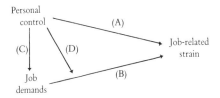

Figure 6.1 A general model of control.

this control in order to reduce job demands to a comfortable level. Job demands (stressors), in turn, are hypothesized to have some direct impact on job-related strain (path B). This path more or less represents the working hypothesis underlying most of the occupational stress literature. Thus, control is hypothesized to have an indirect effect on strain through its impact on job demands. Finally, as represented by path D, control may interact with job demands to affect strain. This last path represents the Karasek (1979) job decision latitude hypothesis. Clearly, these do not represent mutually exclusive hypotheses. However, given appropriate research designs, the relative effects of each of these pathways can be independently estimated. Below I would like to discuss several research questions that could be explored within this general framework.

Direct effects of control

Path A in Figure 6.1 asserts that personal control directly affects strain. The term 'strain' in this context is used quite broadly, and is meant to encompass both psychological and physiological reactions of the worker. These reactions would include such responses as anxiety, tension, depression and elevated levels of physiological and biochemical responses. The underlying assumption is that chronic strain has effects on mental and physical health.

That actual or perceived personal control has some direct effects on strain is a hypothesis that has been receiving some support for a long time. For example, Haggard (1943) found that physiological indicants of strain were reduced when subjects could control the onset and termination of aversive stimulation. Studies employing yoked controls suggest that it is the control itself which produces decrements in strain, and not a reduction in the duration or intensity of aversive stimulation. That is, unexercised control reduces strain. Research on control has examined a number of different types of stressors, such as electrical shocks (Szpiler and Epstein, 1976), loud noise (Glass and Singer, 1972), the administration of an intelligence test (Stotland and Blumenthal, 1964), cold pressors (McCaul, 1980) and aversive photographs (Geer and Maisel, 1972).

Why should control, even when it is not exercised, reduce the stressfulness of aversive or threatening events? Miller (1979) posits one explanation in the form of the 'Minimax hypothesis'. According to this explanation, an individual with a control response available believes that the situation will not become unbearable. With control, one will be able to minimize maximum danger. Thus, an individual with control will tolerate higher levels of stressful stimuli than one without control.

Some data in the occupational stress literature are consistent with the hypothesis that control has a direct effect on strain. For example, Caplan *et al.* (1975), in their study of 23 occupations, found participation to be one of the better predictors of job dissatisfaction and boredom. Margolis *et al.* (1974), with a national sample of workers, also found participation to be significantly related to job satisfaction and depressed mood. These and many other findings showing a relationship between participation and a variety of strain variables, while consistent with the main effect hypothesis of control, do not provide strong support for it. For one, these findings cannot rule out the explanation that participation may lead to a change in job demands which, in turn, leads to a reduction of strain. Evidence more suggestive of a Minimax mechanism was provided by Quinn (1972) and Cohen (1976), who found that mental health indicators were lower for workers who felt they were 'locked in' to stressful and dissatisfying jobs.

Indirect effects of control

As denoted by path C in Figure 6.1, workers with personal control may indeed influence the level of job demands that they face. Presumably, workers would either increase or decrease job demands to better suit their preferences. The resultant level of demands would then induce a lower level of strain. In this view, then, control does not lead directly to strain, but rather indirectly through its effects on experienced job demands. This hypothesis is also consistent with the person–environment fit model of job stress (Caplan *et al.*, 1975). In this model, job demands are hypothesized to be strain-inducing when there is a misfit between the level of the demand and the level desired by the worker. Control could thus decrease strain by allowing the worker to improve person-environment fit.

Is there evidence that when workers have control over demands they exercise that control to make their jobs less demanding? Unfortunately, there is not much experimental evidence that directly addresses this question. From survey studies there is suggestive evidence that more control leads to adjustments of job demands. For example, in the Caplan *et al.* (1975) survey, self-reports of participation are associated with better person–environment fit for job complexity and responsibility for persons. In addition, participation is negatively correlated with under-utilization of skills (one of the most important stressors found in the study) and with ambiguity about the future. While such data are suggestive of an indirect role for control, making causal inferences is tenuous at best. Because there was no experimental control, we cannot determine whether the relationships between participation and stressors are spurious. Additionally, while we might hypothesize that those who report more participation are apt to feel that they have more control over events at work, there are no data to indicate whether this is true.

Recently, Jackson (1983) reported a field experiment in which she randomly assigned 126 workers to either a condition in which they received increased participation in decision-making or a control condition. The participation manipulation consisted of instituting a new policy that staff meetings would be held twice a month. Participation in decision-making led to higher reported influence at both 6-month and

9-month post-tests. The only job demands or stressors that Jackson measured were role conflict and ambiguity, but both the manipulation of participation and the self-reports of influence were significantly negatively correlated with them, especially at the 9-month post-test. Again, these data are suggestive of an indirect effect of control on strain through job demands. But given the paucity of data on job demands, the evidence for the indirect effect is no more convincing than for a direct effect of influence on emotional strain ($r = -0.42$ in the 9-month post-test).

There is also evidence that workers with control will *increase* job demands. For example, studies of participation in the goal-setting process (Latham *et al.*, 1978) indicate that individuals tend to set higher and more difficult performance goals for themselves than would have been set by their supervisors. Whether these higher performance goals represent strain-inducing job demands we do not know.

Control as a moderator of job demands

Much of the experimental laboratory evidence regarding the effects of control suggests that control lessens the stressful impact of aversive stimuli. In this sense, findings can be viewed as supporting its role as a moderator variable. In the occupational stress literature, however, this hypothesis has not been much examined. As noted above, this was the thrust of Karasek's research, but his confounding of control with job complexity does not permit a clear interpretation of his data with regard to this hypothesis.

In many ways, control as a moderator of job demands is a compelling proposition. If control in some general sense were really to have such an effect, it implies that we might effectively intervene in the occupational setting by implementing methods of increasing workers' control over their job situation. Testing means of augmenting worker control might be a much more workable approach than the task of attempting to identify the important stressors in a given situation and devising ways of treating them. We should also note, as did Karasek (1979), that this model implies that pursuing the goals of reducing worker strain and increasing productivity are not incompatible. We reduce worker strain not by reducing demands (which presumably affect productivity), but by increasing control. As appealing as this hypothesis might be, I think we have very little convincing evidence that it is valid.

4. Research directions for control

Up to this point this cursory review of the control construct was designed to support the plausibility of two conclusions:

1. Control is potentially a variable of great importance in understanding occupational stress.

2. We do not know very much at all about the specific effects of control in the workplace.

In the remainder of this chapter I shall discuss some research questions and methodological issues that might be addressed concerning the construct of control.

Control domains

Workers can have varying levels of control over different aspects of their occupational environment. Below are different domains in which individuals might have control.

1. *Work tasks*. Can the individual determine the order in which tasks are completed as well as choosing among available methods for accomplishing them? Can the individual choose among a variety of tasks or projects? Can the individual influence the quality of his or her output?

2. *Work pacing*. Can the individual determine the pace of work, or is it controlled by machine? Can the individual determine the scheduling and duration of rest breaks? Can the individual increase or decrease the workload?

3. *Work scheduling*. Can the individual determine his or her working hours (flexitime) so that non-work demands can be better co-ordinated with work demands? Can vacations and other days off be taken when the individual desires? Does the worker have a choice of shift schedules?

4. *Physical environment*. Is the individual able to modify, decorate, or otherwise personalize his or her physical setting at work? Does the individual have some control over lighting, temperature, noise or privacy?

5. *Decision-making*. Does the individual have influence concerning organizational policies, goals or procedures?

6. *Other people*. Does the individual have control over the activities of others? Does he or she have some influence over the training of others or how they are evaluated?

7. *Mobility*. Does the individual perceive that he or she can leave the occupation or the employer? Or does the individual feel locked in to a particular job?

These areas represent some of the domains in which the worker might have control. If control at work is viewed as a multi-dimensional construct, several questions can be posed. Is control in some areas more important in determining strain than control in other areas? Does the importance of different domains of control vary systematically across different occupations or across different types of individuals? Does control in several domains cumulate to determine an individual's overall sense of being in control of their occupational life? Can control in one domain compensate for a lack of control in another domain?

This multi-dimensional perspective suggests a measurement strategy that attempts to tap employee perceptions of these various domains of control. It might be that different domains of control could have different impacts on strain because of the individual's attributions regarding why he or she does or does not have control. Abramson *et al.* (1978), for example, proposed an attributional reformulation of learned helplessness theory which posited that the effects of perceived uncontrollability are determined largely by why people think they lack control. Such control attributions are made on three orthogonal dimensions: (*a*) internal versus external; (*b*) stable versus unstable; and (*c*) global versus specific. There is some evidence that individuals who make internal, stable and global attributions regarding their lack of control are more likely to demonstrate generalized helplessness effects, depression and lowered self-esteem. It is possible that different types of control in the occupational setting might lead to systematic differences in attributions along these dimensions. This perspective suggests that we look not just at workers' perceptions of how much control they have but their attributions regarding the sources of that control.

Predictability versus control

Up to this point control has meant that the individual can actually influence aspects of the work environment—that is, that the individual has behavioural control. The individual can also have information about events at work even though he or she cannot influence them. This is sometimes referred to as informational control, or simply predictability. Clearly, the two are confounded in that behavioural control implies predictability. To the extent that you can control your workload, changes in your workload over time should be predictable. We should note the distinction between control and predictability because some theorists (e.g., Averill, 1973) have argued that it is the predictability inherent in control that accounts for all of the beneficial outcomes of control, and the unpredictability accompanying lack of control that explains all the negative outcomes. Consistent with this argument, Schulz and Hanusa (1980) found that for the elderly in an old people's home, visits on a predictable schedule were just as beneficial as were visits on a predictable schedule that were also controllable by the elderly residents.

Without reviewing all of the evidence regarding the differential effects of predictability and control, it would seem to be a worthy question in the occupational stress domain. If predictability accounts for at least some of the beneficial effects of control, the need for augmenting behavioural control might be obviated. It seems that this is a researchable question, and it requires that we discriminate between control and predictability either psychometrically or experimentally in research on occupational stress.

Moderators of control

The discussion thus far has treated control as something that is beneficial, something that either directly or indirectly leads to reductions in strain. It should be noted, however, that control (or predictability) is not necessarily always positive. Averill (1973) notes, for example, that some investigators have found little or no reduction in stress among subjects who have had control. Moreover, even in studies in which the majority of subjects showed reduced stress with control, typically 10–20% of subjects showed just the opposite reaction. That is, for some subjects control increased experienced stress. Averill (1973) concluded that in order to understand the effects of control on stress, one must account for the meaning of the control response in its context. One implication of Averill's conclusions is that we consider individual differences which might affect the desirability of behavioural control or predictability. Several potential constructs come to mind.

Having specific behavioural control responses in an occupational setting might be stressful if the individual perceives that exercising that control might lead to aversive consequences. Having influence over decisions at work and its concommitant responsibility might entail more threat to the individual than not having such influence if the individual is not confident in his or her ability to make the correct decisions. Thus, a job that leads to perceptions of high skill utilization for one individual may lead to perceptions of qualitative role overload for another. In a very general sense, someone who has a perception of high control in the occupational setting is more apt to have a sense of high responsibility for his or her occupational attainment. To an individual with generally low self-efficacy perceptions, low self-confidence or low self-esteem, high control could be generally stressful. Measures of self-esteem or perceived ability, then, might be expected to moderate the relationship between control and strain. In just the opposite sense, individuals with high levels of the Type A coronary-prone behaviour pattern might be expected to react more positively to increased control than do Type B's, and to react more negatively to losses of control.

Miller (1980) has suggested that the effects of predictability of stressful events will differ depending on the individual's characteristic coping style. She distinguishes between 'monitors', who generally cope by monitoring the details of the situation, and 'blunters', who attempt to blunt the effects of stressors by attending to distracting information. Miller and Mangan (1983) administered a scale which assesses self-reported preferences for information or distraction in stressful situations to patients about to undergo a stressful medical procedure. Some patients were provided with extensive predictive information about the surgery and others were not. They found evidence that providing information to blunters increased pulse rate and subjective distress while it decreased distress for monitors. As Miller (1980) has noted, the highly constrained circumstances of laboratory experiments on control and predictability may have masked the importance of individual differences such as coping style. Following Miller (1980), we might also suspect that in the complexity of occupational settings, the effects of such individual differences in response to control and predictability may be more pronounced than in laboratory studies.

Methodological considerations

There are a number of theoretical and practical implications of control in the work setting, and a host of questions that occupational stress researchers have yet to explore. I will end this discussion of control with a few thoughts about some general methodological issues involved with the investigation of control in the occupational stress context.

Perhaps the most urgent methodological need is for the development of a general psychometric measure for occupational control. Such a measure should incorporate items tapping the relevant domains of control, as enumerated above, and perhaps others as well. Ideally, the items in such a measure would discriminate between behavioural control and predictability. Survey studies using such an instrument could begin to address many of the research questions discussed in here. Moreover, a reliable psychometric measure of control would be valuable in experimental field studies in which control-related variables are manipulated. If nothing else, such a measure could serve as an important manipulation check on various interventions such as partici-pation in decision-making, flexitime, machine-versus self-pacing, and goal-setting.

Survey designs can address questions such as the importance of different control domains, the compensatory nature of different domains, and the general relationships among control, stressors, individual differences and strains. However, to estimate the causal pathways of Figure 6.1, experimental designs are needed. Specifically, in order to test the direct versus indirect effects of control, one would need to experimentally manipulate control while holding constant other job demands. By using reliable measures of job demands both before and after the control interventions, the indirect effects of control through job demands could be estimated. I would argue that deter-mining the effects of control on demands is important insofar as job demands may affect productivity (at least in the short-term). Managers are apt to be reluctant to endorse control-enhancing interventions without some reassurances regarding the effects of control on other factors related to productivity. Even more elegant designs could be used in specific contexts. For example, while yoked-control designs are commonly used in laboratory studies to hold exposure to stressors constant across behavioural control conditions, they are virtually unheard of in organizational settings. Research in the machine-pacing area, for example, might particularly benefit from such designs.

Finally, whether studies are experimental or not, it would be very useful for them to include a longitudinal component. Aside from the usual benefits that are generally attributed to longitudinal designs (though not always accurately), such designs could assess the effects of *losses* of control in addition to gains in control. This is potentially an important distinction, especially in the light of evidence which suggests that loss of control may have much more serious health consequences than never having had control at all (Mineka, 1982). Longitudinal designs could distinguish between those workers who lost control and those who never had it. Finally, the Wortman and Brehm (1975) integration of helplessness and reactance theories incorporates a specific time component. (For a full explanation of reactance theory, *see* Brehm 1972.) In their model, losses of control lead to reactance in the short-term, but continued loss of control leads to helplessness over time as individuals become resigned to their fate. Thus, where loss of control could lead to anger and increased behavioural activity in the short term, it could lead to passivity and depression in the long term. A cross-sectional design in which we cannot distinguish individuals who have lost or gained control, nor distinguish individuals who have recently lost or gained control from those who have had very stable control experiences, may underestimate the relation-ship of control to health outcomes.

References

Abramson, L.Y., Seligman, M.E.P. and Teasdale, J.D. (1978). Learned helplessness in humans: critique and reformulation. *Journal of Abnormal Psychology*, **87**, 49–74.

Averill, J.R. (1973). Personal control over aversive stimuli and its relationship to stress. *Psychological Bulletin*, **80**, 286–303.

Brehm, J.W. (1972). *Response to Loss of Freedom: A Theory of Psychological Reactance* (Morristown, NJ: General Learning Press).

Caplan, R.D., Cobb, S., French, J.R.P., Jr, Harrison, R.V. and Pinneau, S.R. (1975). *Job Demands and Worker Health*. US Department of Health, Education, and Welfare; Publication No. (NIOSH) 75–160.

Cohen, J. (1976). German and American workers: a comparative view of worker distress. *International Journal of Mental Health*, **5**, 138–147.

Gatchel, R.J. (1980). Perceieved control: A review and evaluation of therapeutic implications. In A. Baum and J. Singer (eds), *Advances in Environmental Psychology, Volume 2. Applications of Personal Control* (Hillsdale, NJ: Lawrence Erlbaum).

Geer, J.H. and Maisel, E. (1972). Evaluating the effect of the prediction control confound. *Journal of Personality and Social Psychology*, **23**, 314–319.

Glass, D.C. and Singer, J.E. (1972). *Urban Stress: Experiments on Noise and Social Stressors* (New York: Academic Press).

Gunnar, M. (1980). Contingent stimulation: a review of its role in early development. In S. Levine and H. Ursin (eds), *Coping and Health* (New York: Plenum).

Hackman, J.R. and Oldham, G. (1976). Motivation through the design of work: test of a theory. *Organizational Behavior and Human Performance*, **16**, 250–279.

Haggard, E.S. (1943). Experimental studies in affective processes: I. Some aspects of cognitive structure and active participation on certain automatic reactions during and following experimentally induced stress. *Journal of Experimental Psychology*, **33**, 257–284.

Hurrell, J. (1981). *Psychological, Physiological, and Performance Consequences of Paced Work: An Integrated Review* (Cincinnati, OH: National Institute for Occupational Safety and Health).

Jackson, S.E. (1983). Participation in decision making as a strategy for reducing job-related strain. *Journal of Applied Psychology*, **68**, 3–19.

Karasek, R. (1979). Job demands, job decision latitude, and mental strain: Implications for job redesign. *Administrative Science Quarterly*, **24**, 285–306.

Karasek, R., Baker, D., Marxer, F., Ahlbom, A. and Theorell, T. (1981). Job decision latitude, job demands, and cardiovascular disease: A prospective study of Swedish men. *American Journal of Public Health*, **71**, 694–705.

Latham, G., Mitchell, T. and Dossett, D. (1978). The importance of participative goal setting and anticipated rewards on goal difficulty, goal acceptance, and job performance. *Journal of Applied Psychology*, **63**, 163–171.

Latham, G. and Yukl, G. (1976). The effects of assigned and participative goal setting on performance and job satisfaction. *Journal of Applied Psychology*, **61**, 166–177.

Locke, E. and Schweiger, D. (1979). Participation in decision-making: one more look. In B.M. Staw (ed.), *Research in Organizational Behavior*, Volume 1 (Greenwich, CT: JAI Press).

Margolis, B.L., Kroes, W.H. and Quinn, R.P. (1974). Job stress: an unlisted occupational hazard. *Journal of Occupational Medicine*, **16**, 659–661.

McCaul, K.D. (1980). Sensory information, fear level, and reaction to pain. *Journal of Personality*, **48**, 394–404.

Miller, S.M. (1979). Controllability and human stress: method, evidence, and theory. *Behavior Research and Therapy*, **17**, 287–304.

Miller, S.M. (1980). When is a little information a dangerous thing? Coping with stressful life-events by monitoring vs. blunting. In S. Levine and H. Ursin (eds). *Coping and Health* (New York: Plenum).

Miller, S.M. and Mangan, C.E. (1983). Interacting effects of information and coping style in adapting to gynecologic stress: Should the doctor tell all? *Journal of Personality and Social Psychology*, **45**, 223–236.

Mineka, S. (1982). Depression and helplessness in primates. In H.E. Fitzgerald, J.A. Mullins and P. Gage (eds), *Child Nurturance Series, Volume 3. Studies of Development in Nonhuman Primates* (New York: Plenum).

Quinn, R.P. (1972). *Locking-in as a Moderator of the Relationship between Job Satisfaction and Worker Health* (Ann Arbor, MI: University of Michigan, Survey Research Center).

Quinn, R., Mangione, T. and Seashore, S. (1975). *1972-73 Quality of Employment Survey (Codebook)* (Ann Arbor, MI: University of Michigan, Institute for Social Research).

Rodin, J. and Langer, E.J. (1980). The effects of labelling and control on self-concept in the aged. *Journal of Social Issues*, **36**, 12–29.

Rodin, J., Rennert, K. and Solomon, S.K. (1980). Intrinsic motivation for control: Fact or fiction. In A. Baum and J. Singer (eds), *Advances in Environmental Psychology, Volume 2. Applications of Personal Control* (Hillsdale, NJ: Erlbaum).

Rotter, J.B. (1966). Generalized expectancies for internal versus external control of reinforcement. *Psychological Monographs*, **80**(1), No. 609.

Schulz, R. and Hanusa, B.H. (1980). Experimental social gerontology: a social psychological perspective. *Journal of Social Issues*, **36**, 30–46.

Stotland, E. and Blumenthal, A.L. (1964). The reduction of anxiety as a result of the expectation of making a choice. *Canadian Journal of Psychology*, **18**, 139–145.

Szpiler, F.A. and Epstein, S. (1976). Availability of an avoidance response as related to autonomic arousal. *Journal of Abnormal Psychology*, **85**, 73–82.

Thompson, S.C. (1981). Will it hurt less if I can control it? A complex answer to a simple question. *Psychological Bulletin*, **90**, 89–101.

White, R.W. (1959). Motivation reconsidered: the concept of competence. *Psychological Review*, **66**, 297–333.

Wortman, C.B. and Brehm, J.W. (1975). Responses to uncontrollable outcomes: an integration of reactance theory and the learned helplessness model. *Advances in Experimental Social Psychology*, **8**.

7

Conceptualization and Measurement of Personality in Job Stress Research

Suzanne C. Ouellette Kobasa

1. Introduction

Stress is not a single concept with a single correct definition. In using the term or its more specific forms like job stress, most contemporary reseachers have in mind a complex person–environment process that includes a number of different concepts having psychological, social and/or physiological manifestations. Required preliminary steps in any new stress project are the specification of concepts to be investigated and the explication of the relationships between the selected concepts.

This chapter discusses the relevance of personality to the preliminary steps. The aim is to demonstrate the advantage of making personality an essential concept in any stress model and of observing its role in dampening the negative effects of environmental stress stimuli, or what Selye calls 'stressors', on health. In my view, exploratory questions and hypotheses-for-testing that include personality variables as moderators or buffers in the stress process stand to contribute a great deal to our understanding of human behaviour and health in the workplace.

Personality is defined here as a person's characteristic and general orientation toward self and world (and the interaction between self and world) that endures across time and varying life situations. Allport provides a more formal definition: personality is that "dynamic organization within the individual of the psychosocial systems that determine his unique adjustments to his environment" (Allport, 1937, p. 48). Personality is said to matter for job stress in its influence on the way a person feels, thinks, and acts in the face of work stressors. In other words, personality shapes the coping responses to what Holmes labels stressful life events and understands as demands for readjustment from the environment (Holmes and Masuda, 1974), as well as to what Lazarus and Folkman (1984) prefer to view as a relationship between the person and the environment that is interpreted by the person as exceeding his or her available resources and a threat to well-being. When personality promotes the sort of coping that prevents or cuts short negative stress consequences, i.e., the excessive physiological arousal and activation that is said to leave one vulnerable to disease, personality is said to be a source of stress-resistance.

Most of this chapter is a presentation of some of my own work in the area of personality and job stress, work that is usually referred to as hardiness research. It is described here with an emphasis on the importance of prospective designs for the development of personality and stress notions. I then refer briefly to related stress and personality projects by other investigators. The closing section offers two criticisms of existing research and suggests directions for future personality work.

2. Hardiness research

The conceptualization of hardiness forms the basis of my research on stress resistance (Kobasa, 1982). Hardiness is a personality style that expresses commitment, control and challenge.

Commitment is the ability to believe in the truth, importance and interest value of who one is and what one is doing; and thereby, the tendency to involve oneself fully in the many situations of life, including work, family, interpersonal relationships, and social institutions.

Control refers to the tendency to believe and act as if one can influence the course of events. Persons with control seek explanations for why something is happening with an emphasis on their own responsibility and not simply in terms of others' actions or fate.

Challenge is based on the belief that change, rather than stability, is the normative mode of life. People with 'challenge' seek out change and new experiences and approach them with cognitive flexibility and tolerance for ambiguity.

The basic proposition in the hardiness model is that among people facing significant stressors, those high in hardiness will be significantly less likely to fall ill, either mentally or physically, than those who lack hardiness or who display alienation, powerlessness and threat in the face of change. Hardiness facilitates a form of coping that includes:

1. Keeping specific stressors in perspective. Hardy individuals' basic sense of purpose in life allows them to ground events in an understandable and varied life course.

2. Knowing that one has the resources with which to respond to stressors. Hardy individuals' underlying sense of control allows them to appreciate a well-exercised coping repertoire.

3. Seeing stressors as potential opportunities for change. Challenge enables hardy individuals to see even undesirable events in terms of possibility rather than threat.

A number of retrospective studies involving working adults support the hardiness model. Although stressors are conceptualized and measured as stressful life events from all life areas, the most frequently reported events in our studies are work or job events. The most important retrospective study was the initial observation of Midwestern telephone company executives (Kobasa, 1979). Beginning with all of the male middle- and upper-level executives from a single operating company, we were able to identify through questionnaires, 100 executives who reported significantly high levels of stressful life event experiences and high levels of general physical symptoms and illnesses, and 100 executives with comparably high stressful life event experiences who were not showing the same physical debilitation.

The primary measure of stressors was a modified Schedule of Recent Events (Holmes and Rahe, 1967) and its associated list of stressfulness weights. Modifications included the better specification of ambiguous events and the addition of job stress events important to a telephone company sample. The primary measure of physical debilitation was the Seriousness of Illness Survey (Wyler, *et al.*, 1970). The high stress/high illness executives formed the group one expected to find based on the stress research popular before the mid-1970s. The early research emphasized a simple correlation between stressful life event occurrence and illness reports. The high stress/low illness executives, however, formed the group in which we expected to find higher hardiness.

To test our prediction, we had all the executives complete a lengthy personality questionnaire designed to assess all three hardiness components, as well as questions about demographic and job characteristics. The personality questionnaire included some newly developed items and adaptations of parts of all of the following instruments: the Personality Research Form (Jackson, 1974), the Internal–External Locus of Control Scale (Rotter *et al.*, 1962), the California Life Goals Evaluation Schedules (Hahn, 1966), and the Alienation versus Commitment Test (Maddi *et al.*, 1979). Discriminant function analysis established that high stress/low illness executives did differ significantly from high illness counterparts and that personality made the crucial difference. Scales representing operationalizations of hardiness discriminated between those falling sick in the face of work and non-work stressors and those staying healthy, whereas demographic characteristics such as age did not. To establish the generalizibility of these findings, other executives from the same company participated in a cross-validation study. The discriminant function coefficients for the hardiness indicators were again significant predictors of health status.

These retrospective results suggested the importance of looking for individual differences in response to stressors and the possibility of systematically raising a personality question in stress research. They fell far short, however, of answering questions about psychological aetiology and causal priority among stress variables. They did not permit rejection of the alternative explanation that personality hardiness results from, rather than causes, health for executives in the wake of stressful life events.

Consider the situation of the men in the retrospective study. An executive fills out a questionnaire noting frequency of occurrence of stressful events at work and home during the last three years; he then goes on to engage in a health review from which he may conclude that he is in pretty good shape (low illness). The high levels of commitment, control and challenge that he later tells us about may be more a reflection of the glow that he feels from having remained symptom-free in the face of pressures than the actual source of his successful coping.

Even more troublesome is the case of the executive who tells us about frequent and serious health problems (e.g., high blood pressure and recurring migraine headaches), as well as significant stressors. His low hardiness profile may indicate the blow to his self-esteem that he has suffered because of his weakened physical state. It is a sign of the psychological debilitation that sometimes accompanies health problems. The alternative explanation charges that he was not alienated, powerless and threatened by change *before* his bouts with illness.

We had to put the hardiness model to a prospective test. We decided to continue to follow members of the original executive pool (Kobasa *et al.*, 1982a). Two hundred and fifty-nine executives from whom personality, stressor and health data had been collected in 1975 provided yearly stress and illness reports for the next two years. A new hardiness score was created for each subject, from the 1975 data, by creating a composite from the five scales (out of the original 15) that appeared on conceptual and empirical grounds to be the best indicators of the hardiness construct. These scales were the work, self and powerlessness subscales from the Alienation Test, the Rotter locus of control scale, and the security scale from the California Life Goals test. The intercorrelations among these five scales were significant in the expected directions.

We summed executives' follow-up physical symptom and illness reports in such a way as to ensure at least one month and up to two years time lag between self-reports of personality and the onset of illness. Equally crucial to our prospective intentions, we utilized what we knew about executives' health status at the initial assessment. We ran an analysis of covariance with total follow-up or later illness as the dependent variable, the hardiness component and stressful life event reports entered as independent variables, and executives' prior illness scores from 1972 to 1975 served as the covariate. This last step had the effect of controlling for prior illness. We thereby put hardiness to the test of predicting *changes* in executives' illness scores. The results offered prospective support for our earlier results. Even when prior illness is controlled for, stressful life events (work and non-work) lead to an increase in debilitation and hardiness predicts a decrease. A significant stress and hardiness interaction indicates that being hardy is especially important for one's health when one is undergoing an intensely stressful time.

It is important to emphasize here that a prospective design addresses the problem of confounding that plagues not only personality but most of the moderators that researchers have chosen to include in their stress and stress-resistance studies. For example, reports of perceived social support (the most frequently investigated buffer in the current literature) can easily be contaminated in retrospective studies. The need for prospective designs is especially clear when one attempts to predict psychological distress from the interaction of social support and stressors. Monroe (1983) makes this point well.

Utilizing multiple regression and a comparison of retrospective and prospective studies, he finds that what one observes about the relationship between social support and reported debilitation significantly depends on the design employed, the variables used as controls (notably, prior symptom levels), and the type of disorder studied (psychological versus physical). For example, after controlling for prior symptoms, social support no longer predicts follow-up psychological symptoms in his data. With regard to physical symptoms, however, even after prior symptoms are controlled, social support continues to be highly related to outcome. Monroe reviews these and other findings to help explain who so much confusion exists in the work on stress-resistance, and to encourage continued prospective longitudinal research.

Other studies of hardiness have concentrated on examining its joint effects with other stress-resistance resources. Most interesting among these have been attempts to link hardiness and social support. In one assessment period with our telephone company executives, they completed measures designed to tap both objective social resources and subjective or perceived social support (from work and home sources). The former was assessed through the Luborsky social assets scale (Luborsky *et al.*, 1973), and the latter through the peer cohesion, staff support, family cohesion and family expressiveness subscales of the work environment and family environment scales developed by Moos *et al.* (1974).

The Luborsky scale taps current social resources or assets such as current income and marital status, as well as early life resources such as occupation and education of parents. From the Moos work scales, the peer cohesion subscale measures the degree to which co-workers are seen as friendly and supportive to each other; the staff support subscale measures the extent to which one's superiors in the company are perceived as supportive. From the Moos family scales, the family expressiveness subscale measures the degree to which family members are perceived as being allowed and encouraged to act openly and express their feelings directly; the family cohesion subscale measures the extent to which family members are perceived as concerned about preserving the family as a working unit.

Since there was no correlation between hardiness and objective social resources and far-from-perfect positive correlations between hardiness and perceived forms of social support ($r = 0.17$, $P < 0.10$ for the combined family scales, and $r = +0.28$, $P < 0.05$ for the combined work scales), we decided to look at the differential impact of hardiness and social support on response to stressors. Three-way analyses of variance with stressful life events at work and home, hardiness and objective social resources serving as independent variables, and with general physical illness as the dependent variable, produced significant effects only from stressful events and hardiness. Objective social resources had neither a main nor interaction effect on executives' health status. The same form of analysis, however, involving perceived social support provided more interesting results as well as a more complicated picture of the function of social support than that suggested in earlier research. Two of these analyses, one involving a composite family environment measure (expressiveness plus cohesion) and the other involving the work staff support scale, are most provocative.

In the three-way analysis with perceived family support, main effects on illness are found for only stressful life events (taken as work events and work plus non-work events) and hardiness and *not* for social support. But there are interaction effects. A significant two-way interaction between hardiness and family support establishes that being low in hardiness and at the same time perceiving high expressiveness and cohesiveness in one's family increases an executive's illness score. Further, a significant three-way interaction suggests that executives with high stressful events be treated as a group distinctive from those with low stressful events. Indeed, the executives who report the most symptoms and illnesses are those scoring high on perceived family support, high on stressful life events (again taken as work events and work plus non-work events) and low on hardiness. From these results, one can claim that family support is positively related to health only for people who are hardy while beset by environmental stressors. For people scoring low on commitment, control and challenge and high on stressors, family support is negatively related to health.

The three-way analysis of variance involving perceived staff support at work presents social support as less dependent on pesonality for its effectiveness in stress resistance, but still only indirectly protective of health. Again, only stressful life events and hardiness have main effects on illness. Social support at work emerges as significant only in a two-way interaction between it and stressful life events. When stressful life events are high for executives, regardless of their hardiness scores, perceiving support from superiors, including top management, reduces illness reports.

Explanations for these findings are offered elsewhere (e.g., Kobasa, 1982; Kobasa and Puccetti, 1983). They draw on what we know about the kind of stressors our executives experience, the kind of coping strategies that work superiors rather than family members encourage, and the problems with receiving too much support. These explanations are too lengthy for repetition here. What should be noted here, however, is the importance of looking at more than a single stress-resistance resource at a time. In the work on social support, as well as in other studies that pair hardiness with family medical history (Kobasa *et al.*, 1981) and physical exercise (Kobasa *et al.*, 1982b), the role of personality in the complex process that is stress is clarified in a way that would not be possible if personality were looked at in isolation.

3. Other personality variables relevant to stress

The personality construct, or as many of its investigators prefer to call it, behaviour pattern, most frequently linked to stress is Type A. This psychological style, described as consisting of some combination of extreme competitiveness and achievement striving, a strong sense of time urgency and impatience, hostility and job involvement, has been found to increase significantly one's chances of suffering coronary disease.

Most promising for the stress researcher arguing for the value of a personality concern is the impressive amount of prospective longitudinal and laboratory data on the Type A construct and health. Also relevant and promising is the current work on the early life experiences and socialization of individuals who show Type A pattern as adults (e.g., Matthews, 1982) and those studies seeking to link changes in Type A with organizational and sociocultural changes (e.g., Totman, 1979). Most troubling to the personality and stress researcher are the many unanswered questions about what Type A is and what psychological processes underlie it. As a review by Matthews (1982) makes clear, if Type A researchers are not preoccupied with developing the best possible questionnaire to assess Type A, they are busy varying situational characteristics in an experiment. There is relatively little attention being paid to the sort of concern that traditional personality psychologists such as Gordon Allport or Henry Murray would have found interesting. Recent efforts to alter Type A, however, may force a greater concern with psychological structures and processes.

There is space here only briefly to describe some of the other personality variables that have been brought to stress research. Lefcourt (1981) found that locus-of-control constructs, as assessed by Rotter's I–E (introvert–extrovert) scale and Lefcourt's own multidimensional–multiattributionally causality scale affiliation measure in college students, operate significantly as moderator variables between negative life events and mood disturbance over a 4-week period. The higher the students' externality, the greater the distress. Another and different sort of empirical support for locus-of-control is Langer and Rodin's (1976) finding that a belief in control moderates the stresses encountered in senior citizens' residences. Residents allowed belief in their own control over desired outcomes are healthier and live longer.

For David McClelland, it is a personality style consisting of a high inhibited need for power and low need for affiliation that interacts with stressful environments to provoke illness. He assesses this personality style through the Thematic Apperception Test (TAT). Working with samples of students and male prisoners (e.g., McClelland *et al.*, 1982), he observes the personality interaction as well as what might be a critical physiological mediator of the personality and stress process. McClelland finds that following their experience of stressful life events, people high in inhibited need for power show low concentrations of salivary immunoglobulin A.

A very recent contribution to the personality and stress cause is dispositional optimism (Scheier and Carver, 1985). Defining optimism in terms of generalized outcome expectancies and operationalizing it through a 12-item Likert scale, Scheier and Carver found that students who initially report being highly optimistic are subsequently less likely to report being bothered by physical symptoms than are students who initially report being less optimistic. This result stands even after correcting for initial symptom report levels.

A final example brings us closer to the field of job stress. Although still in its early stages of conceptual and methodological development, the construct of 'John Henryism' proposed by Sherman James and his colleagues stands to clarify the impact of job stressors on black male workers. 'John Henryism' is defined as the predisposition to cope actively with environmental stressors and to believe that one can control such stressors through hard work and determination. It is also assessed through a 12-item Likert scale. Although originally proposed as a direct and uniform source of stress resistance in the workplace, 'John Henryism' has been observed to have a more complicated interaction with other psychosocial factors in its impact on health.

An initial study (James *et al.*, 1983), for example, demonstrates that among working class black men, those scoring below the sample median on education but above the median on 'John Henryism' have higher diastolic blood pressure than men who score above the median on both education and the personality variable. In later work (James *et al.*, 1984), 'John Henryism' moderates the job stressor and blood pressure relationship in even less of a straightforward way. For example, James reports interactions between 'John Henryism' and perceived job success: with high 'John Henryism', diastolic blood pressure values change little with changes in job success; but for men showing low 'John Henryism', high job success is associated with a sharp decline in diastolic blood pressure. If this work could be extended to include prospective designs and to take greater care about confounding between variables, it might help us understand something about that which we now know very little, i.e., the psychological pathways through which job stressors negatively influence the health of black men.

4. Suggestions for future personality and job stress research

Although the literature includes many positive and reliable findings about the significance of personality variables as stress-resistance resources, it also includes some negative and inconsistent personality results. One also has to admit that personality is not obviously at the forefront of developments in stress research. If the study of the role of personality in job stress is not to go the way of psychosomatic specificity theories, we may need to consider some serious bolstering of our field. I would like to suggest two directions for research to help keep the personality endeavour viable.

The first of these has to do with the conceptualization of personality as personality-in-context. Too many studies have failed to take into account the interpersonal, small group and broader social and cultural contexts in which personality resides. In order to understand the difference that a subject's personality makes for the job stress he or she experiences, one has to know something about matters such as the expectations of the others with whom he or she interacts, the values of the organization for which he or she works, and the socialization practices of that organization, as well as how all of these influence his or her personality. For me, this contextual approach has proved essential in attempts to make sense of personality and stress resistance data collected across different professional and occupational settings. For those more interested in treatment applications, this contextual approach should serve as a warning against 'blaming the victim'—an error too often found in individual-based stress studies that ignore the multidimensional and multidisciplinary nature of stress phenomena.

A second suggestion has to do with measurement. Although there are many ways of collecting personality data and a case has been well made for using more than one in a single project, studies of personality as a stress-resistance resource have relied almost exclusively on one-shot paper and pencil self-report questionnaires. My personal communications with researchers interested in including a personality measure in their stress research lead me to conclude that the essential criteria for scale inclusion are ease of administration, length and time required for completion. The current cut-off points appear to be 15 items and five minutes.

I recognize that this hesitation about more elaborate forms of personality measurement may stem from a somewhat justified scepticism about the variance in stress-related physical illness that will be explained through personality. I also think, however, that there is reason to look a little more seriously and carefully. A good deal of my research on hardiness was done while painting with a very broad brush. Having found some personality effects through these approaches, however, justifies and requires a more detailed and complex investigation in my future work. Hopefully, this will include the longitudinal observation of personality through interviews, performance measures, projective reports, ratings by significant others, as well as questionnaire assessments.

References

Allport, G.W. (1937). *Personality: A Psychological Interpretation* (New York: Holt).

Hahn, M.E. (1966). *California Life Goals Evaluation Schedules* (Palo Alto, CA: Western Psychological Services).

Holmes, T.H. and Masuda, M. (1974). Life change and illness susceptibility. In B.S. Dohrenwend and B.P. Dohrenwend (eds). *Stressful Life Events: Their Nature and Effects* (New York: John Wiley).

Holmes, T.S. and Rahe, R.H. (1967). The social readjustment rating scale. *Journal of Psychosomatic Research*, **11**, 213–218.

Jackson, D.N. (1974). *Personality Research Form Manual* (Goshen, NY: Research Psychologists Press).

James, S.A., Harnett, S.A. and Kalsbeek, W. (1983). John Henryism and blood pressure differences among black men. *Journal of Behavioral Medicine*, **6**, 259–278.

James, S.A., LaCroix, A.Z., Kleinbaum, D.G. and Strogatz, D.S. (1984). John Henrysim and blood pressure differences among blck men. II. The role of occupational stressors. *Journal of Behavioral Medicine*, **7**, 259–275.

Kobasa, S.C. (1979). Stressful life events, personality, and health: an inquiry into hardiness. *Journal of Personality and Social Psychology*, **37**, 1–11.

Kobasa, S.C. (1982). The hardy personality: toward a social psychology of stress and health. In G.S. Sanders and J. Suls (eds), *The Social Psychology of Health and Illness* (Hillsdale, NJ: Lawrence Erlbaum).

Kobasa, S.C. and Puccetti, M. (1983). Personality and social resources in stress resistance. *Journal of Personality and Social Psychology*, **45**, 839–850.

Kobasa, S.C., Maddi, S.R. and Courington, S. (1981). Personality and constitution as mediators in the stress-illness relationship. *Journal of Health and Social Behavior*, **22**, 368–378.

Kobasa, S.C., Maddi, S.R. and Kahn, S. (1982a). Hardiness and health: a prospective study. *Journal of Personality and Social Psychology*, **42**, 168–177.

Kobasa, S.C., Maddi, S.R. and Puccetti, M. (1982b). Personality and exercise as buffers in the stress-illness relationship. *Journal of Behavioral Medicine*, **5**, 391–404.

Langer, E.J. and Rodin, J. (1976). The effects of choice and enhanced personal responsibility for the aged. *Journal of Personality and Social Psychology*, **34**, 191–198.

Lazarus, R.S. and Folkman, S. (1984). *Stress Appraisal and Coping* (New York: Springer).

Lefcourt, H.M. (1981). Locus of control and stress life events. In B.S. Dohrenwend and B.P. Dohrenwend (eds), *Stressful Life Events and Their Contexts* (New Brunswick, NJ: Rutgers University Press).

Luborsky, L., Todd, T.C. and Katchen, A.H. (1973). A self-administered social assets scale for predicting physical and psychological illness and health. *Journal of Psychosomatic Research*, **17**, 109–1 20.

Maddi, S.R., Kobasa, S.C. and Hoover, M. (1979). An alienation test. *Journal of Humanistic Psychology*, **19**, 73–76.

Matthews, K.A. (1982). Psychological perspectives on the Type A behavior pattern. *Psychological Bulletin*, **91**, 293–323.

McClelland, D.C., Alexander, C. and Marks, E. (1982). The need for power, stress, immune function and illness among male prisoners. *Journal of Abnormal Psychology*, **91**, 61–70.

Monroe, S.M. (1983). Social support and disorder: toward an untangling of cause and effect. *American Journal of Community Psychology*, **11**, 81–98.

Moos, R.H., Insel, P.M. and Humphrey, B. (1974). *Family Work and Group Environment Scales Manual* (Palo Alto, CA: Consulting Psychologists Press).

Rotter, J.B., Seeman, M. and Liverant, S. (1962). Internal vs. external locus of control of reinforcement: a major variable in behaviour theory. In N.F. Washbourne (ed.), *Decisions, Values, and Groups* (London: Pergamon).

Scheier, M.F. and Carver, C.S. (1985). Optimism, coping, and health: assessment and implications of generalized outcome expectancies. *Health Psychology*, **4**, 219–249.

Totman, R.G. (1979). *Social Causes of Illness* (London: Souvenir Press).

Wyler, A.R., Masuda, M. and Holmes, T.H. (1970). The seriousness of illness rating scale: reproducibility. *Journal of Psychosomatic Research*, **14**, 59–64.

8

Stress Research: An Interventionist Perspective

Patricia Shipley and Vanja Orlans

1. Introduction

In this chapter, we put the case for adopting an interventionist perspective in the planning and carrying out of research concerned with the problems of stress. This is a perspective which we have been working with and developing for some time at the Stress Research and Control Centre at Birkbeck College. It is founded on a different set of philosophical assumptions than those which underlie the bulk of the research in this field. It leads to a reconsideration of what might constitute an appropriate methodology, as well as the broader research skills which would be required in order to implement such an approach. In the following pages we develop the case for adopting a different approach to research on stress, provide an outline of our 'interventionist perspective', and conclude with some recent examples from our own work at the Stress Centre.

2. Paradigms in stress research

Even at a time of current widespread anxiety about a potential AIDS epidemic, acute sickness is far less of an economic drain than the steadily rising tide of chronic disease. As in other developed countries, the health service in Britain is a massive insatiable consumer of resources, especially for chronic disease. Many of these diseases are periodically referred to as the diseases of 'affluence' and 'civilization'. A large number are often also referred to as 'stress' diseases. While we do not pretend that all the answers to chronic disease patterns lie in stress control, stress is nevertheless recognized as playing a key role in the aetiology of many of these diseases, and in the development of chronic ill health, whether mental or physical. Stressful experiences in accumulation, accompanied by continually unhealthy coping behaviour, may lay the foundation at an early stage for subsequent, perhaps irreversible, disease.

It follows that stress control, that is, the prevention and management of 'bad' stress, should be of concern to policy-makers, to the general public, and to stress researchers themselves. Occupational experiences, and the workplaces where many of us live out

110

much of our lives, are potential sources of stress and bad coping, and by the same token, potential sources of good health promotion. Those who manage our work-places have a responsibility for the viability of their organizations. They also have a duty to care for the health and welfare of employees. Our own view is that this duty should extend to include the return to the community of those employees, when their days' and lives' work is over, in a state which does not reflect the ravages of continuous and avoidable workplace stress. Indeed, the UK 1974 Health and Safety legislation implies this, although the emphasis in our legislation is largely on physical rather than mental factors. Stress researchers who adopt an interventionist perspective can also play a key role in the attainment of these aims.

There are two broad attitudes to 'stress' as a concept: that it is misleadingly vague, attracting too many of the available scarce resources for research; or that it is a useful and cohesive idea with potentially productive and practical results. As stress researchers we are, by definition, committed to the latter view. We must then demonstrate the usefulness of such research to managers of economies which contain many competing claims for research expenditure. At a time of economic recession, moreover, we are increasingly being challenged to address the socio-economic relevance of what we do.

No one delving into the research literature on stress can fail to detect a mounting unrest about the quality of the research, as well as its value to policy-makers and other consumers. This is encapsulated in phrases such as 'whither stress research?' (Payne *et al.*, 1982). The unrest should be viewed against a background of findings from empirical research studies. While these studies are often of sophisticated design rooted in the traditional paradigm, they have disappointingly predictive value (*see*, for example, Fletcher and Payne, 1980, in relation to work stress).

We are not alone in believing that a breakthrough is needed, and that we may be at a cross-roads. It seems to us that the choices open to researchers in this field are whether to apply themselves to produce more of the same, conducting further studies in the old mould, to seek to make such studies more relevant, or to reject the more traditional paradigm in favour of an approach which ensures relevance at the outset. Without wanting to disparage some of the competent work that has gone into many of the more traditional studies, we would argue for proportionally fewer resources to be devoted in future to traditional research into stress, and for more interest to be taken in, and support given to, what we would refer to as an 'interventionist' paradigm in stress research.

Our argument is predicated on the knowledge that stress research in the traditional mould is not well suited to change and intervention outcomes because it does not emphasize action at the outset. One way of explaining this state of affairs is by reference to the unintended consequences of research based on the expert, as opposed to the subject-centred or collaborative model (*see* Shipley, 1987). In the traditional approach, stress is defined by the expert, rather than self-defined by the 'client'. The expert retains control, seeking normative outcomes and universal laws, and thus remains at some distance from the problems and individuals being researched. In traditional terms this is seen as promoting 'objectivity' and thus the validity of the research. The notion of validity itself however, is one that has been defined and agreed by a scientific community; it is not something that has been imposed from the outside. The onus is on stress researchers themselves to continually assess their own work in terms of a model of validity which is appropriate to the problems under analysis.

In the expert mode, the subject or client is treated as the object by the (supposedly) detached observer, a serious consequence being the risk of underestimation of the potency of the subject as a social actor, possessing the capacity for self-awareness, self-management and change-agency. Passive reaction is taken for ganted, or is sometimes induced as a form perhaps of 'learned helplessness' (*see* Milgram, 1974 for an interesting example of this). The effect of this is to emphasize the status quo rather than the dynamics of the change process.

3. Key aspects of the interventionist approach phenan

A valuable conceptualization of stress as a dynamic transactional process has been advanced by the American cognitive psychologist Richard Lazarus and his colleagues (e.g., Lazarus, 1966; Lazarus and Launier, 1978). In this model, stress depends on people evaluating their relationships with the environment as potentially harmful or threatening; i.e., the environmental demands are perceived to exceed potential coping resources (*see* Shirom, 1986, for an important recent empirical validation of this). A danger with this approach is that it may attract attention away from the environment as a source of stress which is amenable to change. Its value lies in the way it highlights the experiential quality of stress, reminding us that people vary in their interpretation of experience, and that people's experiences are never quite the same. Individual variation is truly vast and immense in all its richness and complexity, and this aspect is inevitably lost in the reductionist methods employed by traditional researchers.

When we combine this 'phenomenological' view of stress with what we shall call 'social action' theory we have a powerful tool which is useful for both diagnostic and interventionist purposes. It steers us towards an exploration of the personal meanings stress can hold for different people, as well as towards self-definition. When coping practices and potential changes are reviewed, the individual as social actor is also construed as a potential locus and instrument for change. In the dynamic transactional process the person–environment relationship is fluid, and attributions are fluid as to the source of stress and the locus of intervention. The dualistic entities of person and environment are dissolved and merged; the individual mirrors the environment; the environment is the product of individual minds which constitute its membership. We are part of the environment and it is part of us.

Yet another powerful dimension is added when social action theory is combined with learning theory. The latter presupposes that much of what we do and think is learnt from others, and is therefore capable of unlearning and modification (*see*, e.g., Bandura, 1977). Much of behaviour therapy and cognitive therapy is predicated on such assumptions. Meichenbaum is an American clinical psychologist who focuses in his therapy on the distortions and misperceptions in an individual's mind as the springs of inappropriate coping. In his book (Meichenbaum, 1983) there is a step-by-step approach to self-help, an important underlying principle of which is self-awareness: getting to know yourself, the situations that cause you stress, and your typical reactions. The self-care philosophy is currently attractive to policy-makers who have to make increasingly difficult decisions about the allocation of scarce resources. Dealing with (as opposed to dabbling in) self-awareness and self-help is not a matter to be taken light-heartedly. It is certainly not being advocated here as the panacea. It can be abused as well as used constructively.

Seeking to change awareness levels presumes that we often do things unthinkingly; that we can get locked into a behavioural chain under stress which is so automatic and habitual that we do not stop to think about it. Implicit here is a recognition of the sub-conscious as a potent force. This dimension, the subconscious, represents yet another important aspect of our interventionist model. To bring such processes into awareness is to render them potentially amenable to change.

4. Levels for analysis and change

Cochrane's thesis (1983) concerning the social creation of mental illness, is a sober reminder of our duty to find the most appropriate intervention at the right level, indi-vidual or environment. Stress is viewed by him as an important link between circum-stances and illness. While Herzlich (1973) utilized the Durkheimian notion of 'social representation' to understand the meanings of stress and illness in samples from urban and rural France, Cochrane is more concerned with emphasizing the material and structural circumstances, constraints and deprivations in different individual's lives. These circumstances may be due to such socio-economic factors as the differential access to wealth and status, and their potential for generating stress, poor coping and ill health. Under these conditions, structural rather than behavioural interventions may be theoretically more relevant, if difficult to achieve in practice.

The cognitive therapists, on the other hand, work with individual clients whose circumstances are usually more fortunate than the subjects of Cochrane's studies. Their aim is to re-empower those clients to recover lost self-control. Such awareness-raising could also lead to clients becoming effective agents for changing their environ-ments.

Fisher is a British cognitive psychologist whose publications on stress, strategy and control elucidate some of the cognitive biases which can make us more or less vulner-able to threat and the victims of poor coping habits (Fisher, 1984). Our perceptions of reality may be quite realistic (in the case of the most deprived members of society, for example), although 'learned helplessness' and chronic depression are not necessarily the consequence. On the other hand, we may be unrealistic in our control attributions. We may have more power to change ourselves or our environment than we first thought. Some of our stress may be self-inflicted, although reinforced socially by others. In Type A societies with their rewards for competition and aggressive striving to achieve status and recognition, extreme Type A individuals need not be helpless puppets. They can stop to think and evaluate their behaviours, and the subconscious motives which propel them. They can choose to continue to be Type A or to modify themselves. But the choice is theirs, not the experts'. Self-help is just one form of stress control complementing other strategies, and is sometimes the only available solution.

Interventions for stress control may take place at levels wider than that of the individual, for example, at the group and organizational levels. Initiatives of the 'stress control' and 'quality of working life' kind in British companies are likely to be self-generated, if they occur at all, as there is negligible external pressure on them for change of this kind. Unlike, say, the 1977 Swedish Work Environment Act, there is no UK legislation that gives explicit directives about stress control and the quality of working life, although the 1974 Health and Safety statute imposes a general duty of care on employers to include protection from mental as well as physical injury. The scope of the latter, however, has hardly been comprehensively tested out in the courts. Although we do hear from time to time of successful cases against employers for mental stress, the usual practice is to settle out of court for relatively trivial sums of money. Until such time as the legislative environment becomes more stringent, quality of working life and stress control initiatives in Britain will continue to rely on the autonomous efforts of more humanitarian employers, or the clear demonstration of the productivity benefits which accrue when employers take an interest in employee well-being.

Although there is currently some evidence of a slow cultural shift towards a greater organizational interest in stress management and prevention, this is being hampered by the present economic and political climate. Changes at the organizational level are far fewer in practice than those at the more micro, individual level. The latter are easier to effect, and are often superficially cheaper to execute, although they may reflect a short-sighted, somewhat palliative, policy. Individual-level interventions, designed to remain at this level, are sometimes the result of powerful influences resisting wider change programmes. Resistance to changes in management style and decision-making structures may occur if entrenched interests are threatened. The stress researcher who adopts the interventionist perspective needs to assess such influences in the delicate process of setting up a project. Relevant organizational 'gatekeepers' must be identified whose commitment is required if there is to be a chance of success in implementing relevant changes (see Handy, 1986).

This is not to deny the value of change located at the level of the individual, or the fact that many individuals bring their stress problems with them into the organization. Strategies such as the introduction of counselling programmes and relaxation training can be extremely helpful. Our concern, however, is that diagnoses and interventions are made at the appropriate levels, and that organizational problems, for example, do not masquerade as individual mental ill health.

It is true that powerful influences which resist important relevant changes may be outside the control of the interventionist. On the other hand, the narrow training of many stress researchers and other professionals, coupled with an unwillingness to explore methods and approaches which go beyond this, often result in research doing no more than supporting the status quo at best, and at worst, dealing with trivial questions which may have neither theoretical interest nor practical relevance. Such 'diagnostic error' is encapsulated in the old joke about the drunkard fruitlessly searching for his keys under the lamp post, because that is where the light is. A narrow diagnostic scan may be welcomed by a management which defines stress problems in an equally narrow way. However, where a good relationship is established with an organization, a stress project may be the way in to an analysis of wider organizational problems, and possibly to 'organizational development'.

This is not to suggest that all employee stress problems will be rooted in organizational ills. Rather, there is the recognition that problems will manifest themselves within the work setting whatever their source, and that the caring organization will act as a support to those who carry their stress burdens into the workplace from outside, rather than adding work stresses on top of personal and family problems. Within the organizational setting, however, problems may often mirror each other at different levels of analysis: individual, group or organizational. Stress at the top of the organization, for example, will percolate down through these levels, highlighting the potential diagnostic errors which may arise if problems are artificially separated from the environments in which they are occurring.

One of the most important reasons for adopting a broad perspective of this kind is that, without such a perspective, prevention is unlikely to be attained. Limited competence on the part of researchers and helping professionals in general can exacerbate the problem, and adds to the disillusionment about stress research. Perhaps we need to understand and deal with the problems of these professionals themselves. In coping with their own stresses, a strategy of self-protection can lead to poor diagnostic scan, resulting in intervention at inappropriate levels, and in irrelevant ways. This is reflected in wanting to 'hide behind the white coat' in order to play the defensive expert's role. In such a setting, an organization's counselling programme can become a 'dumping ground' for a range of organizational problems.

5. Taking appropriate action

Prevention of physical and mental ill-health is much talked about but is often not attained, particularly in relation to mental health problems in the organizational setting. Yet economic necessity and unremitting pressure for improved quality of life require that preventative goals be achieved. We would argue for a greater involvement on the part of stress researchers in the goals of prevention. Such an involvement, however, requires a paradigm shift to methods of enquiry and intervention which place the locus for stress control with potentially stressed individuals who are regarded as possessing the capacities for acquiring good as well as poor coping habits. Such methods are effective also at group and organizational levels, where there may be a greater possibility of promoting good stress management and prevention practices by enabling changes to be made in procedures, practices and structures, and to the beliefs and socio-organizational norms and values therefore which are embodied in them.

In our research studies in recent years we have attempted to develop a 'theory of practice' in relation to stress problems, by conducting interventionist research with client groups in a collaborative way. By seeing our 'clients', whether individuals or groups, as social actors and thus potential change agents, we have sought both to understand stress better as a complex process, while at the same time working with these clients in a joint identification of their own problems, their coping habits, and the possibilities for self-initiated change. The stress problems are theirs, not ours, and the solutions are theirs also. In this collaborative mode the expert's mantle is cast aside as the different parties jointly share in trying to reach a mutual understanding of what is going on, and what might be done in a creative way to effect potentially beneficial changes. In this research process, priority is given to individual and organizational learning. Furthermore, 'learned resourcefulness' is a potentially constructive alternative to 'learned helplessness' (*see*, e.g., Rosenbaum, 1983).

A way forward for change is to work with the stresses of those groups who are already public and organizational 'gate-keepers', such as teachers, social and community workers, managers and trade unionists. Such individuals and groups are well placed, in a positional and influential sense, to take appropriate preventive action on identified problems, and to publicize and promote such actions within other settings. Effective interventions can be planned at different levels, as individuals take steps to manage their own stress problems, as well as working together to change unhealthy institutional norms and practices.

Didactic pleas and exhortations by official health education bodies are not sufficient to persuade people to make profound changes in their life-styles or their coping strategies. People have to be committed to change. To do so requires incentive. Awareness as a basis for informed choice is part of that complex process. Expert definition, with its concomitants in the control and management of the problems under analysis by experts, does not seek to change awareness there and then. Instead, it creates and reinforces alienation between experts and subjects, and between the latter and their stress problems.

Before we can begin to meet these challenges however, a change in our collective consciousness as researchers is required. Sometimes unthinkingly we research only in reaction to the pressures on us to publish, in outlets read only by the elite. Well-intended, conscientious researchers devote many hours to the self-perpetuation of a process which threatens to lead to the disillusionment of colleagues and potential consumers alike. This may be partly because of the paucity of new ideas and approaches in the area of stress research, as well as the perceived lack of relevance of much research to social problems, and the fact that many researchers are not prepared, or are not capable of, taking an interventionist role in the problems which they address. In only exceptional cases, in some recent Swedish action research for example, are positive attempts being made to break through this cycle (*see*, e.g., Gardell, 1983 and Gardell, in press, with reference to findings on stress, working conditions and workplace change).

We contend that good interventionist research is more difficult to execute than research of a more traditional kind. It cannot be carried out in a hurry, and its principles lead to a hardening, not a softening up of the data. The demands placed on the researchers are far greater than those which are required in the more traditional mould. It demands a greater level of interpersonal skill, as well as the capacity to confront both theoretically and philosophically such aspects as 'data contamination' and the meaning and nature of 'subjectivity'. When working in the organizational setting, we are required to be much more than just 'occupational psychologists'. We need also to be counsellors, managers, politicians, collaborators and friends. The fact that a traditional training, at least as far as the occupational psychologist is concerned, may fall short of the requirements 'in the field' has also been highlighted in the *Bulletin of the British Psychological Society* where a recent article (Cooper, 1986) refers to the emergent role of the 'clinical occupational psychologist'. Apart, however, from the requirement for a wider range of skills of such researchers, we would suggest that their aims would also need to be somewhat different. Interventionist research is set up to lead, where appropriate, to changes which can play a preventative role, and the researchers themselves are therefore involved in these changes, and are actively prepared to accept joint responsibility for the success or failure of these.

6. Stress studies at Birkbeck

In our recent studies of organizational stress, we have adopted and developed the interventionist perspective outlined above, incorporating definitions of stress and diagnostic tools which recognize individuals as active learners with the potential for helping themselves as well as operating as change agents within their organizational settings. Instead of selecting 'objectivity' and 'generalizability' as our goals, we have approached the problems of stress psychologically, utilizing the concepts of the 'subjective' and the 'intersubjective'. While we have also on occasion utilized medical screening data, an important focus has been the meanings of such data to the individuals and groups with which we have worked, and the links between such data and client self-awareness.

Our interventionist perspective is not one which we have arrived at by 'armchair theorizing', but rather it has been developed experientially in the course of our work. A mounting dissatisfaction with the research output in the field of stress, coupled with a sense that we had a duty as researchers to do something more than just 'generate data' of an impartial kind, led to the initial considerations of what a different approach might look like. To start with, we began working with the notion of stress as a complex phenomenological process, and began to consider the methodological implications of such a view. Although we have used both qualitative and quantitative data collection methods, we have avoided as far as possible the temptation of 'objectifying' the latter in order to appear more 'scientific'.

In the course of a three-year programme designed to develop a stress assessment procedure which would be appropriate for use within the organizational setting (Orlans and Shipley, 1986), we had the opportunity to develop our ideas in a more systematic way. An important initial step was the design and use of a survey methodology within organizational settings, and the more detailed selection and testing of a number of structured questionnaires with professional samples. The scores derived from these questionnaires were compared with data derived from an in-depth semi-structured interview with each participant. This enabled us to assess the suitability and validity of such a questionnaire package for a sample of that kind. Our assessment package was subsequently modified in the light of the research data, and was tested out in its final form within one organizational setting where we had access to all levels in the organizational structure. As a result of these studies, we have been able to produce a framework for the assessment of stress at individual, group and organizational levels.

In the course of our work on the assessment of stress within organizations, we came to recognize the limitations, from a research perspective, of relying too heavily on data derived from a set of structured instruments, even where these are used in a 'client-centred' way. Apart from the role of such instruments in the ordering and controlling of reality (*see*, e.g., Dale and Payne, 1976), their use can never tap the whole of a respondent's 'world view', being based as they are on a set of *a priori* categories. Furthermore, their use in conjunction with the 'random stratified sampling' approach can ensure that certain key people in the system are never identified. The latter group includes those who could provide particularly important insights as to 'what is going on' (sometimes referred to as the 'expert witnesses'), and whose commitment to change might be crucial from an interventionist standpoint. As a result, we always use a variety of data collection methods which include the completion of inventories and questionnaires, the carrying out of semi-structured and unstructured interviews, the analysis of conversations and group meetings, and the analysis of our own self-awareness as researchers, and our own experiences of 'being in the organization'.

We place particular emphasis on 'researcher awareness', as we believe that an understanding of the relationship of the researcher to her/his subjects or clients, and to the variety of data collection methods in use, will enable us to make better judgements as to the validity of the data derived from the research. This places a continual demand on the researcher, which does not exist within more conventional approaches, to 'know thyself' (*see*, e.g., Devereaux, 1967). Our experiences in the field of stress research have thus led us to broaden our conception of what constitutes 'valid data, and have enabled us to be less technical and more process-orientated in our research efforts.

The emphasis on process is also mirrored at the level of the research content. As outlined earlier, we treat our clients as active and insightful human beings, who have a natural capacity for learning and unlearning. The experiential learning cycle (*see* Figure 8.1) as delineated by Kolb (*see*, e.g., Kolb and Fry, 1975) has been shown to be a useful model of this process. While learning may theoretically begin at any point in the cycle, Kolb highlights the experiential nature of the process by 'postulating concrete experience' as the starting point. From the individual perspective, a person will reflect on her/his experience, and will then continue to make sense, in a more abstract or conceptual way, of what has occurred. This 'search for meaning' then enables the person to take (either consciously or subconsciously) some active steps in order to test a particular hypothesis.

This process of experiencing, making sense and testing is fundamental to every human being. It is probably, however, more easily recognized in young children, as the adult world in general, and educational systems in particular, have tended to over-emphasize the rational and analytical, leading to the 'abstract conceptualization' of problems in a somewhat static way.

The experiential learning cycle has emerged from our interview data as important in relation to the process of stress at both individual and organizational levels, and reflects the kind of process which is implicit in Argyris and Schoen's notion (1978) of 'organizational learning'. In addition, it is relevant to the research and intervention process itself, and thus provides a useful link between the researcher and the researched.

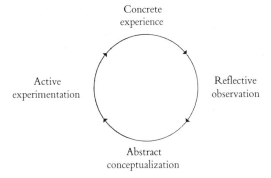

Figure 8.1.   The experiential learning cycle (adapted from Kolb and Fry, 1975).

7. A case study example

Some of our recent work with a trade union organization provides a good illustration of the way in which our interventionist perspective works in practice in the context of research on stress. The organization approached us initially because a number of its senior people had died of heart attacks, and there was a general feeling that stress may have had something to do with it. At one level, we were being asked to investigate the problem, while at another level we were already being presented with 'the solution'. The latter was envisaged by the client to be an occupational health service with the emphasis especially on screening for potential heart disease.

During a series of group meetings, we worked at jointly defining and re-defining the problem on which we might all work, while also, at a process level, concentrating on building the trust which would be required to enable us to collect 'high quality data' on an issue (job stress) which was potentially threatening both to individuals and to the organization as a whole. As a result of these meetings alone, we made several journeys around the learning cycle. Working with representatives from the organization, we planned each stage of the data collection exercise, which included both physiological and psychological assessments. At all stages, our 'subjects' were treated as collaborators on the project, and therefore their feelings and views about the assessments, as well as the emerging technical data, were also recorded. In a very important sense, this enabled us to validate our data as we went along.

Using a variety of both quantitative and qualitative methods within this overall collaborative framework, we collected data which related to many different levels within the organization as a whole. These methods included 'stress indicators' (as illustrated by the probable prevalence level for mental ill health using the General Health Questionnaire, for example), lifestyle factors, medical assessments, historical and cultural aspects of that particular organization, communication patterns and other important procedures and processes, as well as structural factors which were considered to be relevant. When all the data had been collected they were discussed and analysed further in group meetings which were attended by researchers and organizational representatives. Only then was the final report produced. A copy of this report was sent by us to all participants in the project, together with a request for comments and criticisms, and was subsequently also distributed more widely within the organization.

Working with an interventionist approach enabled us to conduct the research process in a way which was likely to be most helpful to participants in the project. For example, as well as asking people to complete a number of inventories and questionnaires, we also conducted lengthy semi-structured interviews with each individual. While these interviews enabled us to become closer to organizational members, and thus to understand better their subjective world, they were also approached as counselling sessions by both researchers and participants. Individuals had two or more hours in which they could explore their stressful experiences in confidence, and to consider some ways in which they might be able to cope more effectively. Whereas we could not offer individuals an extended counselling service, we did undertake, if requested, to see people a second time, and to suggest other potential resources as required.

All participants in the project received individual, confidential summaries of the interview discussions, as well as detailed results from, and explanations of, both medical and psychological assessments. Subsequent follow-ups revealed that a large majority of participants reported benefits as a result of the counselling session. Many were grateful for the rare opportunity provided to discuss their problems so openly in a confidential setting. Others reported that they had made subsequent lifestyle changes, or modifications within the work setting, which enabled them to cope more effectively.

At the more macro level, we used the project as a whole to model some of the components of a possible occupational health programme: it would include both medical and psychological assessments; counselling sessions would be offered to employees; it would be run independently of the company, in a way which guaranteed complete confidentiality; and its overall orientation would be client-centred rather than expert-centred. By modelling a potential programme in this way, participants could make judgements about the value of such a programme to them, and could decide whether they would want to continue to utilize such facilities on an on-going basis.

We believe that our emphasis on the process of the research, and our preparedness to act in an interventionist and collaborative mould, enabled two important outcomes to be achieved: first, the report was not 'shelved', or left like many such reports to gather dust in the company's 'no action' file; and second, because of the client involvement at all stages of the project, there was a very high level of commitment and energy to act on the results and conclusions arrived at. These were *their* data, and *their* solutions.

At present, we are continuing to work with this particular client organization. We have undertaken to plan collaboratively the implementation of a radical occupational health programme along the lines we had modelled in the course of the feasibility project, and also to discuss the ways in which it could be evaluated on a continuing basis. The first stage of this exercise is already underway. As a result of the project, we have learned much about ourselves as researchers and also about the functioning of trade union organizations. Our clients have learned many new concepts, and have taken on board some of our research language, which will be helpful to them in the next stage of their efforts to improve the health of their organization.

8. Some final comments

We are continuing to work with many other client organizations in the way outlined above, and are continually learning more about ourselves and the research process. The interventionist perspective which we have adopted is thus being continually developed and modified in the light of experience. While it may be difficult to convince some of our more traditional and expert-oriented colleagues that this may be a way forward in the field of stress research, we can only state that: the approach works for us; it addresses relevant theoretical and philosophical issues; it is exciting; and it produces the possibility of changes which can enhance both individual and organizational health.

References

Argyris, C. and Schoen, D.A. (1978). *Organizational Learning: A Theory of Action Perspective* (Reading, MA: Addison-Wesley).

Bandura, A. (1977). Self-efficacy: towards a unifying theory of behavioural change. *Psychological Review*, **84**, 191–215.

Cochrane, R. (1983). *The Social Creation of Mental Illness* (London: Longman).

Cooper, C.L. (1986). Job distress: recent research and the emerging role of the clinical occupational psychologist. *Bulletin of the British Psychological Society*, **39**, 325–331.

Dale, A. and Payne, R. (1976). Consulting interventions using structured instruments: a critique. Working paper prepared for the seminar on Client-Consultant Relationships, Groningen, Holland.

Devereaux, G. (1967). *From Anxiety to Method in the Behavioural Sciences* (The Hague: Mouton).

Fisher, S. (1984). *Stress and the Perception of Control* (London: Lawrence Erlbaum).

Fletcher, B.C. and Payne, R.L. (1980). Stress and work: a review and theoretical framework, I. *Personnel Review*, **9**, (1), 19–29.

Gardell, B. (1983). Worker participation and autonomy: a multilevel approach to democracy at the workplace. In C. Crouch and F. Heller (eds), *International Yearbook of Organizational Democracy*, Volume 1 (Chichester: John Wiley).

Gardell, B. (in press). Effectiveness and health hazards at work. In J.C. Quick, J.D. Quick, R. Baghat and J.E. Dalte (eds), *Work Stress: The Role for Health Care Delivery Systems* (New York: Praeger).

Handy, J.A. (1986). Considering organizations in organizational stress research: a rejoinder to Glowinkowski and Cooper and to Duckworth. *Bulletin of the British Psychological Society*, **39**, 205–210.

Herzlich, C. (1973). *Health and Illness* (London: Academic Press).

Kolb, D.A. and Fry, R. (1975). Towards an applied theory of experiential learning. In C.L. Cooper (ed.), *Theories of Group Processes* (London: John Wiley).

Lazarus, R.S. (1966). *Psychological Stress and the Coping Process* (New York: McGraw-Hill).

Lazarus, R.S. and Launier, R. (1978). Stress-related transactions between person and environment. In L.A. Pervin and M. Lewis (eds), *Perspectives in Interactional Psychology* (New York: Plenum).

Meichenbaum, D. (1983). *Coping with Stress* (London: Century Publishing).

Milgram, S. (1974). *Obedience to Authority: An Experimental View* (New York: Harper & Row).

Orlans, V. and Shipley, P. (1986). Stress: individual and organizational assessment. A report for the Stress Research and Control Centre, Birkbeck College, London.

Payne, R., Jick, T.D. and Burke, R.J. (1982). Whither stress research?: an agenda for the 1980s. *Journal of Occupational Behaviour*, **3**, 131–145.

Rosenbaum, M. (1983). Learned resourcefulness as a behavioural repertoire for the self-regulation of internal events: issues and speculations. In M. Rosenbaum, C.M. Franks and T. Jaffe (eds), *Perspectives on Behaviour Therapy in the Eighties* (New York: Springer).

Shipley, P. (1987). The methodology of applied ergonomics: validity and value. In J.R. Wilson, E.N. Corlett and I. Manenica (eds), *New Methods in Applied Ergonomics* (London: Taylor & Francis), pp. 13–22.

Shirom, A. (1986). On the cross-environment generality of the relational view of stress. *Journal of Environmental Psychology*, **6**, 121–134.

PART II
PHYSIOLOGICAL
CONSEQUENCES OF JOB STRESS

9

Physiological Indices of Job Stress

J. Alan Herd

1. Introduction

The realization that behaviour influences cardiovascular and metabolic functions has drawn observers to suppose that psychological factors contribute to cardiovascular disease. In addition, epidemiological studies have demonstrated relationships between cardiovascular disease and various social, psychological, and behavioural factors. From these clinical and epidemiological observations, the concept of stress has arisen. By common usage, the concept of stress implies a psychological effect of some influence that is usually considered undesirable or even harmful in some way. In addition, notions of perception, meaning, and previous experience influence personal uses of the concept.

The concept of job stress arises naturally from the realization that behaviour is influenced by occupational conditions, and many individuals can identify influences in the workplace they consider undesirable and possibly harmful. The difference between job stress and other occupational hazards is the contribution from social and psychological factors as distinct from purely physical factors. Because psychological factors are more difficult to measure than physical factors, they have assumed a somewhat mysterious quality. The attempt to identify physiological indices of job stress arises from the proposition that physical effects of social and psychological factors may allow us too quantitate job stress more readily and identify those most susceptible to any adverse physical effects.

The physiological indicators of greatest interest are those related to cardiovascular and metabolic functions most likely to contribute to cardiovascular disease. Other medical conditions have been associated with social and psychological factors, but the prevalence and severity of cardiovascular diseases draws our attention. Peptic ulcer disease, bronchial asthma, and rheumatoid arthritis are strongly influenced by social and psychological factors, but the prevalence of these conditions is less than for cardiovascular diseases, and individuals afflicted usually have physiological and psychological characteristics which put them at a greater risk of illness than most other individuals not so afflicted. In addition, the realization that cardiovascular diseases progress for many years before clinical manifestations appear brings us to make great efforts to prevent these diseases at an early stage.

The search for physiological indicators of job stress arises because individual perceptions of stress and stressful situations are not well defined and are not consistent between individuals. If there were no observable physiological consequences and no apparent relations between job stress and cardiovascular disease, measurement of stress could be as simple as questions concerning subjective effects. Our intention is to avoid discussions about terminology concerning stress and attempt to identify adverse effects of social and psychological factors present in occupational settings.

2. Risk factors for cardiovascular disease

The most prevalent cardiovascular diseases in Western industrialized societies are arterial hypertension and ischaemic heart disease. Although some individuals with arterial hypertension may succumb to heart or kidney failure, the majority of those who are not properly treated succumb to stroke or ischaemic heart disease. The risk factors for stroke and ischaemic heart disease are very similar, and arterial hypertension contributes to the risk of both diseases.

Major risk factors

The cardiovascular risk factor concept derives from epidemiological evidence on cardiovascular mortality rates among countries and from epidemiological evidence concerning prospective long-term studies. The major risk factors for both stroke and ischaemic heart disease are hypertension, high values for concentrations of cholesterol and other lipoproteins in blood, and cigarette smoking. Additional risk factors which have been implicated are glucose intolerance, psychosocial factors and physical inactivity. Interactions between these risk factors have been observed as well as independent effects, and a multifactorial basis for stroke, arteriosclerosis and coronary heart disease has been established.

Results of epidemiological studies in the USA among several thousand middle-aged men demonstrated that high serum cholesterol levels, high blood pressure and cigarette smoking were important risk factors for coronary heart disease (Inter-Society for Heart Disease Resources, 1970). Men with all three of these risk factors had over six times the chance of developing a first major coronary attack than men with none of the risk factors. However, only 14% of the men with all three of the risk factors developed coronary heart disease during 10 years of observation. Furthermore, of all the men who developed coronary heart disease over the 10-year follow-up, only 17% had all three risk factors and only 58% had two or more risk factors. Results of these studies suggest that other risk factors also are important in the aetiology and pathogenesis of arteriosclerosis.

Sociocultural influences

Sociocultural mobility has been implicated as a risk factor for coronary heart disease (Syme *et al.*, 1975). Japanese were studied in Japan, Hawaii and California using comparable study methods. A gradient in coronary heart disease morbidity (Marmot *et al.*, 1975) was observed with the lowest rates in Japan, the highest rates in California and intermediate rates in Hawaii. The gradient was not explained by differences in serum cholesterol, diet, blood pressure or cigarette-smoking patterns. However, a further study of Japanese living in California (Marmot and Syme, 1976) revealed that migrants who had adopted Western lifestyles had coronary heart disease rates between 2.5 and 5 times higher than a second group of migrants who had retained traditional Japanese ways. The differences were evident in childhood, upbringing and adult commitment to the Japanese community. Thus, the group of migrants who retained traditional Japanese ways were relatively protected from the effects of sociocultural mobility.

Socioeconomic status also is known to be associated with morbidity and mortality from coronary heart disease in industrialized societies. Recently, trends have shown a change from a direct to an inverse association of socioeconomic status with mortality from coronary heart disease (Morgenstorn, 1980; Rose and Marmot, 1981; Marmot, 1984). Although people in lower socioeconomic positions currently have higher blood pressures, smoke more cigarettes, have higher serum cholesterol levels and are more obese, the gradient of coronary heart disease by socioeconomic level is not explained totally by these differences in cardiovascular risk factors or by use of medical care services. The possible importance of education and social support resources in accounting for this gradient is suggested by a recent report (Ruberman *et al.*, 1984). In a study of men who had survived a first myocardial infarction, men with lower levels of education had mortality rates twice as high as men with more education. Men with low education also tended to be more socially isolated and to have experienced more life stress, whereas men with more education had more social support. Also, the Multiple Risk Factor Intervention Trial (MRFIT) identified low educational achievement as a strong risk factor for incidence of coronary heart disease (Berkman and Breslow, 1983). Results of these studies indicate the possible importance of education and socioeconomic status on risk for coronary heart disease.

Recently, studies of occupational influences on coronary heart disease have been reported. Studies conducted by Karasek *et al.* (1981, 1982) demonstrated that individuals experiencing demanding work with few opportunities to control the job situation had increased prevalence of coronary heart disease and increased incidence of mortality. Similarly, Alfredsson *et al.* (1982) conducted a case-controlled study of incident myocardial infarction cases and reported that work and occupations characterized by hectic work and low control over work tempo and skill variety had an increased risk of myocardial infarction. The relationship of occupation to development of coronary heart disease also was tested in the Framingham Heart Study by Lacroix. Self-reported perceptions of work and job titles were used to classify exposure to high demand and low control work. Employed women who described their jobs as high demand and low control exhibited a three-fold greater risk of coronary heart disease compared to women reporting low demand job situations. The associations persisted after controlling for standard coronary risk factors. Thus, occupational titles and perceptions of work can be used to classify jobs into high demand and low control categories which have a predictive relation to cardiovascular risk factors and development of coronary heart disease.

Several studies have reported an increased risk of coronary heart disease among people with weak social support. Among 6 928 men and women in Alameda County, California followed for nine years, mortality rates from coronary heart disease were twice as high in those with few social connections (Berkman and Syme, 1979; Berkman and Breslow, 1983). This relationship persisted after controlling for socio-economic status, cigarette smoking, alcohol intake, obesity, physical activity, race and health status. A Social Network Index was developed according to marriage, contacts with extended family and close friends, church group membership, and other group affiliations. Contacts with friends and relatives were also measured by the number of close friends and relatives a respondent reported and the frequency with which they visited. The likelihood of dying from other causes also was reduced in those with high scores for network and social support characteristics.

In the Israeli Ischemic Heart Disease Study, a prospective cohort study of almost 10 000 Israeli male civil service and municipal employees has been reported (Medalie and Goldbourt, 1976). In this study, men aged 40 and over were followed intensively for five years. A relationship was reported between psychosocial problems and the love and support of the wife as important predictors of the development of angina pectoris. However, these same variables did not predict myocardial infarction (Goldbourt *et al.*, 1975).

Although results of these studies suggest that sociocultural factors influence the development of coronary heart disease, further research is necessary. Evidence linking social support with coronary heart disease is provocative but weak. Furthermore, the underlying mechanisms by which support influences coronary heart disease have not been studied. In addition, conceptualizations and measurements of social support need to be standardized.

Psychological influences

The psychological characteristics that have been evaluated most critically for their relation to coronary heart disease are Type A coronary-prone behaviour pattern, anger and hostility. In recognition of the fact that the Type A coronary-prone behaviour pattern is a multidimensional construct, many investigators have attempted to identify various components of the behaviour pattern and determine their relationship to various clinical manifestations of coronary heart disease. In addition, the reliability of measurement techniques and the stability of populations in which the measurements have been made have been studied.

The Type A coronary-prone behaviour pattern has been studied as a possible risk factor for coronary heart disease. Assessment of this behaviour pattern has usually been based on, or correlated with, results of structured interviews. The Framingham Type A Scale (Rosenman *et al.*, 1964) has also been used to assess Type A behaviour pattern. Validations of these assessment techniques have been obtained in the Western Collaborative Group Study (Rosenman *et al.*, 1964) and the Framingham Study (Haynes *et al.*, 1978, 1980). It should be noted that, even among populations similar to the original validation population, the percentage of Type A's is increasing (Haynes *et al.*, 1980). Since an increasing number of individuals are being classified as Type A at a time when coronary heart disease rates are decreasing, the specificity of the assessment techniques for prediction of cardiovascular diseases has been lessened.

An additional prospective study regarding the influence of Type A behaviour on coronary heart disease morbidity and mortality is the clinical trial, the Multiple Risk Factor Intervention Trial (MRFIT, 1979, 1982). The MRFIT was designed to test the effects of a multifactor intervention programme on coronary heart disease mortality in men aged 35–57 years at high risk for coronary heart disease. As part of the MRFIT, a structured interview was administered to participants at eight of the 22 centres and all men were followed for a minimum of six years and an average of seven years. Univariate and multivariate analyses of the MRFIT data showed that no relationship existed between Type A behaviour pattern assessed by the structured interview and coronary heart disease morbidity and mortality. The participants in the AMIS were assessed using the Jenkins Activity Survey at 18 of the 30 centres, and results of data analysis showed that the Jenkins Activity Survey was not predictive of recurrence of a major coronary event in the study sample. Results of these studies have elicited a great deal of controversy concerning assessment of Type A coronary-prone behaviour patterns and their association with coronary heart disease.

In addition, the Type A coronary-prone behaviour pattern is a complex mixture of several common behaviour tendencies including competitiveness, hostility and impatience. Several studies have demonstrated that overall Type A assessment by the structured interview can be predicted from subjective ratings of the subjects' voice stylistics (Schuker and Jacobs, 1977; Scherwitz et al., 1977). Moreover, a study by Howland and Siegman (1982) has shown that objective, semi-automated procedures for measuring speech variables were effective in predicting Type A–Type B classifications. Further studies are necessary to determine the relationship between components of the Type A behaviour pattern and development of coronary heart disease.

Although the structured interview does elicit Type A behaviour, it does not provide information concerning the frequency with which similar types of elicitors occur during normal daily activities of any particular individual. Presumably, an individual with a higher frequency of challenging situations would be at higher risk for any damaging effects of Type A behaviour. Thus, assessment of Type A behaviour should probably include an assessment of the frequency of events that might elicit the coronary-prone behaviour pattern.

Measures of anger and hostility have also been used to assess psychological influences on coronary heart disease. High levels of hostility as assessed by the Cook–Medley Hostility Inventory, a sub-scale derived from the Minnesota Multiphasic Personality Inventory (MMPI), predicted incidence of coronary heart disease as well as total mortality in a 25-year follow-up study of 255 physicians who completed the MMPI while in medical school (Barefoot et al., 1983). This relationship was independent of the effect of smoking status, age, family history of hypertension and current hypertensive status taken individually in the analyses. In a second study, the Western Electric Study, Cook-Medley Hostility scores also were related to 10-year incidence of major coronary heart disease events (Shekelle et al., 1983). In general, the available prospective studies show a relationship between measures of anger and hostility and cardiovascular events, including coronary heart disease and stroke as well as total mortality from causes other than coronary heart disease.

Recently, Dembroski and colleagues have demonstrated through multivariate analyses that several psychological characteristics were significant predictors of coronary artery disease in patients referred for coronary arteriography (Dembroski *et al.*, 1983). Data from these angiographic studies showed that characteristics such as irritability, anger, and cynicism coded from the structured interview were related to the extent of coronary artery disease. In addition, the mode of anger expression also appeared to be a significant correlate of coronary heart disease, in that patients who were judged to hold anger in and be high in hostility had greater levels of coronary artery disease than those patients judged to directly express anger outwardly. These relationships were evident after controlling for the presence of major risk factors such as serum level of cholesterol, level of arterial blood pressure, history of cigarette smoking and family history of coronary heart disease.

3. Pathophysiological mechanisms

Arterial hypertension

Many comparative studies of sympathetic nervous system activity have been carried out in human subjects with essential hypertension and those with average levels of blood pressure. Although many indicators have been used to estimate relative sympathetic nervous system activity, plasma norepinephrine levels are the physiological variable accepted by most investigators as the most valid measure available in human subjects. Many comparative studies have reported higher levels of norepinephrine in hypertensive groups than in normotensive controls, but the differences have been small when blood has been sampled under resting conditions. However, results of several studies suggest that patients with essential hypertension show exaggerated norepinephrine responses to physiological stimuli associated with orthostasis, isotonic and isometric exercise, exposure to cold, hypoglycaemia, hypoxia or pain, and to psychological stimuli eliciting emotional responses such as anxiety or anger (Goldstein, 1981, 1983).

The first detailed studies of cardiovascular and renal function during psychological testing were performed by Brod *et al.* (1959). They used mental arithmetic as a psychological stimulus administered in both normotensive and hypertensive subjects. During the stimulus of mental arithmetic, the systolic, diastolic and mean blood pressures rose in association with an increase in cardiac output and a reduction in total peripheral vascular resistance. Renal clearance of *para*-aminohippurate decreased, indicating an increase in renal vascular resistance, forearm skin temperature fell, indicating skin vasoconstriction, and blood flow through skeletal muscle in the forearm rose to more than six times its original value. Cardiovascular and renal function returned to original values within a few minutes after stopping mental arithmetic. Subsequent studies by other investigators (Obrist *et al.*, 1974) have also focused attention on skeletal muscle blood flow, while effects of behavioural stimuli on renal function have been less thoroughly studied.

The influence of psychological stimuli on heart rate and contractility in human subjects has been studied by Obrist and his colleagues (Obrist *et al.*, 1974, 1978; Light and Obrist, 1980). In one set of experiments, a reaction-time task was imposed in which a visual preparatory signal was followed by an auditory response signal. A correct and rapid response produced a monetary reward, and a slow or incorrect response occasionally caused delivery of an electrical shock to the leg. During the preparatory phase, heart rate and blood pressure rose, then returned towards the baseline until the time of responding occurred. Then heart rate rose by approximately 6 bpm until the time that the electrical shock might be delivered, while systolic and diastolic blood pressures returned to baseline values. Other investigators reported that human subjects varied markedly in reactivity to psychological stimuli. However, magnitude of individual responses for heart rate, systolic blood pressure and diastolic blood pressure showed consistency over two experimental sessions separated by an interval of one week.

Individual variability in renal responses to psychological stimuli has been demonstrated in relation to patients with essential hypertension and normal subjects with a family history of hypertension. Hollenberg *et al.* (1981) used a non-verbal IQ test to demonstrate the influence of a mild psychological stimulus on arterial blood pressure, heart rate, renal blood flow, plasma renin activity and plasma aldosterone concentration in normal subjects with no family history of hypertension, in normal subjects who had a parent with hypertension and in patients with essential hypertension. Transient moderate increases in heart rate and blood pressure were more common in patients with hypertension. Renal blood flow fell in each of the patients with essential hypertension and rose in the majority of subjects with normal blood pressure. Plasma renin activity rose in most patients with essential hypertension and fell in a majority of normal subjects with a negative family history. Both the renal vascular response and the change in plasma renin activity were intermediate in normal subjects with a family history positive for hypertension. Results of these studies indicate an abnormality in the control of both renal circulation and renin release in patients with essential hypertension, and in some normotensive subjects whose parents have hypertension.

Exposure to psychological stimuli has also been shown to reduce urinary excretion of sodium and water. Light *et al.* (1983) used a water-loading procedure in young men with normal levels of blood pressure with and without a family history of hypertension and men with borderline levels of systolic hypertension. A reaction-time task with monetary incentives was effective in evoking increases in heart rate and blood pressure. None of the men with normosensitive parents reduced their excretion of sodium while performing the task, while those with borderline hypertension or hypertensive parents retained sodium and water. The greatest reductions in excretion were seen in those with the greatest increases in heart rate. Thus, psychological stimuli induced sodium retention in subjects with evidence of increased sympathetic nervous system activity.

Psychological mechanisms influencing cardiovascular responses to stimuli depend upon degree of active coping responses during behavioural challenges (Frankenhaeuser and Rissler, 1970; Obrist, 1976; Light and Obrist, 1980; Light, 1981). Intensity of efforts to cope have been shown to be influenced by the role of perceived controlability

(Obrist *et al.*, 1978; Light and Obrist, 1980). Thus, greater changes in heart rate and blood pressure occurred in patients with control over aversive stimuli where they continued their efforts to control them than in subjects without control. However, reduced cardiovascular responses occurred when attempts to control were easy to execute and a favourable outcome was guaranteed (DeGood, 1975). Intense efforts to cope are postulated to facilitate sympathetic nervous system activity and to enhance cardiovascular responses to stimuli. Contrada *et al.* (1982) reported that subjects provided with an opportunity to avoid aversive stimulation displayed shorter response time latencies than subjects for whom aversive stimulation was unrelated to their performance. Greater reactivity in blood pressure and plasma levels of epinephrine occurred when aversive stimulation was contingent upon reaction-time speed. These investigators also reported that subjects with a Type A behaviour pattern who displayed high levels of competitiveness, time urgency and hostility had greater systolic blood pressure and heart rate responses than subjects displaying a Type B behaviour pattern, having less competitiveness, time urgency and hostility. The results of these experiments indicate that behaviour patterns, perception of controlability and active coping all influence the magnitude of cardiovascular responses to behavioural challenge. As a general indication of responsiveness, Light has proposed that subjects with the greatest sympathetic nervous system response to behavioural challenge display greater than average increases in heart rate during active coping with behavioural challenge.

Further studies of interactions between task incentives and behaviour pattern have been conducted by Blumthal *et al.* (1983). Behaviour of subjects was categorized as Type A or B by using a Structured Interview Technique. Results indicated that the presence or absence of explicit incentives affected task performance for subjects with Type A behaviour, but not for those with Type B patterns. In particular, those with Type A behaviour patterns gave more responses more quickly when offered monetary reward. In contrast, the effects of incentive on cardiovascular responses were observed in subjects with the Type B behaviour patterns but not in those with the Type A patterns. Those with the Type A behaviour patterns showed increased systolic blood pressure, heart rate and skeletal muscle vasodilation in both conditions, while those with Type B patterns showed increased heart rate and systolic blood pressure only when incentives were offered. Thus, it would appear that subjects with Type A behaviour patterns had increased cardiovascular response under all conditions, whereas those with Type B behaviour patterns showed enhanced cardiovascular responses only when the opportunity for reward was made explicit. These results suggest that cardiovascular responses may be dissociated from psychomotor behaviour in some individuals more than others.

Evidence that central neurochemical changes may occur in response to psychological factors has been presented in studies of serum prolactin levels. Subjects anticipating anaesthesia and surgery have been shown to have increased serum prolactin levels (Corenblum and Taylor, 1981). The elevation in serum prolactin levels in anticipation of the surgical procedure was enhanced by administration of a dopaminergic antagonist, Pimozide. Studies of medical students undertaking written examinations showed a rise of plasma prolactin levels that continued throughout the examination

(Nguyen *et al.*, 1982). Results of all these studies are consistent with the observations in spontaneously hypertensive rats in which the dopamine agonist Bromocriptine reduced plasma catecholamine levels and plasma renin activity as well as blood pressure following stress of immobilization. These results suggest that cardiovascular, behavioural and psychological mechanisms may be influenced by central dopaminergic and noradrenergic activity.

Atherosclerosis and coronary heart disease

Physiological influences

The majority of studies directed towards physiological influences on coronary heart disease have been concerned with the major risk factors of hypertension, serum total cholesterol concentration and cigarette smoking. Recently, emphasis has been placed on lipoproteins transporting cholesterol and on glucose intolerance (Gotto, 1982). The plasma lipoproteins are complexes of lipid and protein that function to transport the plasma lipids in a stable, soluble form (Verdery and Nichols, 1975). The triglyceride-rich lipoproteins are the chylomicrons and very low density lipoproteins (VLDL). These are attacked by the enzyme lipoproteins lipase, which catalyses the hydrolysis of triglyceride to fatty acid and diglyceride. The enzyme, which is attached to the surface of endothelial cells, can be released into the circulation by intravenous heparin. Its synthesis depends on insulin, and its activity is increased by oestrogen, physical exercise and probably by alcohol. It is positively correlated with the concentration of high density lipoproteins (HDL) and is a key enzyme in regulating lipoprotein metabolism. Chylomicron remnants in HDL are formed through the action of lipoprotein lipase. The surface components of the triglyceride-rich lipoproteins are incorporated into HDL, resulting in the conversion of the smaller HDL_3 to HDL_2.

Relationships between atherosclerosis, glucose intolerance and insulin activity have been reported by many investigators. Physiological studies have shown that plasma insulin levels are higher after an oral glucose load in subjects with coronary or peripheral arteriosclerosis. Epidemiological studies have demonstrated a relationship between plasma insulin levels and the incidence of coronary heart disease. Ducimetiere *et al.* (1980) measured serum cholesterol, serum triglycerides, systolic blood pressure, body weight and height, as well as recording history of cigarette smoking. In addition, they measured plasma glucose and plasma insulin levels before and two hours after a 75 g oral glucose load. The population was 7246 non-diabetic working men aged 43–54 years who were initially free from heart disease and were followed for 63 months, on average. They demonstrated that the fasting plasma insulin level and the fasting insulin/glucose ratio were positively associated with risks for myocardial infarction and coronary heart disease mortality independent of all other factors. They concluded that high insulin levels constituted an independent risk factor for coronary heart disease complications in middle-aged non-diabetic men.

Stout (1977, 1982) has reviewed the scientific literature concerning relationship of abnormal circulating insulin levels and atherosclerosis. He reviewed the evidence that hyperinsulinaemia occurs in patients with arteriosclerosis and is a risk factor for those without clinical manifestations. The high insulin levels associated with obesity, hyper-triglyceridaemia and adult onset diabetes mellitus may be a cause for atherosclerosis in some of those individuals. In addition, he reviewed the evidence that insulin results in proliferation of vascular smooth muscle cells, inhibition of lipolysis and synthesis of cholesterol, phospholipids, and triglycerides. These effects of insulin might promote atherogenesis. Consequently, the combination of clinical and experimental evidence suggests that high levels of circulating insulin may have a role in the development of atherosclerosis.

A combination of elevated cortisol secretion, hyperinsulinaemia, and hypertri-glyceridaemia may create a vicious cycle with atherogenic potential. Steiner and Vranic (1982) reviewed the evidence that hypertriglyceridaemia can interfere with metabolic processes involving insulin even without concomitant obesity or diabetes mellitus of adult onset type. They concluded that hyperinsulinaemia can stimulate triglyceride-containing lipids with atherogenic potential, and the combination constitutes a vicious cycle. Insulin apparently has direct effects on vascular smooth muscle proliferation and triglyceride-containing lipids with atherogenic potential would hasten the process of atherosclerosis. Elevated secretion of cortisol may influence the metabolic response to insulin.

Vascular smooth muscle cells have been studied for effects of insulin on proliferation in cell cultures. Stout *et al.* (1975) compared the growth of cells in culture medium to which insulin had been added in combination with serum. There was a significant linear relationship between the logarithm of the insulin dose and cell growth. In addition, vascular smooth muscle cells showed a diminished response to serum when insulin was extracted from it. However, the highest concentration of insulin produced only 50% of the effect observed following incubation in 5% serum. Results of these experiments suggest that insulin had growth-promoting properties, but that it was not the only growth-promoting factor in serum. Both lipoproteins (Ross and Glomset, 1983) and platelets (Ross *et al.*, 1974) may also have the potential of stimu-lating proliferation of vascular smooth muscle cells.

It has been known for some time that glucocorticoid excess prolongs the removal of glucose during a glucose tolerance test in normal humans (Fajans and Conn, 1954). Also, hypersecretion of adrenal cortical hormones in Cushing's disease has a diabeto-genic effect. However, the mechanism whereby glucocorticoids may influence removal of glucose from blood is poorly understood. Shamoon *et al.* (1980) examined the influ-ence of cortisol on glucose metabolism during continuous infusion of cortisol during a period of five hours. Normal adult men and women were studied after consuming a standard carbohydrate diet and fasting overnight before observations were made. Infusion of cortisol increased levels of glucose in plasma without influencing rates of glucose production. Removal of glucose from blood was reduced, which resulted in cortisol-induced hyperglycaemia. These effects of cortisol on glucose metabolism occurred in the absence of significant changes in plasma insulin or glucagon concentrat-ions. Concomitant effects on fatty acid and amino acid metabolism suggested that cortisol interfered with the cellular action of insulin.

Similar studies of epinephrine also have been performed in human subjects. Soman *et al.* (1980) studied the effects of epinephrine infused intravenously into normal young men and women during a period of four hours. They reported a prompt 45% rise in glucose output and a 120% rise in free fatty acid levels, both of which declined to basal levels within 90 minutes. No significant effect on plasma insulin or glucagon levels was observed. Rate of removal for glucose from plasma decreased by 25% and remained suppressed throughout the 4-hour experiment. The authors concluded that epinephrine had a persistent effect in decreasing removal of glucose, but only transiently increased the output of glucose and free fatty acids. No effect of epinephrine infusion on β-adrenergic binding to lymphocytes was observed. Although no direct measurements of insulin activity were made, results of these experiments are compatible with an interference by epinephrine in the influence of insulin on metabolic processes associated with glucose and lipid metabolism.

Further studies of the effects of epinephrine on lipid metabolism were reported by Dimsdale *et al.* (1982). These investigators produced physiological elevations of plasma epinephrine levels in cynomolgus monkeys. A suspension of epinephrine was injected subcutaneously twice each day, produced increases in epinephrine levels for approximately six hours each day. During the 2-week period of study, the diets remained constant and no change in animal weight was observed. After two weeks, the cholesterol levels in plasma increased by an average of 15 mg%. Four animals also studied during treatment with saline injections showed no increase in plasma cholesterol levels. Although no studies of the mechanism for increasing cholesterol levels were performed, results are consistent with a stimulation of lipid metabolism caused by the reduced influence of insulin on glucose and lipid metabolism.

Insulin sensitivity and levels of insulin in blood may also be altered in patients with mild essential hypertension. These abnormalities may contribute to renal retention of sodium, and they may provoke lipid accumulation in arterial walls. These abnormalities of insulin function and glucose metabolism may contribute to arterial hypertension, and they may also contribute to the increased risk of coronary heart disease observed in patients with essential hypertension.

Singer *et al.* (1985) performed glucose tolerance tests and measured the levels of glucose, insulin, free fatty acids, triglycerides, total cholesterol and high density lipoprotein cholesterol every hour during the day in eight men with mild arterial hypertension and 20 men with normal levels of blood pressure. They reported that insulin response after a glucose load and after each meal was significantly increased in hypertensive men as compared to the controls. Glucose tolerance and postprandial glucose levels were not different between groups. However, the levels of free fatty acids were higher in the postabsorptive phase of men with hypertension than in controls. Levels of triglycerides and cholesterol were the same in both groups. Apparently, men with essential hypertension had increased levels of insulin and decreased insulin sensitivity compared to men with normal levels of blood pressure, and treatment with drugs to lower blood pressure to normal levels may not restore insulin function to normal.

Studies in non-human primates have demonstrated a relationship between physiological reactivity and severity of coronary arteriosclerosis (Manuck *et al.*, 1983). In this investigation, cynomolgus monkeys that were moderately atherogenic were identified as either 'high' or 'low' heart rate reactive animals based on their responses to threat of capture. Following necropsy, the higher heart rate reactive animals were found to have developed nearly twice the coronary atherosclerosis of their low heart rate reactive counterparts. Also, the high heart rate reactors were those who had the greatest aggressive tendencies during social interactions with other monkeys.

In a prospective study of physiological reactivity in human subjects, the relationship between response to the cold pressor test and coronary heart disease has been reported (Keys *et al.*, 1971). Those investigators reported that the magnitude of subjects' diastolic blood pressure responses to cold immersion was associated significantly with the development of coronary heart disease during a 23-year follow-up. Retrospective and case-controlled studies contrasting the psychophysiological responses of pesons with and without coronary heart disease have also been reported (Nestel *et al.*, 1967; Schiffer *et al.*, 1976; Dembroski *et al.*, 1979; Sime *et al.*, 1980; Krantz *et al.*, 1981; Corse *et al.*, 1982). Most of these studies demonstrated a heightened reactivity to laboratory challenges in patients with histories of coronary heart disease when these individuals were compared with subjects who did not have coronary heart disease. Autonomic and neuroendocrine response characteristics of subjects with Type A coronary-prone behaviour patterns have been reported on exposure to diverse psychological and physical challenges. In the majority of studies, Type A subjects were found to exhibit larger increases in blood pressure, heart rate, plasma catecholamines and plasma cortisol levels relative to Type B subjects when exposed to laboratory challenges. These effects were seen most consistently when subjects were faced with threat of failure, harrassment or competitive task demand during personal interactions and when instructional sets were designed to ensure high levels of task involvement (Krantz and Manuck, 1984).

Behavioural influences

NEUROENDOCRINE FUNCTION

Many investigators have reported results of experiments concerning behavioural influences on physiological processes. The majority of studies performed have demonstrated effects on cardiovascular function. In particular, changes in heart rate and blood pressure have been studied under a variety of behavioural conditions. Other investigators have studied behavioural influences on neuroendocrine processes. In general, psychological factors have been shown to influence secretion of cortisol, epinephrine and norepinephrine. Although the psychological characteristics of experimental conditions used to test behavioural influences are not well defined, some general characteristics of situations influencing secretion of cortisol and epinephrine can be stated.

One characteristic of situations provoking increased secretion of cortisol is novelty of an experimental situation. Davis *et al.* (1981) tested normal young men under a graded exercise tolerance procedure. One group of subjects was experienced with exercise testing and the other group had no previous experience with the procedure. The subjects in both groups had similar capacities for physical work. No significant relationship could be demonstrated between maximal oxygen uptake, venuous lactate concentrations, Borg ratings of perceived exertion or serum cortisol responses during exercise. However, the post-exercise increase in serum cortisol levels was greater in the naive subjects. Serum cortisol increased by 59% in the experienced subjects and 138%

in the naive subjects. The authors concluded that novelty was the major determinant in the increased cortisol response in naive subjects compared to experienced subjects. Furthermore, this cortisol response bore little relationship to maximal oxygen uptake, heart rate or venous lactate concentrations. Apparently, the magnitude of response observed in cortisol concentrations was influenced more by psychological factors than the physiological effects of exercise.

The adaptation of response to psychological factors such as novelty or fear of failure has also been studied. Ursin *et al.* edited a monograph concerning the process of coping in young men under training in the Norwegian Army Parachute School (Ursin *et al.*, 1978). The authors postulated that coping would be a crucial dimension for coping with fear and amelioration of physiological responses. All men were asked to record a self-rating of fear before and after each jump from a practice tower used in the early stages of training for parachute jumping. There was a gradual reduction in fear levels reported. At the time of each jump from the practice tower, instructors kept records of the jumps and rated each jump as accepted or not accepted. As training proceeded, a few more criteria were added in the evaluation of each jump, and the irregularities in, the curve reflect these changes in criteria for acceptable jumps.

Plasma levels of cortisol also were obtained during repeated experiences with parachute training. For each jump day, two samples of blood were obtained, one immediately after the jump and one 20 minutes later. Values obtained immediately after the jumps showed a highly significant change on successive days and there was a significant fall from day to day until the third sample day, when the levels seemed to plateau. Similar results were reported for blood levels of glucose and free fatty acids. Measurements of epinephrine and norepinephrine in urine demonstrated increased levels during the first jump day with a return to basal levels at the time of the third sample day, i.e., jump days. The authors interpreted these results as demonstrating that improved performances and reduction of fear reduced the magnitude of physiological responses during parachute training.

Another psychological characteristic of test situations is mental task demand and efforts to cope with those demands. Brandenberger *et al.* (1980) measured plasma levels of catecholamines and pituitary adrenal hormones in normal healthy male college students while they performed a short-term memory task under quiet or noisy conditions. Performing the task led to significant increases in the plasma levels of cortisol. Similarly, there were significant increases in plasma levels of epinephrine and norepinephrine. Cortisol responses in all subjects were greater during the first experimental session than during the second session. Exposure to noise did slightly amplify the cortisol response to the task, but had little effect on the plasma levels of epinephrine and norepinephrine. In addition, a significant correlation was found between individual plasma cortisol increments and error rates assessed from an accuracy of recall variable. The relation between individual errors and plasma cortisol persisted in the second session, and the increments in plasma cortisol were greatest during the first experimental session. The authors interpreted these results as demonstrating a relationship between sympathoadrenomedullary activity and intentional demand with an additional relationship between adrenocortical activity and success in coping with the mental task.

Behavioural influences on catecholamine responses to test situations can be further defined according to differential responses of epinephrine and norepinephrine. Psychological factors have a greater effect on epinephrine responses than in norepinephrine responses, whereas physical factors have a greater effect on norepinephrine responses. LeBlanc *et al.* (1979) measured plasma epinephrine and norepinephrine levels as well as blood pressure and heart rate in 12 normal young men. They were studied before, during and after a cold hand test, a mental arithmetic test and a combination of both of these tests. Systolic blood pressure increased during immersion of one hand in cold water, during the mental arithmetic test, and when both tests were given simultaneously. No significant difference in systolic blood pressure response was seen during any of these trials. In contrast, the response of plasma epinephrine was substantially greater during the mental arithmetic test than during the cold hand test. Plasma epinephrine increased during the mental arithmetic test and when both tests were given simultaneously but showed little increase during immersion of one hand in cold water. A third pattern of response was observed in levels of plasma norepinephrine. Plasma norepinephrine increased during immersion of one hand in cold water, during the mental arithmetic test and when both tests were given simultaneously. In contrast to the pattern observed with systolic blood pressure and plasma epinephrine levels, plasma levels of norepinephrine remained elevated for at least 10 minutes after beginning each trial, whereas levels of systolic blood pressure and plasma epinephrine had returned to basal levels within this period of time. Thus, responses of systolic blood pressure and plasma levels of norepinephrine were similar during trials involving either psychological or physical factors. In contrast, response of plasma epinephrine was greater during mental arithmetic than during immersion of one hand in cold water. Apparently, elevations in plasma levels of epinephrine reflect a physiological response to psychological factors.

Additional influences of psychological factors on neuroendocrine secretion have been demonstrated in studies of plasma renin activity. Januszewicz *et al.* (1979) studied normal men and women with essential hypertension who were hospitalized and maintained on a standard hospital diet with normal sodium intake. These subjects were studied during a mental arithmetic test combined with noise. Concentrations of plasma and urine catecholamines and their metabolites as well as plasma renin activity before and after the test were measured. Measurements of plasma demonstrated significant increases in epinephrine, norepinephrine and plasma renin activity after mental arithmetic. These investigators did not find any substantial differences in the response of catecholamines between hypertensive and normotensive subjects. Elevations in plasma renin activity after mental arithmetic were actually greater in normal subjects than in those with hypertension. Thus, although the authors were not able to detect substantial differences between responses of normal subjects and patients with essential hypertension, they were able to demonstrate a substantial effect of psychological factors on plasma renin activity as well as plasma levels of epinephrine and norepinephrine.

The effects of psychological factors on healthy individuals over longer periods of time than in those investigations cited above have also been studied. Although many experiments conducted under laboratory conditions suggest a rapid adaptation of psychological responses to psychological factors, observations of normal subjects in natural situations indicate that chronic exposure to psychological factors may have enduring effects on neuroendocrine processes. Timio and Gentili (1976) and Timio *et al.* (1979) have studied the neuroendocrine responses in industrial workers under different working conditions. In one set of experiments, serial measurements of urinary epinephrine, norepinephrine and 11-OH-corticosteroid excretion were performed on men during four days of work under a payment-by-results schedule of compensation and during days of similar work compensated by a fixed salary (Timio and Gentili, 1976). Compared to working under a fixed salary schedule, subjects showed an increase in mean daily urinary excretion of epinephrine, norepinephrine and 11-OH-corticosteriods. Similar experiments with another group of workers showed that men had higher levels of urinary epinephrine, norepinephrine and 11-OH-corticosteriods while working on an assembly line than when working off the assembly line. The authors interpreted these results as indicating that psychosocial factors common to normal activities have significant effects on neuroendocrine function.

Persistence of behavioural influences on neuroendocrine processes was demonstrated by Timio *et al.* (1979) in studies of similar groups of workers under payment-by-results, fixed daily wage, assembly-line conditions and ordinary work conditions off the assembly line. Working under alternating schedules consisting of 4-day periods in each work condition did not ameliorate the pattern of greater neuroendocrine responses observed during the payment-by-results and assembly-line conditions. The authors interpreted results of their experiments as indicating that industrial workers experienced enhanced neuroendocrine responses to psychosocial factors during normal working conditions which also persisted for long periods of time.

Studies of Air Traffic Controllers conducted over long periods of time have also demonstrated the enduring effects of psychological factors on endocrine activity. Rose *et al.* (1982) measured levels of cortisol and growth hormones in blood on at least three different occasions in 201 controllers at work. Comparing controllers with themselves, the three largest endocrine studies showed a consistent but modest relationship between increases in workload and increases in cortisol levels. In addition, behavioural measurements revealed that on days with higher cortisol levels, the controllers did more work and showed more aroused behaviour. They also reported more subjective difficulty, more unusual events and more depression and fatigue at the time of their arrival at work. However, the controllers with the greatest increases in workload did not necessarily have the greatest increases in levels of cortisol. These results suggest that cortisol secretion was not closely associated with the amount of work done or the behavioural response to that work. Apparently, some adaptation to psychological factors occurred during work. Rose *et al.* (1982) also reported that some men showed a substantial increase in cortisol levels as workload increased. Behavioural measures also indicated that these controllers performed very well during periods of increased workload. They were generally judged by their peers to be more competent than average, and they were more likely than average to describe themselves as satisfied with their work. Apparently, they were highly motivated in their work, and this involvement may have facilitated their increase in levels of cortisol with increasing workload.

LIPID METABOLISM

Levels of cholesterol and lipoproteins in blood have strong relationships to nutritional status and inherited characteristics. These relationships have demonstrated in numerous clinical and epidemiological studies. However, lipid metabolism is also strongly influenced by psychological factors, and their effects on lipid metabolism can cause elevations in levels of cholesterol and lipoproteins in blood.

Dimsdale and Herd (1982) reviewed results of 60 studies in which plasma lipid levels were observed to respond to psychological factors. The majority of studies involved effects of psychological factors over short periods of time such as a few minutes or a few hours. However, some studies involved the effects of psychological factors over days, weeks or months. In all studies, the effects of unpleasant, novel or arousing situations were observed in relation to levels of free fatty acids, triglycerides and cholesterol in blood.

In these studies, levels of free fatty acids were almost invariably elevated. The percentage elevation ranged from 5% to more than 150%. Demonstration of elevation depended on obtaining a baseline measurement before the test situation was imposed.

Levels of triglycerides also responded to test situations, but they increased more slowly. Often they were not elevated during the test experience but increased several hours after the test. Unfortunately, this sequence of measurements in relation to test exposure was not consistent among all studies and results reported were inconsistent.

Most studies also found that levels of cholesterol increased during a response to psychological challenge. The percentage elevation ranged from 8% to 65% above baseline values. These effects were particularly evident in subjects exposed to natural situations for several weeks or months. In several studies, the percentage increase in level of cholesterol was greatest when subjects identified their own periods of greatest psychological distress.

Psychological techniques for lowering levels of cholesterol in blood have also been reported. Cooper and Aygen (1979) reported results of a study to determine the effect of a relaxation technique. Levels of cholesterol in blood were measured at the beginning and end of an 11-month period, in which 12 hypercholesterolaemic subjects regularly practised meditation. A control group of 11 hypercholesterolaemic subjects who did not use the technique were also followed for 11–13 months. Paired comparisons showed a significant reduction in levels of cholesterol in blood of those subjects who regularly practiced meditation. These results suggest that psychological factors can reduce as well as increase levels of lipids in blood.

4. Physiological indices of job stress

Heart rate and blood pressure

Measurement in blood pressure and heart rate have been used by many investigators to assess cardiovascular responses to physical and psychological factors. Since levels of blood pressure are a risk factor for cardiovascular disease, the situations which influence levels of blood pressure may contribute to the development of arterial hypertension and coronary heart disease. Many investigators have assumed that subjects with large and rapid changes in blood pressure and heart rate might be at greater risk of developing cardiovascular disease than subjects who have lesser changes in similar situations. The evidence available at present suggests that large rapid changes in blood pressure and heart rate are an index of individual responsiveness to test situations but are probably not pathological by themselves.

Measurements of blood pressure and heart rate have been a basic part of psycho-physiological studies by investigators for many years. A variety of physical stressors such as dynamic exercise under exercise tolerance testing and isometric work are examples of test situations demonstrating responses to physical stressors. Cognitive challenges such as mental arithmetic have been used to elicit changes in blood pressure and heart rate as measures of response to psychological stressors. The cold pressor test has been used as a test which combines effects of physical and psychological stressors. Using these tests, it has been possible to show a wide range of normal responses in blood pressure and heart rate.

The measurement of blood pressure and heart rate as physiological indices of job stress provides a rapid and sensitive measure of response to physical and psychological stressors. Results from previous studies indicate that some subjects are responders and some are non-responders, and that the intensity of response is fairly stable for each subject. With progress in electronic, mechanical and hydraulic devices, it is possible to monitor blood pressure automatically over long periods of time with minimal inconvenience to the subject and obtain automatic recordings of the results.

Although individual differences between subjects in response to physiological and psychological stressors are interesting in determining susceptibility to stressors, it is also a source of difficulty in assessing effects for subjects who simply do not respond in a test situation. In addition, blood pressure and heart rate are influenced by posture, physical activity, intake of caffeine, absorption of nicotine and dietary intake of sodium. Levels of blood pressure and responses of blood pressure and heart rate are also influenced by heredity and body composition. Although levels of blood pressure and heart rate and their responses to test situations are fairly reproducible within individuals, many of these factors may influence results differently under different conditions.

Under ideal conditions, measurements of blood pressure and heart rate provide sensitive indices of physical and psychological stress. Ideal conditions include measurements under baseline conditions with subjects resting comfortably in a bland environment. The most restful conditions would be obtained while subjects were on relief from usual daily activities such as during vacation. In addition, measurements should be made repeatedly to obtain reliable resting values. Once reliable baseline measures are obtained, the potential for response in each subject should be tested using physical and psychological stressors. Physical stressors may include the cold pressor test, isometric hand grip and dynamic work under an exercise tolerance test. Response to psychological stressors also should be measured using standard procedures such as mental arithmetic with measures of competence and performance included. These procedures would indicate the potential each subject has for response in test situations.

The response to test situations such as job conditions should be made during 24-hour periods. The periodic measurement of both blood pressure and heart rate during this time should be recorded automatically and correlated with features of the test situation objectively measured, perceptions of impact on a subject by self-report, and behaviour of the subject observed and measured objectively by others. In addition, the relationship between heart rate and blood pressure should be tracked and analysed.

Using this approach, it becomes possible to use responders as probes of test situations. Even those subjects who do not respond vigorously to physical and psychological stressors can be observed for their response to job situations, but the intensity of response may be less. Ultimately, the long-term rise in average level of blood pressure is more important than short-term responses. Consequently, the average level of blood pressure in a test situation during periods of several hours on several different days will be the most important measure of response to a job situation.

Although the ideal study of blood pressure and heart rate can be specified, there are many constraints imposed under normal conditions. Baseline values are difficult to obtain during rest and repeated measures are frequently difficult to obtain. The measurement of blood pressure and heart rate during 24-hour periods is expensive and analysis of data is time-consuming. Furthermore, all subjects must be used as their own controls, since each will respond more or less vigorously than others in similar situations. In fact, some subjects simply do not respond to physical and psychological stressors, and assessing the impact of test situations becomes difficult if blood pressure and heart rate are the only measures available.

In practical applications, baseline measures must be obtained under the best possible resting conditions. Since level of blood pressure is a risk for cardiovascular disease, individuals with sustained high levels would be those most worthy of intense study. During such studies, the influence of posture, physical activity, sodium intake, coffee consumption and nicotine absorption should be considered and kept as constant as possible. Also, the correlations of blood pressure and heart rate with the situation, individual perception and behaviour should be recorded. Since sustained high levels of blood pressure elicited in a job situation would be more important than large rapid but brief changes, periodic measurements using a standard blood pressure cuff can be satisfactory for good research investigation of physical and psychological stressors in test situations.

In the future, investigations of blood pressure and heart rate may be combined with other measures. In particular, the ECG wave-form components can be analysed for relations between heart rate, blood pressure and Q-T intervals (the time between the Q wave and the end of the T wave). Also, correlations can be made with respiratory rate, and cycle relationships between heart rate, blood pressure and respiratory rate provide information concerning the autonomic control of cardiovascular function. Additional information can be obtained from measurements of body temperature, both central and peripheral.

Catecholamines

Levels of epinephrine, norepinephrine and their metabolic products in blood and urine are the end result of complex physiological processes. Since the majority of epinephrine and norepinephrine released from adrenal medulla and adrenergic nerve terminals is

taken up by those nerve terminals, the levels of catecholamines in blood are not necessarily correlated with rates of secretion. However, the amount of epinephrine secreted
by the adrenal medulla does influence the proportion of epinephrine to norepinephrine
in blood. Epinephrine is normally 10–20% the concentration of norepinephrine in
blood, and increasing release of epinephrine from the adrenal medulla increases the
relative proportion of epinephrine even if re-uptake mechanisms maintain levels of catecholamines at low concentrations. Investigations indicate that secretion of epinephrine
from the adrenal medulla is influenced more by psychological factors, whereas
secretion of norepinephrine from adrenergic nerve terminals is influenced more by
physical factors.

Measurement of catecholamine levels in blood and urine has contributed a great deal
of information concerning physical and psychological stressors in test situations.
Results of many investigations have shown that, as intensity of psychological response
increases, the levels of epinephrine and norepinephrine in blood and urine also increase.
The recent development of sensitive and accurate measurements of catecholamines and
their metabolic products has enhanced the potential for their use in assessing responses
to physical and psychological stressors.

Results of many investigations have shown that catecholamines are secreted rapidly
in response to physical and psychological stressors. However, there are many individuals who respond very little and other individuals who respond with large increases
in levels of catecholamines in blood and urine. At present, information concerning the
neuroendocrinology of catecholamine function is well advanced. In addition, pharmacology has provided many compounds that are highly specific in mimicking or
blocking effects of catecholamines. Consequently, there are many opportunities for
sophisticated analysis of catecholamine secretion in test situations.

Many difficulties do arise in the interpretation of results. Many factors influence
rates of secretion and levels of concentrations in blood and urine. The amount of
sodium in the diet, subjects' posture, their physical activity, their intake of caffeine and
their absorption of nicotine influence rates of secretion and levels of concentration in
blood. In addition, the amount of norepinephrine in urine is influenced not only by fil-
tration from blood into the urine, but also by secretion of norepinephrine from adrenergic nerve terminals in the kidney itself. Furthermore, collection of urine frequently is
difficult because of poor understanding and co-operation by subjects in providing
specimens. Although it is possible to obtain a great deal of sophisticated information
concerning adrenergic nerve activity using measurements of catecholamines, these are
some of the difficulties which must be overcome.

In the ideal situation, very useful information can be obtained. The baseline values
must be obtained under resting conditions and values should be obtained on several
different days to ensure that baseline values are reliable and as low as possible. After
baseline values have been obtained, the potential for response should be evaluated
under standardized laboratory situations using both physical and psychological
stressors. Physical stressors such as isometric muscle contraction, dynamic exercise
under exercise tolerance testing and postural stress on a tilt table are useful to assess the
potential for response to physical stressors. In addition, turnover rates of epinephrine
and norepinephrine can be measured using labelled substances injected intravenously

by continuous infusion during several hours and then the rate of their disappearance measured as the infused substances are degraded or absorbed into adrenergic nerve terminals. Effects of psychological stressors also can be tested using mental arithmetic for cognitive challenges and psychological stress interviews to elicit emotional responses. In natural settings, continuous measurements of levels in blood can be obtained using a constant withdrawal pump and periodic sampling of blood obtained. Urine can be sampled frequently and measurements made on samples obtained at precise times during a 24-hour period. These measurements of levels in blood and urine can be related to situations which are evaluated objectively, to perceptions reported by subjects concerning their effect, cognitive effort and sense of competence, and behaviour can be measured by other observers. In each of the samples of blood and urine, the proportion of epinephrine to norepinephrine should be determined, both in the free hormone levels and their metabolic products. From these measurements, a thorough appreciation of catecholamine secretion in relation to physical and psychological stressors could be obtained.

Although the ideal situation might provide substantial information, many constraints are found in test situations. The 24-hour urine collections are difficult to obtain, and the use of a continuous withdrawal pump is costly and difficult to operate. All subjects must be used as their own controls, and responses to test situations must be repeated several times to overcome effects of novelty or fear of an experimental situation. The ideal conditions of the laboratory seldom can be obtained in natural settings.

In practical applications, the baseline measures obtained are usually the best available and should be repeated as often as possible. Since venipuncture and collection of blood is troublesome, collection of urine can suffice if the amounts of epinephrine, norepinephrine and their metabolites can be determined precisely. The influences of posture, physical activity, intake of caffeine, absorption of nicotine, ambient temperature and intake of sodium must be controlled. Complete collection of urine can be checked by using measurements of creatinine to estimate the total volume expected. Using precautions and observing test conditions carefully, it should be possible to obtain good information concerning effects of physical and psychological stressors in job situations.

Cortisol

The levels of cortisol in blood also are affected by both secretion and removal mechanisms. However, the pituitary ACTH secretion provides a feedback mechanism operative in relation to cortisol levels. Thus, the levels of cortisol are of significance, since they represent the end result of this feedback process. A complication for interpreting results of studies involving levels of cortisol in blood and urine is the pattern of diurnal secretion rates as well as absolute amounts secreted. Consequently, the maximal and minimal levels of secretions are important as well as the average levels or integrated values during a 24-hour period.

Most investigators concerned with studies of cortisol secretion have measured concentrations of cortisol in blood at two or three points during the day to assess the levels and patterns of secretion. In addition, some investigators include measurements of

17-OH- or 11-OH-corticosteroids as metabolic products representative of cortisol secreted into the blood. Recently, measurements of free cortisol concentrations have been made to determine the concentrations of active hormone present in blood and filtered into urine. In general, the levels of cortisol in blood and urine have been taken as an index of the intensity of cognitive effort elicited in some psychological test situations. In addition, levels of cortisol have been noted to increase under intense physical stimulations such as maximal dynamic exercise. Results of these studies by many investigators have provided a solid base of information concerning the effects of physical and psychological stressors on secretion of cortisol.

The recent advances in techniques for measuring cortisol in blood and urine have enhanced our understanding of its dynamics. In addition, the effects of cortisol on glucose metabolism, lipid metabolism, renal function and electrolyte balance have increased the potentials for understanding effects of physiological and psychological stressors on physiological function. For example, cortisol has a strong influence on potassium rhythm. The potassium tide released from skeletal muscle corresponds to the high levels of cortisol in blood, and the drop in cortisol during the day is followed by a reduction in potassium movement from muscle into blood and ultimately into urine. In addition, the effects of cortisol on exchange of sodium and potassium in the renal tubule influences the patterns of renal electrolyte excretion. The effects of cortisol on several systems can be used to assess the intensity of its effects in various test situations.

There are many difficulties encountered in studies involving measurements of cortisol. The diurnal pattern precludes the measurement of a steady baseline state during minutes or hours under resting conditions. Repeated measures on several different days can provide some confidence that baseline values have been obtained. However, any changes observed must be interpreted against a background of constant change in relation to the diurnal pattern. Other effects—eating meals, physical activity, changes in posture, and change in ambient temperature—must be noted and considered when analysing results. Finally, difficulties of collecting urine and obtaining complete samples are ever-present hazards in conducting studies of cortisol secretion.

In the ideal experimental situation, cortisol levels in blood and urine would be obtained under restful conditions over periods of several hours on several different days. In addition, sufficient number of samples must be obtained to fully document the diurnal pattern and to capture the maximal and minimal values for concentration of cortisol in blood at the appropriate times of day. After determining the diurnal pattern and its reliability, the potential for response should be obtained using both physical and psychological stressors. As in studies of catecholamines, the physical stressors commonly used are cold pressor test, isometric muscle contraction and dynamic exercise under exercise tolerance testing. The cold pressor test is also an effective means of eliciting endocrine responses and should be studied for its effects on secretion of cortisol. The psychological stressors that have been tested include mental arithmetic, and some assessment of competence, effort, motivation and adaptation should be obtained. Upon completion of measurements under controlled laboratory conditions, measurements in natural settings should be made during 24-hour collections. A constant withdrawal pump provides frequent samples of blood so that small changes in concentration can be detected. In addition, frequent samples of urine provide estimates of amounts filtered into urine. Along with measurements of cortisol and its metabolites, measurements of potassium in blood and urine and sodium in urine provide information concerning the effects of cortisol on electrolyte metabolism. All of these measurements, in the ideal situation, would provide a thorough assessment of cortisol function in test situations.

As with studies of cardiovascular function and catecholamines, there are many constraints on the ideal test situation. The use of a constant withdrawal pump is artificial and intrudes on normal daily activities. Its operation is cumbersome and costly. All subjects must be used as their own controls, and studies must be repeated on as many days as possible to overcome effects of novelty and to determine the adaptation which might occur in test situations. The result is that the ideal test situation seldom can be obtained. The most practical way to measure cortisol and its metabolites to assess physical and psychological stressors is in urine. By frequent sampling, the pattern of the diurnal rhythm can be obtained and the 24-hour sample provides an integrated measure of plasma levels. The combination of hormone levels with patterns of electrolytes provides information concerning the effects of cortisol on physiological systems. By combining measurements of creatinine with measurements of electrolytes and cortisol, it is possible to check on the adequacy of complete collection. The appropriate use of these measurement techniques should provide substantial information concerning the effects of physical and psychological stressors on cortisol secretion.

Lipids

Lipid metabolism is profoundly affected by neuroendocrine function. Adrenergic nerve stimulation causes release of free fatty acids from adipose tissue, and corticosteroids influence the balance between glucose and lipid metabolism at least partly through effects on sensitivity to insulin in muscle, adipose tissue and liver. Thus, lipid levels reflect adrenergic and corticosteroid activity while supplying the substrate for metabolic processes. Under ideal physiological conditions, the free fatty acids released from adipose tissue are metabolized to supply energy under aerobic metabolism. Under some conditions, the amounts of free fatty acids liberated exceed the requirements of metabolic processes, and the subsequent path of those lipid substances may enhance the risk of cardiovascular disease.

Results of many epidemiological and clinical investigations have demonstrated the relationship of lipid metabolism to risk of cardiovascular disease. In particular, the total levels of cholesterol concentration in blood have been demonstrated to increase the risk of atherosclerosis and coronary heart disease. Effects of heredity, nutrition and physical activity on levels of total cholesterol concentration in blood have been demonstrated. Effects of various interventions on cardiovascular risk have been assessed through measurements of free fatty acids, total cholesterol, high and low density lipoproteins and triglycerides. Effects of psychological factors have seldom been considered.

Measurements of lipid substances in blood provide rapid and sensitive indices of physiological and psychological stressors. The most rapid responses can be observed in levels of free fatty acids but within a few hours after free fatty acids have been released, the effects on concentrations of triglycerides can be observed. As in other physiological systems, many individuals have large and rapid responses to physiological and psychological stressors. Other individuals have little response, even under the most severe conditions. This difference between individuals allows us to identify individual characteristics which may increase risk for cardiovascular disease.

The major difficulties encountered in studying lipid responses to physical and psychological stressors are the responses to many different factors. These include heredity, gender, body composition, dietary intake of fat, physical activity and cigarette smoking. All of these factors influence lipid responses in test situations.

Under ideal conditions, the baseline measures would be obtained from individuals under resting conditions on several different days under constant conditions of nutrition, physical activity and other factors. In addition to responses that would be elicited by physical and psychological stressors, the metabolic responses to glucose and triglycerides would be observed. In this way, assessment of clearance and secretion would be obtained. The obvious importance of cholesterol level in its low-density lipoprotein and high-density lipoprotein components makes the measurement of these substances most important for assessing risk induced by test situations. Although the response of free fatty acids, β-OH-butyrate and glucose give important information concerning neuroendrocrine effects on metabolic function, ultimately the effects of test situations on lipoproteins provide the most important information. Accordingly, experiments should be designed to measure the gradual changes occurring over several weeks with as much control exerted as possible over physical activity, nutrition and other factors known to influence lipid metabolism.

The individuals most likely to be responsive will be those with high levels of cholesterol in low density lipoproteins and high levels of triglycerides in blood. In these individuals, changes in neuroendocrine function will have an effect on insulin sensitivity and degradation of triglycerides into high density and low density lipoproteins. Any individuals with low levels of cholesterol and triglycerides in blood will probably be unresponsive to most physical and psychological stressors.

Insulin function

Conditions which interfere with the influence of insulin on metabolic processes are said to increase insulin resistance. When insulin resistance was first defined it was measured by determining the rate of insulin–glucose uptake in patients with non-insulin-dependent diabetes mellitus or patients with severe obesity. The inference that insulin action was reduced was obtained by measuring the effects of insulin injected intravenously on levels of glucose in plasma or by combining administration of glucose and insulin intravenously and measuring plasma glucose concentrations during the next 60 minutes (Reaven, 1983). More recently, the mechanism and significance of insulin resistance has been studied from the perspective of receptor physiology (Flier, 1983). Insulin, like many other hormones, binds to specific receptors located on the surface of cells. Consequently, the number of receptors on target cells and the affinity of receptors for insulin determine the influence of insulin on metabolic processes. Direct measurements of insulin receptors on target tissues in several disease states indicate that decreased receptor concentration and affinity are responsible for insulin resistance (Roth *et al.*, 1975; Flier *et al.*, 1979). Also, the number of insulin receptors in tissues removed from patients with several diseases correlated inversely with the concentration of insulin present in plasma of those patients (Bar *et al.*, 1979). Many modulators of receptor concentration or affinity have been reported. These include the influence of diet, exercise, hormones and metabolic factors (Merimee *et al.*, 1976; Muggeo *et al.*, 1977; Thomopoulos *et al.*, 1977).

Ultimately, an important manifestation of insulin resistance is elevated levels of glucose in plasma, levels that are higher than would be expected in proportion to concentrations of insulin in plasma. A useful indicator of the average blood sugar concentration in an individual over a period of several weeks is the concentration of haemoglobin $A1_c$. This form of haemoglobin is present in red blood cells of normal subjects in a proportion of up to 5% of the total concentration of haemoglobin. In patients with diabetes mellitus and elevated plasma levels of glucose, concentrations of haemoglobin $A1_c$ may rise to 15%. Since haemoglobin synthesis is a slow and nearly irreversible reaction in red blood cells, the level of haemoglobin $A1_c$ reflects concentrations of glucose at the time the red blood cell was formed. Because red blood cells remain in the circulation for approimately 120 days, it takes several weeks for the concentration of haemoglobin $A1_c$ to reflect abrupt changes in levels of glucose in blood. Thus, measurement of haemoglobin $A1_c$ gives an objective assessment of the average concentration of glucose over long periods of time (Koenig and Cerami, 1980; Cesana *et al.*, 1985).

A relationship between haemoglobin $A1_c$, concentrations of lipoproteins in plasma and administration of insulin in patients with adult onset diabetes has demonstrated a relationship between diabetic control and lipoprotein profile. Schmitt *et al.* (1982) found that levels of cholesterol in serum of diabetic patients under poor control were substantially reduced when these patients were treated with insulin. The reduction in cholesterol paralleled the reduction in haemoglobin $A1_c$ concentrations. Levels of triglycerides in serum also were markedly reduced following treatment with insulin. Results of these experiments indicate not only the influence of insulin on lipid metabolism but also the value of measuring haemoglobin $A1_c$ in assessing average levels of glucose in plasma over long periods of time.

Another approach to studies of insulin resistance has been shown by Bar *et al.* (1976) who measured the concentration of insulin receptors on monocytes. A deficiency of receptors was observed that was inversely related to the basal insulin level, and diet was effective in restoring insulin binding to near-normal levels. Similar studies in obese subjects (Kolterman *et al.*, 1980) demonstrated that insulin receptor deficiency contributed to insulin resistance in obese subjects. Apparently, measurements of receptor concentration and affinity provide an index of average concentrations of insulin in blood. However, studies of receptor physiology indicate they have a half-life that can be measured in hours. Apparently, measurements of receptor concentration and affinity would not provide information about average concentrations of insulin over durations of several days or weeks.

Improving insulin sensitivity can be achieved through several therapeutic measures. The effect of physical training on insulin production in obesity has been demonstrated by Bjorntorp *et al.* (1970). They studied obese patients during a physical training programme which increased maximal oxygen uptake and increased muscle strength. Body weight actually increased during the training programme due primarily to an increase in body fat. A normal glucose tolerance test performed before and after the training programme showed no change in blood glucose values. However, there was a substantial reduction in the concentrations of insulin in plasma following the administration of glucose. The results of these studies were interpreted as indicating an increased insulin sensitivity of tissues. Since body fat mass was not decreased, the effect of physical training on insulin sensitivity apparently occurred independently of any change of adipose tissue function.

The observation that non-diabetic obese individuals had high circulating levels of insulin (Koram *et al.*, 1963; Bagdade *et al.*, 1967) suggests a resistance to the action of insulin. Studies of animal models of obesity indicate that a reduction in fat mass through diet corrects the insulin resistance (Kahn *et al.*, 1973).

5. Conclusions

The study of behavioural influences on physiological processes is influenced strongly by individual variation. Consequently, ipsative analysis must be performed in which all subjects serve as their own controls. A corollary of this is the need to compare all subjects under different conditions with well-established baseline measurements followed by thorough studies under test conditions.

An appreciation of the physiological processes under study is imperative for interpreting results. Levels of substances in blood and amounts appearing in urine often have little relation to rates of secretion or metabolic influence. An appreciation of turnover rates, metabolic pathways and physiological consequences must be obtained for each system under study.

The most compelling feature in all studies of individual responses to physical and psychological stressors is the enormous range of individual variability. Although each subject may have similar responses under similar situations on different days, the differences between subjects are frequently large. Some individuals can be termed responders in one system or another, but little information is available to determine whether individuals respond with similar intensity in all physiological systems. The capacity for physiological response must be determined under standardized test conditions to satisfy our concern for assessing intensity of response in natural test situations.

Three measures might prove useful for screening subjects during normal daily activities in natural situations. The first of these is the ratio of epinephrine to norepinephrine in urine or blood. It is expected that psychological factors would stimulate epinephrine secretion more than norepinephrine secretion, and the ratio of the catecholamines and their metabolic products should change under the varying influences of psychological and physical factors. The second of these measures is the ratio of potassium to sodium in urine. It is expected that the diurnal pattern of this ratio would be flattened when cortisol secretion is high and stays high without the usual diurnal pattern for its secretion when psychological factors have a strong influence over physiological function. The third of these measures involves lipoproteins, both total cholesterol and triglyceride levels in blood. It is expected that triglyceride levels would be high and HDL-cholesterol levels would be low when cortisol and catecholamine secretions are elevated under the influence of strong psychological factors. These measures are worth exploring to determine whether subjects are responding to situations with intense cognitive effort, strong emotional effects, or psychological distress.

The progress that has been made in physiology, psychology and biobehavioural technology makes it possible to study physiological indices of job stress. However, attention must be paid to the myriad of processes influencing the variables under study.

References

Alfredsson, L., Karasek, R. and Theorell, T. (1982). Myocardial infarction risk and psychosocial work environment: An analysis of the male Swedish working force. *Social Science and Medicine,* **16**(4), 463–467.

Bagdade, J., Bierman, E. and Porte, D. (1967). The significances of basal insulin levels in the evaluation of the insulin response to glucose in the diabetic and nondiabetic subjects. *Journal of Clinical Investigation,* **46**, 1549–1557.

Bar, R., Gorden, P., Roth, J., Kahn, C. and DeMeyts, P. (1976). Fluctuations in the affinity and concentration of insulin receptors on circulating monocytes of obese patients. *Journal of Clinical Investigation,* **58**, 1123–1135.

Bar, R., Harrison, L. and Muggeo, M. (1979). Regulation of insulin receptors in normal and abnormal physiology in humans. *Advances in Internal Medicine,* **24**, 23–52.

Barefoot, J.C., Dahlstrom, W.G. and Williams, W.B. (1983). Hostility, CHD incidence and total mortality: A 25-year follow-up study of 255 physicians. *Psychosomatic Medicine,* **45**, 59–64.

Berkman, L. and Breslow, L. (1983). *Health and Ways of Living: Findings from the Alameda County Study* (New York: Oxford University Press).

Berkman, L. and Syme, S.L. (1979). Social networks, host resistance and mortality: A nine-year followup study of Alameda County Residents. *American Journal of Epidemiology,* **109**, 186–204.

Bjorntorp, P., DeJounge, K., Sjostrom, L. and Sullivan, L. (1970). The effect of physical training on insulin production in obesity. *Metabolism,* **19**, 631–638.

Blumenthal, J.A., Lane, J.D., Williams, R.B., McKee, D.C., Haney, T. and White, A. (1983). Effects of task incentive on cardiovascular response in Type A and Type B individuals. *Psychophysiology,* **20**, 63–70.

Brandenberger, G., Follenius, M., Wittersheim, G. and Salame, P. (1980). Plasma catecholamines and pituitary adrenal hormones related to mental task demand under quiet and noise conditions. *Biological Psychology,* **10**, 239–252.

Brod, J., Fencl, V., Hejl, Z. and Jirka, J. (1959). Circulatory changes underlying blood pressure elevation during acute emotional stress (mental arithmetic) in normotensive and hypertensive subjects. *Clinical Science,* **18**, 269–279.

Cesana, G., Panza, G., Ferrario, M., Zanettini, R., Arnoldi, M. and Grieco, A. (1985). Can glycosylated hemoglobin be a job stress parameter? *Journal of Occupational Medicine,* **27**, 357–360.

Contrada, R.J., Glass, D.C., Krakoff, L.R., Krantz, D.S., Kehoe, K., Isecke, W., Collins, C. and Elting, E. (1982). Effects of control over aversive stimulation and Type A behaviour on cardiovascular and plasma catecholamine responses. *Psychophysiology*, **19**, 408–419.

Cooper, M. and Aygen, M. (1979). A relaxation technique in the management of hyper-cholesterolemia. *Journal of Human Stress*, **5**(4), 24–27.

Corenblum, B. and Taylor, P. (1981). Mechanisms of control of prolactin release in response to apprehension stress and anesthesia-surgery stress. *Fertility and Sterility*, **36**, 712–715.

Corse, C.D., Manuck, S.B., Cantwell, J.D., Giordani, B. and Matthews, K.A. (1982). Coronary-prone behavior pattern and cardiovascular response in persons with and without coronary heart disease. *Psychosomatic Medicine*, **44**, 449–459.

Davis, H., Gass, G. and Bassett, J. (1981). Serum cortisol response to incremental work in experienced and naive subjects. *Psychosomatic Medicine*, **43**, 127–132.

DeGood, D.E. (1975). Cognitive control factors and vascular stress response. *Psychophysiology*, **12**, 399—401.

Dembroski, T.M., MacDougall, J.M. and Dimsdale, J. (1984). Components of Type A, hostility, and anger in relationship to angiographic findings. *Psychosomatic Medicine*, **46**, 284.

Dembroski, T.M., MacDougall, J.M. and Lushene, R. (1979). Interpersonal interaction and cardiovascular response in Type A subjects and coronary patients. *Journal of Human Stress*, **5**, 28–36.

Dimsdale, J. and Herd, J.A. (1982). Variability of plasma lipids in response to emotional arousal. *Psychosomatic Medicine*, **44**, 413–430.

Dimsdale, J., Herd, J. and Hartley, L. (1982). Epinephrine mediated increases in plasma cholesterol. *Psychosomatic Medicine*, **45**, 227–232.

Ducimetiere, P., Eschwege, E., Papoz, L., Richard, J., Claude, J. and Rosselin, G. (1980). Relationship of plasma insulin levels to the incidence of myocardial infarction and coronary heart disease mortality in a middle-aged population. *Diabetologia*, **19**, 205–210.

Fajans, S. and Conn, J. (1954). An approach to the prediction of diabetes mellitus by modification of the glucose tolerance test with cortisone. *Diabetes*, **3**, 296–304.

Flier, J.S. (1983). Insulin receptors and insulin resistance. *Annual Review of Medicine*, **34**, 145–160.

Flier, J., Kahn, C. and Roth, J. (1979). Receptors, antireceptor antibodies, and mechanisms of insulin resistance. *New England Journal of Medicine*, **300**, 413–419.

Frankenhaeuser, M. and Rissler, A. (1970). Effects of punishment on catecholamine release and efficiency of performance. *Psychopharmacologia*, **17**, 378–390.

Goldbourt, U., Medalie, J. and Neufeld, H. (1975). Clinical myocardial infarction over a five year period. III. A multivariate analysis of incidence. *Journal of Chronic Diseases*, **28**, 217–37.

Goldstein, D.S. (1981). Plasma norepinephrine during stress in essential hypertension. *Hypertension*, **3**, 551–556.

Goldstein, D.S. (1983). Plasma catecholamines and essential hypertension: An analytical review. *Hypertension*, **5**, 86–99.

Gotto, A.M. (1982). Atherosclerosis today. In S. Lenzi and G. Descovitch (eds), *Atherosclerosis Clinical Evaluation and Therapy* (Lancaster: MTP Press), pp. 3–15.

Haynes, S.G., Feinleib, M. and Kannel. W.B. (1980). The relationship of psychosocial factors to coronary heart disease in the Framingham study: III. Eight-year incidence of coronary heart disease. **111**, 37–58.

Haynes, S.G., Levine, S., Scotch, N., Feinleib, M. and Kannel, W.B. (1978). The relationship of psychosocial factors to coronary heart disease in the Framingham Study: I. Methods and risk factors. *American Journal of Epidemiology*, **107**, 362–383.

Hollenberg, N.K., Williams, G.H. and Adams, D.F. (1981). Essential hypertension: Abnormal renal vascular and endocrine responses to a mild psychological stimulus. *Hypertension*, **3**, 11–17.

Howland, E.W. and Sietman, A.W. (1982). Toward the automated measurement of the Type A behavior pattern. *Journal of Behavioural Medicine*, **5**, 37–54.

Inter-Society Commission for Heart Disease Resources (1970). Primary prevention of the atherosclerotic diseases. *Circulation*, **42**, A55–A95.

Januszewicz, W., Sznajderman, M., Wocial, B., Feltynowski, T. and Klonowicz, T. (1979). The effect of mental stress on catecholamines, their metabolites and plasma renin activity in patients with essential hypertension and in healthy subjects. *Clinical Science*, **57**, 229s–231s.

Kahn, C., Neville, D. and Roth, J. (1973). Insulin receptor interaction in the obese hyperglycemic mouse. *Journal of Biological Chemistry*, **248**, 244–250.

Karam, J., Grodsky, G. and Forsham, P. (1963). Excessive insulin response to glucose in obese subjects as measured by immunochemical assay. *Diabetes*, **12**, 197–204.

Karasek, R., Baker, D., Marxer, F., Ahlbom, A. and Theorell, T. (1981). Job decision lattitude, job demands and cardiovascular disease: A prospective study of Swedish men. *American Journal of Public Health*, **71**, 694–705.

Karasek, R.A., Theorell, T.G., Schwartz, J., Pieper, C. and Alfredsson, L. (1982). Job, psychological factors and coronary heart disease. Swedish prospective findings and U.S. prevalence findings using a new occupational inference method. *Advances in Cardiology*, **29**, 62–67.

Keys, A., Taylor, H.L., Blackburn, H., Brozek, J., Anderson, J.T. and Somonson, E. (1971). Mortality and coronary heart disease among men studied for 23 years. *Archives of Internal Medicine*, **128**, 201–214.

Koenig, R. and Cerami, A. (1980). Hemoglobin A1$_c$ and diabetes mellitus. *Annual Review of Medicine*, **31**, 29–34.

Kolterman, O., Insel, J., Saekow, M. and Olefsky, J. (1980). Mechanism of insulin resistance in human obesity: Evidence for receptor and postreceptor defects. *Journal of Clinical Investigation*, **65**, 1273–1284.

Krantz, D.S., and Manuck, S.B. (1984). Acute psychophysiologic reactivity and risk of cardiovascular disease: A review and methodologic critique. *Psychological Bulletin*, **96**, 435–464.

Krantz, D.S., Schaeffer, M.A. Davia, J.E., Dembroski, T.M., MacDougal, J.M. and Shaffer, R.T. (1981). Extent of coronary atherosclerosis, Type A behavior, and cardiovascular response to social interaction. *Psychophysiology*, **18**(6), 654–664.

LeBlanc, J., Cote, J., Jobin, M. and Labrie, A. (1979). Plasma catecholamines and cardiovascular responses to cold and mental activity. *Journal of Applied Physiology: Respiratory Environment Exercise Physiology*, **42**, 1207–1211.

Light, K.C. (1981). Cardiovascular responses to effortful active coping: Implications for the role of stress in hypertension development. *Psychophysiology*, **18**, 216–226.

Light, K.C., Koepke, J.P., Obrist, P.A. and Willis, P.W., IV, (1983). Psychological stress induces sodium and fluid retention in men at high risk for hypertension. *Science*, **220**, 429–431.

Light, K.C. and Obrist, P.A. (1980). Cardiovascular response to stress: Effects of opportunity to avoid shock, shock experience, and performance feedback. *Psychophysiology*, **17**, 243–252.

Manuck, S.B., Kaplan, J.R. and Clarkson, T.B. (1983). Behaviorally-induced heart rate reactivity and atherosclerosis in cynomolgus monkeys. *Psychosomatic Medicine*, **45**, 95–108.

Marmot, M.G. (1984). Lifestyle and national and international trends in coronary heart disease mortality. *Postgraduate Medicine*, **60**, 3–8.

Marmot, M.G., Syme, S.L., Kagan, A., Kato, H., Cohen, J.B. and Belsky, J. (1975). Epidemiological studies of coronary heart disease and stroke in Japanese men living in Japan, Hawaii and California: Prevalence of coronary and hypertensive heart disease and associated risk factors. *American Journal of Epidemiology*, **102**, 514–525.

Marmot, M.G. and Syme, S.L. (1976). Acculturation and coronary heart disease in Japanese–Americans. *American Journal of Epidemiology*, **104**, 225–247.

Merimee, T., Pulkkinen, A. and Loften, S. (1976). Increased insulin binding by lymphocyte receptors induced by BOH butyrate. *Journal of Clinical Endocrinology and Metabolism*, **43**, 1190–1192.

Medalie, J. and Goldbourt, V. (1976). Angina pectoris among 10 000 men: II. Psychosocial and other risk factors as evidenced by a multivariate analyses of a five year incidence study. *American Journal of Medicine*, **60**, 910–921.

MRFIT (1979). The MRFIT behavior pattern study I. Study design, procedures, and reproducibilty of behavior pattern judgements. *Journal of Chronic Diseases*, **32**, 293–305.

MRFIT (1982). Multiple risk factor intervention trial: Risk factor changes and mortality results. *Journal of the American Medical Association*, **248**, 1465–1477.

Morgenstern, H. (1980). The changing association between social status and coronary heart disease in a rural population. *Soc. Sci. Med.*, **14a**, 191–201.

Muggeo, M., Bar, R. and Roth, J. (1977). Change in affinity of insulin receptors following oral glucose in normal subjects. *Journal of Clinical Endocrinology and Metabolism*, **44**, 1206–1209.

Nestel, P.J., Verghese, A. and Lovell, R.R. (1967). Catecholamine secretion and sympathetic nervous responses in men with and without angina pectoris. *American Heart Journal*, **73**, 227–234.

Nguyen, N.U., Dumoulin, G., Henriet, M.T., Wolf, J.P. and Berthelay, S. (1982). Influence d'une activite intellectuelle associee ou non a une charge emotionnelle sur la prolactinemie chez l'homme. *Comptes Rendus de la Societé Biologique*, **176**, 314–318.

Obrist, P.A. (1976). The cardiovascular–behavioral interaction—as it appears today. *Psychophysiology*, **13**, 95–107.

Obrist, P.A., Lawler, J.E., Howard, J.L., Smithson, K.W., Martin, P.L. and Manning, J. (1974). Sympathetic influences in carotid rate and contractility during acute stress in humans. *Psychophysiology*, **11**, 405–427.

Obrist, P.A., Gaebelein, C.J., Teller, E.S., Langer, A.W., Grignolo, A., Light, K.C. and McCubbin, J.A. (1978). The relationship among heart rate, carotid dP/dt, and blood pressure in humans as a function in the type of stress. *Psychophysiology*, **15**, 102–115.

Reaven, G.M. (1983). Insulin resistance in non-insulin-dependent diabetes mellitus. Does it exist and can it be measured? *Journal of Medicine*, **1983**(3), 17.

Rose, R.M., Jenkins, O., Hurst, M., Livingston, L. and Hall, R.P. (1982). Endocrine activity in air traffic controllers at work. I. Characterization of cortisol and growth hormone levels during the day. *Psychoneuroendocrinology*, **7**, 101–111.

Rose, R.M., Jenkins, C.D., Hurst, M., Herd, J.A. and Hall, R.P. (1982). Endocrine activity in air traffic controllers at work. II. Biological, psychological and work correlates. *Psychoneuroendocrinology*, **7**, 113–123.

Rose, G. and Marmot, M.G. (1981). Social class and coronary heart disease. *British Heart Journal*, **45**, 13–19.

Rosenman, R.H., Friedman, M., Straus, R., Wurm, M., Kositchek, R., Hahn, W. and Werthessen, N.T. (1964). A predictive study or coronary heart disease. Western Collaborative Group Study. *Journal of the American Medical Association*, **189**, 15–22.

Ross, R. and Glomset, J. (1973). Atherosclerosis and the arterial smooth muscle cell. *Science*, **180**, 1332–1339.

Ross, R., Glomset, J., Kariya, B. and Harker, L. (1974). A platelet-dependent serum factor that stimulates the proliferation of arterial smooth muscle cells *in vitro*. *Proceedings of the National Academy of Science of the USA*, **71**, 1207.

Roth, J., Kahn, C., Lesniak, M., Gorden, P., DeMeyts, P., Megyesi, K., Neville, D., Gavin, J., III, Soll, A., Freychet, P., Goldfine, I., Bar, R. and Archer, J. (1975). Receptors for insulin, NSILAS, and growth hormone: Applications to disease states in man. *Recent Progress in Hormonal Research*, **31**, 95–139.

Ruberman, W., Weinblatt, E., Goldberg, J.D. and Chaudhary, B.S. (1984). Psychosocial influences on mortality after myocardial infarction. *New England Journal of Medicine*, **311**, 522–559.

Scherwitz, L., Berton, K. and Leventhal, H. (1977). Type A assessment and interaction in the behavior pattern interview. *Psychosomatic Medicine*, **39**, 229–240.

Schiffer, F., Hartley, L.H., Schulman, C.I. and Ableman, W.H. (1976). The stress electrocardiogram: A new diagnostic and research technique for evaluating the relation between emotional stress and ischemic heart disease. *American Journal of Cardiology*, **37**, 41–47.

Schmitt, J., Poole, J., Lewis, S., Shore, V., Maman, A., Baer, R. and Forsham, P. (1982). Hemoglobin A1 correlates with the ratio of low-to-high density lipoprotein cholesterol in normal weight type II diabetes. *Metabolism*, **31**, 1084–1089.

Schucker, B. and Jacobs, D.R. (1977). Assessment of behavioral risk of coronary disease by voice characteristics. *Psychosomatic Medicine*, **39**, 219–228.

Shamoon, H., Soman, V. and Sherwin, R. (1980). The influence of acute physiological increments of cortisol on fuel metabolism and insulin binding to monocytes in normal humans. *Journal of Clinical Endocrinology and Metabolism*, **50**, 495–501.

Sime, W.E., Buell, J.C. and Eliot, R.S. (1980). Cardiovascular responses to emotional stress (Quiz interview) in postinfarct cardiac patients and matched control subjects. *Journal of Human Stress*, **6**(3), 39–46.

Singer, P., Godicke, W., Voight, S., Hajdu, I. and Weiss, M. (1985). Postprandial hyperinsulinemia in patients with mild essential hypertension. *Hypertension*, **7**, 182–186.

Soman, V., Shamoon, H. and Sherwin, R. (1980). Effects of physiological infusion of epinephrine in normal humans: Relationship between the metabolic response and β-adrenergic binding. *Journal of Clinical Endocrinology and Metabolism*, **50**, 294–297.

Steiner, G. and Vranic, M. (1982). Hyperinsulinemia and hypertriglyceridemia, a vicious cycle with atherogenic potential. *International Journal of Obesity*, **6**, Suppl. 1, 117–124.

Stout, R. (1977). The relationship of abnormal circulating insulin levels to atherosclerosis. *Atherosclerosis*, **27**, 1–13.

Stout, R. (1982). Hyperinsulinemia as an independent risk factor for atherosclerosis. *International Journal of Obesity*, **6**, Suppl. 1, 111–115.

Stout, R., Bierman, E. and Russell, R. (1975). Effect of insulin on the proliferation of cultured primate arterial smooth muscle cells. *Circulation Research*, **36**, 319–327.

Syme, S.L., Marmot, M.G., Kagan, A., Kato, H. and Rhoads, G. (1975). Epidemiologic studies of coronary heart disease and stroke in Japanese men living in Japan, Hawaii and California: Introduction. *American Journal of Epidemiology*, **102**, 477–480.

Thomopoulos, P., Kosmakos, F., Pastan, I. and Lovelace, I. (1977). Cyclic AMP increases in the concentration of insulin receptors in cultured fibroblasts and lymphocytes. *Biochemical and Biophysical Research Communications*, **75**, 246–252.

Timio, M. and Gentili, S. (1976). Adrenosympathetic overactivity under conditions of work stress. *British Journal of Preventive and Social Medicine*, **30**, 262–265.

Timio, G., Gentili, S. and Pede, S. (1979). Free adrenaline and noradrenaline excretion related to occupational stress. *British Heart Journal*, **42**, 471–474.

Ursin, H., Baade, E. and Levine, S. (eds). (1978). *Psychobiology of Stress. A Study of Coping Men* (New York: Academic Press).

Verdery, R.B. and Nichols, A.V. (1975). Arrangement of lipids and proteins in human serum high density lipoproteins: A proposed model. *Chemistry and Physics of Lipids*, **14**, 123.

Worth, R.M., Kato, H., Rhoads, G.G., Kagan, A. and Syme, S.L. (1975). Epidemiologic studies of coronary heart diease and stroke in Japanese men living in Japan, Hawaii and California: Mortality. *American Journal of Epidemiology*, **102**, 481–490.

10

An Assessment of the Physiological Measurement of Work Stress

Kendrith M. Rowland
Gerald R. Ferris
Yitzhak Fried and Charlotte D. Sutton

1. Introduction

An increasing amount of attention is being given by behavioural and organizational scientists (e.g., McGrath, 1976; Cohen, 1980; Schuler, 1980; Schuler and Jackson, 1986) to the investigation of stress in work organizations and the impact of work stress on personal and organizational outcomes (e.g., Cooper and Marshall, 1976; Beehr and Newman, 1978; Beehr and Bhagat, 1985).

Two perspectives have usually been taken to defining and investigating stress (e.g., Cox, 1978; Shirom, 1982; Fleming *et al.*, 1984; Folkman, 1984). One of these, the psychological perspective, views stress as the interaction between the person and his or her environment and the perceived inability of the person to adequately respond to the demands of that environment. Major contributions to this perspective have been made by Lazarus (1966) and McGrath (1976, 1982).

The second perspective is the physiological perspective. This is anchored in the work of Selye (1976). Selye defines stress as a non-specific bodily response to environmental stimuli. He also suggests that physiological responses to environmental stimuli can be made by a person without any subjective assessment of those stimuli. Although Selye's views have received some empirical support (Caplan and Jones, 1975; Eden, 1982), they contain at least two apparent weaknesses. First, it has been shown that an awareness of potential or actual threat is necessary for a stress response to occur (Mason, 1975a, b; Fleming *et al.*, 1984). Second, Selye's approach does not identify the specific physiological responses that can be expected to occur with particular environmental stimuli. In this regard, the need for additional specificity is noted by Mason (1975a, b).

Behavioural and organizational science journals to date have focused almost exclusively on studies and reviews of work stress research from the psychological perspective. Studies dealing with the physiological aspects of work stress rarely appear in these journals and typically are not read by behavioural and organizational scientists. Thus, it appears that for these scientists an assessment of physiologically based work stress research is needed. Ultimately, it is hoped that an integration of this research with the research on work stress currently conducted by behavioural and organizational scientists can be accomplished.

Physiological symptoms of work stress

Among the physiological symptoms associated with stress (McQuade and Aikman, 1974; Frankenhaeuser, 1975; Cox, 1978; Morse and Furst, 1979; Weiner, 1979), the most common are:

1. Cardiovascular symptoms, including heart rate and blood pressure;
2. Biochemical symptoms, such as cholesterol, catecholamines, uric acid, blood sugar, and steriod hormones;
3. Gastrointestinal symptoms, such as peptic ulcer.

Behavioural and organizational scientists have generally assumed that the physiological measures of stress provide more objective data than their self-report or behavioural measures because physiological measures are less susceptible to the influences of a variety of individual and situational factors. This assumption, as this chapter will demonstrate, is less than accurate because physiological measures are also subject to these same sorts of influences.

Research design issues

The research designs of the physiologically based studies of stress included in this assessment used designs quite similar to those found in the psychologically based studies of stress. That is, nearly 50% of the physiologically based studies were cross-sectional in nature. They examined the relationships between stressors and physiological measures of stress at one point in time. A smaller percentage of these studies, sometimes in an experimental framework, examined over a short time interval (i.e., several hours or days) the physiological measures of individuals and groups in stressful and non-stressful conditions. Only a few of them could be classified as longitudinal, in which time the period was extended to several months or years.

Finally, the studies included in this assessment incorporated several types of stressors, among them role stressors (role conflict, ambiguity and overload), occupational stressors (presumably inherent in such groups as managers, pilots and air traffic controllers), and situational stressors (computer shutdowns, plant closings and space vehicle launchings).

2. *The physiological measurement of work stress*

As noted earlier, little physiologically based stress research has appeared in the behavioural and organizational science literatures. Even less research has appeared concerning the potential methodological problems associated with the measurement techniques typically used. Kasl (1978) has suggested that these problems may account for the weak and inconsistent results of studies examining the relationships between work stressors and physiological symptoms. Supporting evidence for this point is provided in Table 10.1. This table identified the most commonphysiological measurement categories (i.e., cardiovascular, serum cholesterol, catecholamines and peptic ulcer) and the potential confounding factors for each category. For the studies listed in Table 10.1, many potential confounding factors were not considered.

3. Potential confounding factors

It was found, during the review of the studies listed in Table 10.1, that the potential confounding or validity threatening factors could be logically grouped into three factor sets: stable or permanent factors; transitory factors; and procedural factors. These factor sets are described below and are then discussed in greater detail for each physiological measurement category.

Stable or permanent factors

These factors represent the differences among people in their susceptibility to specific physiological symptoms. Such individual differences include genetic tendencies, race, sex, age and diet. To illustrate, it has been shown that people with a family history of high blood pressure tend to develop higher levels of blood pressure than people who do not have such a family history (Zinner *et al.*, 1971; Light, 1981).

Transitory factors

Research evidence also indicates that measurement results can be affected by factors such as the time of day, room temperature, the subject's postural position, physical exertion and consumption of caffeine and nicotine. These factors, which are time- and situation-specific, are considered transitory factors. It has been shown, for example, that the level of cholesterol tends to be higher when the subject is standing than when sitting (Statland *et al.*, 1974); that physical exertion prior to or during measurement tends to increase urinary noradrenaline (Christie and Woodman, 1980); and that intake of caffeine or nicotine prior to or during measurement tends to increase the level of cardiovascular activity (Siddle and Turpin, 1980).

Procedural factors

Procedural factors encompass the problems of physiological measurement *per se*, such as the number of times measurements are made or the duration of time between measurements. For example, blood pressure is a dynamic measure, varying with the natural variation in the cardiovascular system. A single measure of blood pressure, therefore, would not be an accurate assessment of the impact of a given stressor (Rosner and Polk, 1979, 1981).

A major argument of this chapter is that research on work stress often fails to control for these three sets of factors or considers their potential effects on physiological measurement. In contrast to cross-sectional studies, for example, one would expect the potential threats of the three sets of factors to be substantially reduced by using short-time interval or longitudinal studies, which compare measurements of

Table 10.1. *Potential confounding factors considered in the physiological measurement of work stress*[a].

(a) *Cardiovascular measures*

Study	Race	Sex	Age	Familial tendency	Health conditions	Postural position	Consumptions of caffeine and nicotine[b]	Humidity	Alcohol consumption	B.P. variability	B.P. technique of measure
Astrand et al. (1973)		+	+								
Aunola et al. (1978, 1979)	+	+	+								
Bernard & Duncan (1975)		+			+						
Brousseau & Mallinger (1981)	+	+	+	+							
Caplan (1971)	+	+	+		+						
Caplan & Jones (1975)		+				+					
Caplan et al. (1975)	+	+	+			+					
Chapman et al. (1966)		+			+		+				
Cobb & Kasl (1972)		+									
Cobb & Rose (1973)	+	+	+								
Crump et al. (1981)		+	+	+							
Dougherty (1967)		+	+								
Eden (1982)	+	+									
Ferris (1983)		+									
French & Caplan (1970)	+	+									
Harburg et al. (1979)	+	+	+								
Hennigan & Wortham (1975)		+	+		+						
House et al. (1979)	+	+				+					
Howard et al. (1976)		+								+	
Kasl & Cobb (1970)	+	+									
Kuorinka & Korhonen (1981)	+	+	+		+						
Orth-Gomér & Ahlbom (1980)		+		+	+	+					
Reeder et al. (1973)	+	+	+		+						
Reynolds (1974)		+	+								
Rose et al. (1978)	+	+				+					
Sales (1970)		+									
Schär et al. (1973)	+	+	+	+							
Shirom et al. (1973)	+	+	+								
Waldron (1978)	+	+									
Warheit (1974)	+	+	+		+						

(b) *Serum cholesterol*

Study	Sex	Age	Familial tendency	Health condition	Diet	Postural position	Consumption of caffeine[b]	Season	Venous occlusion
Caplan (1971)	+		+	+				+	
Caplan et al. (1975)	+	+				+	+		
Chapman et al. (1966)	+			+	+				
Cobb & Kasl (1972)	+	+	+					+	
Crump et al. (1981)	+								
Eden (1982)	+								
French & Caplan (1970)	+				+			+	
Friedman et al. (1958)	+								
Gore (1978)	+								
Howard et al. (1976)	+							+	
Orth-Gomér & Ahlbom (1980)	+							+	
Reeder et al. (1973)	+			+				+	
Rubin & Rahe (1974)	+	+	+	+					
Schär et al. (1973)	+	+	+					+	
Shirom et al. (1973)	+	+						+	

(c) *Catecholamines*

Study	Sex	Health condition	Time of day	Postural position	Consumption of caffeine and nicotine[b]	Physical exertion
Dutton et al. (1978)	+		+	+	+	+
Frankenhaeuser & Gadell (1979)	+		+	+	+	+
Grandjean et al. (1971)	+					
Hale et al. (1971a)	+					
Hale et al. (1971b)	+					
Jenner et al. (1980)	+		+	+	+	+
Johansson et al. (1978)	+		+	+	+	+
Rubin (1974)	+	+				

Table 10.1 Continued

(d) Peptic ulcer

Study	Familial tendency	Longitudinal consumption of caffeine and nicotine	Peptic ulcer definition	Peptic ulcer illness criteria
Caplan et al. (1975)				
Cobb & Kasl (1972)				
Cobb & Rose (1973)			+	
Dunn & Cobb (1962)				
Gosling (1958)				
House et al. (1979)				
Johansson et al. (1978)			+	
Sandberg & Bliding (1976)				

[a] The + sign indicates the confounding factor(s) considered in each study.
[b] Before or during measurement.

physiological symptoms over a period of time, or between one or more experimental groups and one or more control groups. In these studies, one would also expect that many of the threatening contextual factors, such as time of day or familial tendency, would be randomly distributed across both the experimental and control groups and/or among the different points of measurement over time. However, even experimentally designed studies with a number of time measurements cannot remove the procedural problems often encountered in the assessment of stress-related physiological symptoms.

In addition, even an adequate research design may not eliminate such transitory factors as room temperature, the subject's postural position, or time of day. In an analysis of the work stress studies summarized in Table 10.1, it is apparent that researchers tend not to be aware of the need to equalize these factors, and, as a result, such factors are likely in some studies to be dissimilar across the different conditions of measurement. For example, suppose the experimental and control groups are kept in different areas of the research site and the temperatures in these areas are quite different. Such differences in temperature might well affect the physiological measurements that are made.

Researchers might also expect that the randomization of subjects in the experimental and control groups would control for the effects of the potential confounding factors. However, such factors as coffee drinking and smoking are often affected by the level of experienced stress. As a result, subjects in the experimental group might consume more caffeine and nicotine during the period of exposure to work stress simply as a stress-coping mechanism. The resulting higher levels of caffeine and nicotine in the experimental group than in the control group would probably affect some physiological measurements.

Finally, researchers frequently ignore the possible interactions between the potential confounding factors and work stress. For example, subjects with a family history of high blood pressure might experience significantly higher blood pressure under stressful situations than under non-stressful situations because of the interactive effects between stress and the tendency towards high blood pressure. Thus, unless researchers control for high blood pressure tendencies, the results of their studies may lead to invalid conclusions about the effect of work stress on blood pressure, while ignoring the realistic possibility that the interaction between work stress and the tendency towards high blood pressure actually produced the results.

From the above discussion, it is evident that an 'adequate' research design is not enough. Work stress researchers utilizing physiological measures must also deal with the effects of the potential confounding factors. We will discuss these factors and several measures among the most common physiological measurement categories below.

4. *Cardiovascular measures*

Stable or permanent factors affecting blood pressure/cardiac activity

Familial tendency and health disorders

Substantial research has established the effects of familial or genetic tendencies on the level of blood pressure and cardiac activity (Perera *et al.*, 1961; Johnson *et al.*, 1965; Light, 1981; Miall *et al.*, 1967; Schweitzer *et al.*, 1967; Zinner *et al.*, 1971; Shapiro, 1973). Despite the evidence of the effects of familial tendencies, only four of the 30 studies surveyed took into consideration the potential effects of genetic tendencies on cardiovascular measures. Only a few more (eight) considered the impact of the subject's health on the cardiovascular measures used, and even those eight tended to be vague about the definition of 'health'.

Sex, race and age

Although the overall evidence is inconclusive, Siddle and Turpin (1980) concluded that sex, race and age all seem to affect blood pressure and cardiac activity. Only a few studies have separately examined the cardiovascular impact of work stress on men and women (e.g., Aunola *et al.*, 1978, 1979; Harburg *et al.*, 1979). Even fewer studies investigated the relationship between work stress and race. It seems that only Harburg *et al.* (1979) accounted for race in thier study of work stress effects on blood pressure.

As indicated in Table 10.1, approximately 50% of the reviewed studies either ruled out or considered the possible effects of age on the measures of blood pressure or cardiac activity.

Transitory factors affecting cardiovascular measures

Research results have shown that the level of cardiovascular activity is affected by factors such as temperature; humidity; postural change; consumption of caffeine, nicotine, and alcohol prior to or during measurement; exercise before or during the measurement; time of day; and even the time of the subject's last meal (Semler, 1965; Berne and Levy, 1967; Elliott and Thynsell, 1968; Malmstrom, 1971; Cohen and MacDonald, 1974; Siddle and Turpin, 1980; Jennings *et al.*, 1981). However, studies of stress in organizations have generally failed to consider the possible impact of such transitory factors on the cardiovascular system. In fact, of the studies surveyed, only Caplan *et al.* (1975) controlled for the intake of caffeine and nicotine.

Postural position was controlled for in only five of the 30 studies reviewed. It may be that other studies have unintentionally controlled for the potential effects of the subject's postural position by recording the cardiovascular measures with the subject in only one position. However, the remaining studies have failed to describe the specific steps used to control for these factors. Therefore, the postural factor continues as a possible threat to both internal and external validity, as do many of the transitory factors.

Procedural factors affecting cardiovascular measures

Procedural factors, which focus on problems of measurement, also pose a threat to the validity of studies on work stress, particularly studies using cardiovascular measures. Measures of blood pressure are particularly susceptible to procedural problems.

As noted previously, a normal person's blood pressure can vary quite naturally, by as much as 30 mm Hg during a 1-minute recording using a direct blood pressure technique with a catheter inserted into the blood vessel (Tursky, 1984). As a result, a single reading of blood pressure is not sufficient for reliably identifying hypertension. In fact, Rosner and Polk (1979, 1981) concluded as a result of their studies that three visits with two measurements per visit would yield an accurate assessment of hypertension. Although other scholars might choose different schedules, blood pressure should, at the very least, be measured several times over a period of several days. It is also important to note that repeated measurements within a limited period of time on the same day may cause temporary tissue changes and result in different blood pressure readings (Stern *et al.*, 1980).

Except for the study by Kasl and Cobb (1970), none of the studies which investigated the impact of work stress on blood pressure adequately measured blood pressure. In seven of the studies, blood pressure was measured only once, and, in an eighth study, blood pressure was measured only once each year for several years. In six of the studies, multiple blood pressure readings were taken but on only one occasion. In the majority of studies, several measures of blood pressure were taken repeatedly during a short period of time, thus making them susceptible to the problem identified by Stern *et al.* (1980).

5. Serum cholesterol

Fifteen of the studies reviewed here focused on the impact of work stress on cholesterol in the blood. For the most part, these studies failed to consider many of the potential confounding factors.

Stable or permanent factors affecting serum cholesterol levels

Familial tendency

It has rather convincingly been shown that cholesterol levels in children are positively correlated with those of their parents and siblings (Schaefer *et al.*, 1958; Johnson *et al.*, 1965; Mayo *et al.*, 1969; Christian and Kang, 1977; Hennekens *et al.*, 1980). Some researchers have shown that approximately one-half of the variance in plasma cholesterol is genetically related. Yet, despite such findings, only four studies took the subject's familial tendencies into consideration.

Health disorders

In addition to direct familial tendencies, large numbers of inheritable disorders of lipid metabolism can influence cholesterol levels (Sabine, 1977). Other non-inheritable diseases, such as liver disorders, can also affect the level of cholesterol in the blood. Only three blood cholesterol studies considered their subject's health.

Sex and age

Plasma cholesterol usually increases rapidly in individuals after birth and continues to rise slowly throughout life until about the age of 50. From childhood to young adulthood, there appears to be little difference in cholesterol levels between males and females (e.g., Dyerberg and Hjorne, 1973). At about 50, however, differences between the sexes begin to become apparent. At that age, the cholesterol levels in men tend to level off or decrease slightly. In women, the cholesterol level may continue to rise.

Of the stable or permanent factors affecting serum cholesterol levels, age was the factor most often controlled for, being considered in five of the 15 studies. The effects of sex differences were generally controlled for because most of the studies on stress and cholesterol were limited to male subjects.

Diet

Research evidence has confirmed that the quantity and quality of fatty acids in the diet can strongly influence the level of serum cholesterol in men (Kinley and Krause, 1959; Spirts et al., 1965; Sabine, 1977). As a result, the quantity and quality of fatty acids seem to be important factors which should be considered in work stress research focusing on serum cholesterol, particularly because only two of the studies took the diet of their subjects into consideration.

Transitory factors affecting serum cholesterol levels

Seasonal differences

Levels of cholesterol tend to be lowest in the fall and winter months, but rise again in the spring and summer months (Fyfe et al., 1968; Sabine, 1977). Such seasonal differences influence the findings of research in several ways. In longitudinal studies, the varying levels of serum cholesterol may well jeopardize both internal and external validity. In short time interval studies, in which cholesterol is measured only in one season, the research results may have higher internal validity, but the findings cannot be generalized beyond that specific season nor can they be meaningfully compared to studies conducted in other seasons.

Seven studies examined the cholesterol levels of their subjects across different seasons. However, none took the seasonal differences into account. Those researchers who gathered blood samples only in one season typically failed to report the specific season, thus making generalizability and cross-study comparisons difficult.

Smoking, venous occlusion and postural position

Three additional factors need to be considered. Levels of blood cholesterol tend to increase when the subject has smoked before or during measurement (Sabine, 1977). In addition, cholesterol levels tend to be higher while standing than while sitting (Statland *et al.*, 1974). Research results have also shown that venous occlusion, even for a short period, can significantly increase the measured level of cholesterol (Koerselman *et al.*, 1961; Statland *et al.*, 1974). Finally, a second sample taken through the same venupuncture tends to show a slightly higher level of cholesterol than the first (Bokelund *et al.*, 1974).

Few of the studies examining cholesterol and stress explicitly considered any of the above transitory factors. Caplan *et al.* (1975) eliminated the possible impact of smoking before measurement and controlled the postural position of their subjects.

6. Catecholamines

Stable or permanent factors affecting catecholamine levels

Gender

In the past, it has been generally accepted that only minor differences exist between men and women in their catecholamine excretion rates when the excretion rate is expressed in relation to body weight. However, more recent research findings raise questions about those conclusions, at least in regard to adrenaline excretions. Johnson (1972), Johnson and Post (1972) and Frankenhaeuser (1973) have contended that sex differences do appear in adrenaline excretions when subjects undergo psychosocial stress. The research reviewed here can add little information about sex differences, since all the catecholamine studies used male subjects exclusively.

Health disorders

Some health disorders, particularly hypoglycaemia and hypertension, have been found to affect catecholamine levels (Frankenhaeuser, 1975). However, out of the nine studies which investigated the impact of work stress on catecholamine levels, only one controlled for the health conditions of its subjects.

Transitory factors affecting catecholamine levels

A number of factors have been found to affect urinary catecholamine adrenaline and noradrenaline secretion and excretion. Of those factors, four are discussed below:

Time of day, postural position, and consumption of caffeine and nicotine

One of the most important factors which must be considered in the study of stress and catecholamine levels is the time of day during which measurement is made. One study found that urine values of noradrenaline were 50% lower at night than during the day, and adrenaline concentrations were 10% lower.

Catecholamine values also tend to vary depending on the subject's postural position.

Such values tend to be higher when people are in a standing position than in a supine position. Dutton *et al.* (1978) were the only reseachers to control for postural position.

Research evidence has also indicated that the intake of caffeine from coffee, tea or cocoa, as well as cigarette smoking shortly prior to measurement, may produce materials which interfere with the biochemical analysis of catecholamines.

Four of the nine stress studies that measured catecholamine levels controlled for the time of day the samples were collected and the postural position of subjects (Frankenhaeuser and Gardell, 1976; Dutton *et al.*, 1978; Johansson *et al.*, 1978; Jenner *et al.*, 1980).

These four sets of reseachers also controlled for the consumption of caffeine and nicotine. Subjects were asked to refrain from consuming caffeine and nicotine during the study (Frankenhaeuser and Gardell, 1976; Dutton *et al.*, 1978), to keep a record of caffeine intake (Frankenhaeuser and Gardell, 1976; Jenner *et al.*, 1980), or to keep caffeine intake and cigarette smoking during less stressful rest days the same as during work days (Frankenhaeuser and Gardell, 1976; Johansson *et al.*, 1978).

Physical exertion

Urinary noradrenaline levels also tend to increase with physical exertion, particularly if the exertion occurs shortly before the urine sample is collected. Only Dutton *et al.* (1978) controlled for physical exertion. During the study, which involved collecting hourly urine samples from the subjects (firemen and paramedics) during both a work day and a rest day, the subjects were requested to refrain from excessive mental and physical exertion during the rest day.

Procedural factors affecting catecholamine levels

A major problem in the measurement and analysis of catecholamine levels is the natural fluctuations of such hormones. Numerous hormones in the blood, including catecholamines and cortisol, fluctuate so rapidly that hormone levels taken in samples even just a few hours apart can be highly variable, depending on the stage of the secretion–action–breakdown sequence at the time the blood is drawn (Christie and Woodman, 1980).

Of the studies examining stress and catecholamines that have been discussed thus far, all have tested for the level of the hormone in urine rather than in the blood, perhaps to avoid the problem of rapid hormonal fluctuations in the blood.

7. *Peptic ulcers*

Stable or permanent factors affecting the occurrence of peptic ulcers

Two factors appear to have a great deal of influence on the development of peptic ulcers. Research findings support the importance of genetic factors on the development and persistence of peptic ulcers (Yager and Weiner, 1971; Chapman, 1978; Wolf *et al.*, 1979).

Research evidence also suggests that the consumption of caffeine and nicotine over long periods of time increases the probability of duodenal ulcers, a specific type of peptic ulcer. Of the eight studies which examined the influence of work stress on peptic ulcers, none of them considered the influence of either genetic factors or consumption of caffeine and nicotine.

Procedural factors affecting the occurrence of peptic ulcers

The major problems in the study of peptic ulcers are procedural in nature. First, there is a lack of a commonly accepted definition of a peptic ulcer, and, second, criteria for determining peptic ulcer illness are vague.

Definitional problem

'Peptic ulcer' is actually a group of heterogeneous diseases of diverse aetiology and pathogenesis, not a single disease (Wolf et al., 1979). Wolf and his associates have noted that a duodenal ulcer is different from a gastric ulcer and have suggested that these two types of ulcer should be treated separately in research. Of the eight work stress studies examining peptic ulcers, two dealt explicitly with duodenal ulcers, the remaining six appeared to deal with both types of ulcers, or failed to specify the particular type of ulcer studied.

Criteria problem

There also appears to be some vagueness as to which criteria to consider in identifying peptic ulcer illness. Studies such as those conducted by Caplan et al. (1975) and House et al. (1979), which chose patient identification of symptoms as a diagnostic criterion, may be overstating the existence of the illness. Studies which use only surgical evidence may well understate the frequency of the disease.

Most studies have arbitrarily chosen their own criteria for defining peptic ulcers. Dunn and Cobb (1962) defined the disease by the level of serum pepsinogen in the blood, and Johansson et al. (1978) used additional chemical tests. Gosling (1958) used a radiographic examination as the basis for determining the existence of the disease. Cobb and Rose (1973) based their decisions about peptic ulcer occurrence among air traffic controllers on the results of the aero-medical certification examinations. Sandberg and Bliding (1976) used medical records and information from fellow trainees and platoon commanders in the diagnosis of peptic ulcers.

8. Conclusions

The initial assumption of this chapter was that behavioural and organizational scientists could usefully supplement their research of work stress with the inclusion of a variety of physiological measures of stress, which were perceived as being more objective in nature than the psychological measures of stress. This perceptual bubble regarding the objectivity of the physiological measures bursts, however, when the physiologically-based research on work stress is examined. Physiological measures of stress *are* susceptible to the influences of many individual and situational factors.

Furthermore, not only are the physiological measures of stress often less than adequate, but medical and health-care reseachers frequently neglect (unintentionally, it appears) to control for several potential confounding factors in their research, even when conventionally acceptable research designs are used.

An integration of both the physiological and psychological perspectives to work stress research should continue, it seems. What is necessary now is an increased awareness of the need for better measurement techniques and research designs. The ultimate results of efforts in this regard, of course, will be more valid and generalizable findings concerning the work stress phenomenon.

References

Åstrand, I., Fugelli, P., Karlsson, C.G., Rodahl, K. and Vokac, Z. (1973). Energy output and work stress in coastal fishing. *Scandinavian Journal of Clinical and Laboratory Investigation*, **31**, 105–113.

Aunola, S., Nykyri, R. and Rusko, H. (1978). Strain of employees in the machine industry in Finland. *Ergonomics*, **21**, 509–519.

Aunola, S., Nykyri, R. and Rusko, H. (1979). Strain of employees in the manufacturing industry in Finland. *Ergonomics*, **22**, 29–36.

Barnard, R.J. and Duncan, H.W. (1975). Heart rate and ECG responses of fire fighters. *Journal of Occupational Medicine*, **17**, 247–262.

Beehr, T.A. and Bhagat, R.S. (eds) (1985). *Human Stress and Cognition in Organizations*, New York: John Wiley).

Beehr, T.A. and Newman, J.D. (1978). Job stress, employee health, and organizational effectiveness: A facet analysis, model, and literature review. *Personnel Psychology*, **31**, 665–699.

Berne, R.M. and Levy, M.N. (1967). *Cardiovascular Physiology*, (St Louis, MO: C.V. Mosby).

Bokelund, H., Winkel, P. and Statland, B.E. (1974). Factors contributing to intra-industrial variation of serum constituents. Use of randomized duplicate serum specimens to evaluate sources of analytical error. *Clinical Chemistry*, **20**, 1507–1512.

Brousseau, K.R. and Mallinger, M.A. (1981). Internal-external locus of control, perceived occupational stress and cardiovascular health. *Journal of Occupational Behaviour*, **2**, 65–73.

Caplan, R.D. (1971). Organizational stress and individual stress: A socio-psychological study of risk factors in coronary heart disease among administrators, engineers, and scientists. Unpublished PhD thesis, University of Michigan, Ann Arbor.

Caplan, R.D. and Jones, K.W. (1975). Effects of work load, role ambiguity, and type A personality on anxiety, depression, and heart rate. *Journal of Applied Psychology*, **60**, 713–719.

Caplan, R.D., Cobb, S., French, J.R.P., Jr, Harrison, R.U. and Pinneau, S.R., Jr (1975). *Job Demands and Worker Health*. (Washington, DC: NIOSH).

Chapman, M.L. (1978). Peptic ulcer: A medical perspective. In H.D. Janowitz (ed), *The Medical Clinics of North America* (New York: Saunders).

Chapman, J.M., Reeder, L.G., Massey, F.J., Jr, Borun, E.R., Picken, B., Browning, G.D., Coulson, A.A. and Zimmerman, D.H. (1966). Relationships of stress tranquilizers and serum cholesterol levels in a sample population under study for coronary heart disease. *American Journal of Epidemiology*, **83**, 537–547.

Christian, J.C. and Kang, K.W. (1977). Maternal influence on plasma cholesterol variation. *American Journal of Human Genetics*, **20**, 462–467.

Christie, C.W. and Woodman, D.D. (1980). Biochemical methods. In I. Martin and P.H. Venables (eds), *Techniques in Psychophysiology* (New York: John Wiley).

Cobb, S. and Kasl, S.V. (1972). Some medical aspects of unemployment. *Industrial Gerontology*, **12**, 8–16.

Cobb, S. and Rose, R. (1973). Hypertension, peptic ulcer and diabetes in air traffic controllers. *Journal of the American Medical Association*, **224**, 489–492.

Cohen, S. (1980). Aftereffects of stress on human performance and social behavior: a review of research and theory. *Psychological Bulletin*, **88**, 82–108.

Cohen, D.H. and MacDonald, A.K. (1974). A selective review of central and neural pathways involved in cardiovascular control. In P.A. Obrist, A.H. Black, J. Brener and L.V. DiCara (eds), *Cardiovascular Psychophysiology: Current Issues in Response Mechanisms, Biofeedback and Methodology* (Chicago, IL: Aldine).

Cooper, C.L. and Marshall, J. (1976). Occupational sources of stress: a review of the literature relating to coronary heart disease and mental ill health. *Journal of Occupational Psychology*, **49**, 11–28.

Cox, T. (1978). *Stress* (Baltimore, MD: University Park Press).

Crump, J.H., Cooper, D.L. and Maxwell, V.B. (1981). Stress among air traffic controllers: Occupational sources of coronary heart disease risk. *Journal of Occupational Behaviour*, **2**, 293–303.

Dougherty, J.D. (1967). Cardiovascular findings in air traffic controllers. *Aerospace Medicine*, **38**, 26–30.

Dunn, J.P. and Cobb, S. (1962). Frequency of peptic ulcer among executives, craftsmen and foremen. *Journal of Occupational Medicine*, **4**, 343–348.

Dutton, L.M., Smolensky, M.H., Leach, C.S., Lorimer, R. and Hsi, B.P. (1978). Stress levels of ambulance paramedics and fire fighters. *Journal of Occupational Medicine*, **20**, 111–120.

Dyerberg, J. and Hjörne, N. (1973). Plasma lipid and lipoprotein levels in childhood and adolescence. *Scandinavian Journal of Clinical and Laboratory Investigation*, **31**, 473–479.

Eden, D. (1982). Critical job events, acute stress, and strain: A multiple interrupted time series. *Organizational Behavior and Human Performance*, **301**, 312–329.

Eliot, R.S. (1979). *Stress and the Major Cardiovascular Disorders*. (New York: Futura).

Elliott, R. and Thynsell, R.V. (1968). Note on smoking and heart rate. *Psychophysiology*, **5**, 280–283.

Ferris, G.R. (1983). Activation-increasing properties of task performance. *Psychological Reports*, **52**, 731–734.

Fleming, R., Baum, A. and Singer, J.E. (1984). Toward an integrative approach to the study of stress. *Journal of Personality and Social Psychology*, **46**, 939–949.

Folkman, S. (1984). Personal control and stress and coping process: A theoretical analysis. *Journal of Personality and Social Psychology*, **46**, 839–852.

Frankenhaeuser, M. (1973). Sex differences in reactions to psychosocial stressors and psychoactive drugs. In L. Levy (ed), *Society, stress and disease*, Volume 3 (London: Oxford University Press).

Frankenhaeuser, M. (1975). Sympathetic-adrenomedullary activity, behavior and the psychosocial environment. In P.H. Venables and M.J. Christie (eds), *Research in Psychophysiology* (New York: John Wiley).

Frankenhaeuser, M. and Gardell, B. (1976). Underload and overload in working life: outline of a multidisciplinary approach. *Journal of Human Stress*, **2**, 35–46.

French, J.R.P., Jr and Caplan, R.D. (1970). Psychological factors in coronary heart disease. *Industrial Medicine and Surgery*, **39**, 31–45.

Friedman, M.D., Rosenman, R.D. and Carroll, V. (1958). Changes in serum cholesterol and blood clotting time in men subjected to cyclic variation of occupational stress. *Circulation*, **17**, 852–861.

Fyfe, T., Dunnigan, M.G., Hamilton, E. and Rae, R.J. (1968). Seasonal variation in serum lipids, and incidence and mortality of ischaemic heart disease. *Journal of Atherosclerosis Research*, **8**, 591–596.

Gore, S. (1978). The effect of social support in moderating the health consequences of unemployment. *Journal of Health and Social Behavior*, **19**, 157–165.

Gosling, R.H. (1958). Peptic ulcer and mental disorder. *Journal of Psychosomatic Research*, **2**, 285–301.

Grandjean, E.P., Wotzka, G., Schaad, R. and Gilgen, A. (1971). Fatigue and stress in air traffic controllers. *Ergonomics*, **14**, 159–165.

Hale, H.B., Williams, E.W., Smith, B.N. and Melton, C.E., Jr. (1971a). Excretion patterns of air traffic controllers. *Aerospace Medicine*, **42**, 127–138.

Hale, H.B., Williams, E.W., Smith, B.N. and Melton, C.E., Jr. (1971b). Neuroendocrine and metabolic responses to intermittent night shift work. *Aerospace Medicine*, **42**, 156–162.

Harburg, E., Blakelock, E.H. and Roeper, P.J. (1979). Resentful and reflective coping with arbitrary authority and blood pressure. *Psychosomatic Medicine*, **41**, 189–202.

Hennekens, C.H., Levine, R.S., Rosner, B., Klein, B.E., Gourley, J.E., Gelband, H. and Jesse, M.J. (1980). Aggregation of cholesterol among young families of men with premature myocardial infarction. *Journal of Chronic Diseases*, **33**, 359–364.

Hennigan, J.K. and Wortham, A.W. (1975). Analysis of workday stresses on industrial managers using heart rate as a criterion. *Ergonomics*, **18**, 675–681.

House, J.S., McMichael, A.J., Wells, J.A., Kaplan, B.H. and Landerman, L.R. (1979). Occupational stress and health among factory workers. *Journal of Health and Social Behavior*, **20**, 139–160.

Howard, J.H., Cunningham, D.A. and Rechnitzer, P.A. (1976). Health patterns associated with type A behavior: a managerial population. *Journal of Human Stress*, **2**, 24–31.

Jenner, D.A., Reynolds, V. and Harrison, G.A. (1980). Catecholamine excretion rates and occupation. *Ergonomics*, **23**, 237–246.

Jennings, J.R., Berg, W.K., Hutcheson, J.S. Obrist, P., Porges, S. and Turpin, G. (1981). Publication guidelines for heart rate studies in man. *Psychophysiology*, **18**, 226–231.

Johansson, G., Aronsson, G. and Lindström, B.O. (1978). Social psychological and neuro-endocrine stress reactions in highly mechanized work. *Ergonomics*, **21**, 583–599.

Johnson, B.C., Epstein, F.H. and Kjelsberg, M.O. (1965). Distributions and familial studies of blood pressure and serum cholesterol levels in a total community—Tecumseh, Michigan. *Journal of Chronic Diseases*, **18**, 147–160.

Johnson, G. (1972). Sex differences in the catecholamine output of children. *Acta Physiologia Scandinavica*, **85**, 569–572.

Johnson, G. and Post, B. (1972). *Catecholamine Output of Males and Females over a One-Year Period*. Reports from the Psychological Laboratories, University of Stockholm, No. 379.

Kasl, S.V. (1978). Epidemiological contributions to the study of work stress. In C.L. Cooper and R. Payne (eds), *Stress at Work* (London: John Wiley).

Kasl, S.V. and Cobb, S. (1970). Blood pressure changes in men undergoing job loss. A preliminary report. *Psychosomatic Medicine*, **32**, 19–38.

Kinley, L.D. and Krause, R.F. (1959). Influence of vitamin A on cholesterol blood levels. *Proceedings of the Society for Experimental Biology and Medicine*, **102**, 353–355.

Koerselman, H.B., Lewis, B. and Pilkington, T.R.E. (1961). The effect of venous occlusion on the level of serum cholesterol. *Journal of Atherosclerosis Research*, **1**, 85–88.

Kuorinka, I. and Korhonen, O. (1981). Firefighters' reaction to alarm, a ECG and heart rate study. *Journal of Occupational Medicine*, **23**, 762–766.

Lazarus, R.S. (1966). *Psychological Stress and the Coping Process* (New York: McGraw-Hill).

Light, K.C. (1981). Cardiovascular responses to effortful active coping: implications for the role of stress in hypertension development. *Psychophysiology*, **18**, 216–225.

Malmstrom, E.J. (1971). Cross-laboratory comparability of heart rate measures: A reply to Elliott. *Journal of Experimental Research in Personality*, **5**, 151–154.

Mason, J.W. (1975a). A historical view of the stress field. *Journal of Human Stress*, **1**(2), 22–36.

Mason, J.W. (1975b). A historical view of the stress field (Part II). *Journal of Human Stress*, **1**(3), 22–26.

Mayo, O., Fraser, G.R. and Stamatoyannopoulos, G. (1969). Genetic influences on serum cholesterol in two Greek villages. *Human Heredity*, **19**, 86–99.

McGrath, J.E. (1976). Stress and behavior in organizations. In M.D. Dunnette (ed), *Handbook of Industrial and Organizational Psychology* (Chicago, IL: Rand McNally).

McGrath, J.E. (1982). Methodological problems in research on stress. In H.W. Krohne and L. Laux (eds), *Achievement, Stress and Anxiety* (New York: McGraw-Hill).

McQuade, W. and Aikman, A. (1974). *Stress, What it is, What it can do to your Health, How to Fight Back* (New York: Bantam).

Miall, W.E., Heneage, P., Khosla, T., Lovell, H.G. and Moore, F. (1967). Factors influencing the degree of resemblance in arterial pressure of close relatives. *Clinical Science*, **33**, 271–285.

Morse, D.R. and Furst, M.L. (1979). *Stress for Success: A Holistic Approach to Stress and its Management* (New York: Van Nostrand Reinhold).

Orth-Gomer, K. and Ahlbom, A. (1980). Impact of psychological stress and ischaemic heart disease when controlling for conventional risk indicators. *Journal of Human Stress*, **6**, 7–16.

Perera, G.W., Clark, E.G., Gearing, F.R. and Schweitzer, M.D. (1961). The family of hypertensive man. *American Journal of the Medical Sciences*, **241**, 18–31.

Reeder, L.G., Schrama, P.G.M. and Dirken, J.M. (1973). Stress and cardiovascular health: An international cooperative study – I. *Social Science and Medicine*, **7**, 573–584.

Reynolds, R.C. (1974). Community and occupational influences in stress at Cape Kennedy: Relationships to heart disease. In R.S. Eliot (ed), *Stress and the Heart* (Mount Kisco, NY: Futura).

Rose, M., Jenkins, C.D. and Hurst, M.W. (1978). Health change in air traffic controllers: A prospective study. *Psychosomatic Medicine*, **40**, 142–165.

Rosner, B. and Polk, B.F. (1979). The implications of blood pressure variability for clinical and screening purposes. *Journal of Chronic Diseases*, **32**, 451–461.

Rosner, B. and Polk, B.F. (1981). The instability of blood pressure variability over time. *Journal of Chronic Diseases*, **34**, 135–141.

Rubin, R.T. (1974). Biochemical and neuroendocrine responses to severe psychological stress. In E.K.E. Gunderson and R.H. Rahe (eds), *Life Stress and Illness* (Springfield, IL: C.C. Thomas).

Rubin, R.T. and Rahe, R.H. (1974). U.S. Navy underwater demolition team training: biochemical studies. In E.K.E. Gunderson and R.H. Rahe (eds), *Life Stress and Illness* (Springfield, IL: C.C. Thomas).

Sabine, J.R. (1977). *Cholesterol* (New York: Marcel Dekker).

Sales, S.M. (1970). Some effects of role overload and role underload. *Organizational Behavior and Human Performance*, **5**, 592–608.

Sandberg, B. and Bliding, A. (1976). Duodenal ulcer in army trainees during basic military training. *Journal of Psychosomatic Research*, **20**, 61–74.

Schär, M., Reeder, L.G. and Dirken, J.M. (1973). Stress and cardiovascular health: An international cooperative study—II. The male population of a factory at Zurich. *Social Science and Medicine*, **7**, 585–603.

Schaefer, L.E., Adlersberg, D. and Steinberg, A.G. (1958). Heredity, environment and serum cholesterol: a study of 201 healthy families. *Circulation*, **17**, 537–542.

Schuler, R.S. (1980). Definition and conceptualization of stress in organizations. *Organizational Behavior and Human Performance*, **25**, 184–215.

Schuler, R.S. and Jackson, S.E. (in press). Managing stress through PHRM practices: An uncertainty interpretation. In K.M. Rowland and G.R. Ferris (eds), *Research in Personnel and Human Resources Management*, Vol. 4 (Greenwich, CT: JAI Press).

Schweitzer, MD., Gearing, F.R. and Perera, G.W. (1967). Family studies of primary hypertension: Their contribution to the understanding of genetic factors. In J. Stamler and T.N. Pullman (eds), *The Epidemiology of Essential Hypertension* (New York: Grune and Stratton).

Selye, H. (1976). *The Stress of Life* (New York: McGraw-Hill).

Semler, H.J. (1965). Radiotelemetry during cardiac exercise tests. In C.A. Caceres (ed.), *Biomedical Telemetry* (New York: Academic Press).

Shapiro, A.P. (1973). Essential hypertension—Why idiopathic? *American Journal of Medicine*, **54**, 1–15.

Shirom, A. (1982). What is organizational stress? A fact analytic conceptualization. *Journal of Occupational Behavior*, **3**, 21–37.

Shirom, A., Eden, D., Silberwasser, S. and Kellermann, J.J. (1973). Job stresses and risk factors in coronary heart disease among five occupational categories in a Kibbutzim. *Social Science and Medicine*, **7**, 875–892.

Siddle, D.A.T. and Turpin, G. (1980). Measurement, quantification and analysis of cardiac activity. In I. Martin and P.H. Venables (eds), *Techniques in Psychophysiology* (New York: John Wiley).

Spirts, N., Ahrens, E.H., Jr and Grundy, S. (1965). Sterol balance in man as plasma cholesterol concentrations are altered by exchanges of dietary fats. *Journal of Clinical Investigation*, **44**, 1482–1493.

Statland, B.E., Bokelund, H. and Winkel, P. (1974). Factors contributing to intra-individual variation of serum constituents. 4. Effects of posture and tourniquet application on variation of serum constituents in healthy subjects. *Clinical Chemistry*, **20**, 1513–1519.

Stern, R.M., Ray, W.J. and Davis, C.M. (1980). *Psychophysiological Recording*. (New York: Oxford University Press).

Tursky, B. (1974). The indirect recording of human blood pressure. In P. Obrist, A.N. Black, J. Brener and L. DiCara (eds), *Cardiovascular Psychophysiology* (Chicago, IL: Aldine).

Waldron, I. (1978). The coronary-prone behavior pattern, blood pressure, employment and socio-economic status in women. *Journal of Psychosomatic Research*, **22**, 79–87.

Warheit, C.J. (1974). Occupation: a key factor in stress at the manned space center. In R.S. Eliot (ed), *Stress and the Heart* (Mount Kisco, NY: Futura).

Weiner, H. (1979). *Psychobiology of Essential Hypertension* (New York: Elsevier).

Wolf, S., Almy, T.P., Bachrach, W.H., Spiro, H.M., Sturdevant, R.A.L. and Weiner, H. (1979). The role of stress in peptic ulcer disease. *Journal of Human Stress*, **5**, 27–37.

Yager, J. and Weiner, H. (1971). Observations in man. In H. Weiner (ed.), *Advances in Psychosomatic Medicine (Duodenal Ulcer)* (Basel: S. Karger).

Zinner, H.S., Levy, P.S. and Kass, E.H. (1971). Familial aggregation of blood pressure in childhood. *New England Journal of Medicine*, **284**, 401–412.

11

Cognitive Stress and Cardiovascular Reactivity: Relationship to Hypertension

Paul M. Cinciripini

1. Overview

Cardiovascular reactivity refers to the difference (Δ) in heart rate, blood pressure or other measures of cardiovascular function observed between periods of rest and during the presentation of an external stressor. Reactivity may be conceptualized as a quantitative, physiological variable, such that certain individuals will show greater reactivity than others. The majority of reactivity studies have measured changes in heart rate and systolic blood pressure. To a lesser extent, reactivity has also been studied by measuring changes in ST segment depression of the ECG, rate pressure product, pulse pressure, pulse transit time, cardiac output, total peripheral resistance and left ventricular ejection time, as well as other measures of cardiac performance and circulating levels of catecholamines and cortisol. The paradigms for studying reactivity have involved a broad class of experimental stressors and designs.

The evaluation period used to establish resting levels of physiological activity may be a separate relaxation baseline, conducted on a different day than the stress session, or it may be a pre-stress baseline, conducted on the same day as the stress session. The physical stressors may involve the cold pressor test, isometric hand grip and exercise. Cognitive stressors may involve one or more of the following: mental maths, the Stroop Color Word Test, complex analytical or concept formation tasks, a stressful interview, i.e., a structured interview for Type A behaviour, choice reaction time, video games, or naturalistic stress, e.g., job environment.

The saliency of the situation for a particular subject may be enhanced by including such factors as pressure to respond quickly, threat of aversive consequences for errors, e.g., shock, incentives for successful completion of the task, competition and harassment. Different methodological permutations of task and measurement characteristics may elicit patterns of arousal, which accentuate reactivity in one or another measure(s). Suffice it to say, however, that the extent of a subject's reactivity to a particular measure, e.g., heart rate (HR) response to mental maths or a video game, is usually reproducible and stable over time. Correlations between different response measures on different tasks are more variable, but moderately high (Krantz and Manuck, 1985).

Unless otherwise specified, this review will concentrate on studies of cardiovascular reactivity using cognitive stressors. Cognitive stressors may represent an important laboratory analogue which can be used to assess the effects of acute psychological stress on the cardiovascular system. Laboratory stressors are easily administered and the physiological changes which accompany them may have relevance for the future development of cardiovascular disease.

The relationship between laboratory induced cognitive stress and cardiovascular reactivity has been studied in several ways. Early research examined the extent of reactivity in people with manifest cardiovascular disease. These studies typically did not involve comparisons to normal controls but were aimed at linking the presence of an abnormal cardiac event, e.g., excessive oxygen consumption or hypertension, to acute cognitive stress. Later studies of reactivity did include comparisons between normals and patients with cardiovascular disease. It soon became clear that the magnitude of stress induced changes in blood pressure or heart rate was not uniform across all subjects and that certain otherwise healthy subjects, as well as some patients, could be described as cardiovascular reactors. The central question, however, is whether the high reactors are at increased risk for the development of future cardiovascular disease.

This chapter reviews the pathophysiological and epidemiological significance of acute cardiovascular reactivity as it relates to cardiovascular disease. Long-term prospective studies bridging the gap between the initial observation of excessive reactivity to acute stress and the development of future cardiovascular disease are at present few in number. However, several hypotheses have been advanced which link the acute effects of cognitive stress, e.g., increased heart rate, catecholamines, etc., to known pathogenetic factors in cardiovascular disease. Research on subjects who do not yet have manifest cardiovascular disease, but who are excessively reactive to stress, may be particularly important since it could reveal the mechanisms which link the pathophysiology of future diseae to the episodic stress experienced during the preclinical period of a disorder. The reader is referred to the reviews of Krantz and Manuck (1984, 1985) for an in-depth discussion of reactivity research design and methodological issues.

2. Relevance of reactivity to cardiovascular disease: epidemiological, family history and experimental considerations in hypertension

Research on reactivity has the potential for making a unique contribution to the study of hypertension. Traditional epidemiological studies have focused on the association between resting levels of a suspected risk factor, such as heart rate, cholesterol or blood pressure, and the future development of cardiovascular disease. On the other hand, studies of reactivity have attended to the magnitude of change for a particular cardiac event during periods of rest and behavioural (or physical) challenge. The focus on change versus casual measures may be an important distinction. For example, recent studies of hypertension (Perloff et al., 1983) have indicated that average ambulatory blood pressure (BP) readings may be more predictive of future hypertensive complications than casual blood pressure measures. This finding might be due to the inclusion of the daily stress-related blood pressure peaks (reactivity) in the ambulatory readings. However, casual BP measurement is the most typically used method for assessing future blood pressure status.

A positive association between reactivity and future hypertension is also partially supported by research showing that BP obtained during work (Devererex *et al.*, 1983) is more predictive of future hypertension than BP obtained at rest. A most interesting prospective example of this comes from the Air Traffic Controller Study (Rose *et al.*, 1978; Jenkins *et al.*, 1984), which showed that relative to rest, the BP of some controllers rose dramatically while they were actually controlling aircraft. The magnitude of the BP rise (reactivity) was predictive of future hypertension. In the only other prospective study in this area, Falkner *et al.* (1981) noted that the degree of systolic blood pressure reactivity to mental mathematics among borderline adolescent hypertensives was predictive of future hypertension, five years later.

The presence of enhanced reactivity to psychological stressors among borderline hypertensives who later develop hypertension suggests that reactivity may act synergistically with other risk factors, or that it may act as a trait marker for subjects at preclinical levels of the disorder. Support for this argument has been received in studies which show enhanced blood pressure (or heart rate) reactivity among adult (Light and Obrist, 1980) and adolescent (Falkner *et al.*, 1979) normotensive males with a positive family history of hypertension. The degree of BP reactivity appears to increase when both parents are hypertensive (Hewitt *et al.*, 1982).

Recently, Manuck *et al.* (1981) helped clarify the relationship between reactivity and family history of hypertension by evaluating heart rate and blood pressure reactivity to a concept formation task (Feldman Visual-Verbal Test). Relative to a resting baseline, subjects with a parental history of hypertension showed a significant rise in systolic blood pressure ($+20\,mm\,Hg$). Subjects showing a high heart rate reactivity ($+18\,bpm$) and a positive family history of hypertension showed a larger SBP rise than those without a family history of hypertension. Among low heart rate reactors, with and without a parental history of hypertension, only modest and non-significant SBP changes were observed. Results for diastolic blood pressure showed a significant effect of the stress task, but no reactor/family history interaction was observed.

Thus, cardiovascular reactivity appears to be enhanced in subjects with a parental history of hypertension. However, no difference in SBP reactivity is observed among low heart rate reactors, with or without a family history of hypertension. A parental history of hypertension seems to act synergistically with heart rate reactivity when reactivity is observed. But, a history of parental hypertension does not necessarily ensure that high levels of cardiovascular reactivity will be observed. Perhaps heart rate reactivity among normotensives contributes something to the overall risk of hypertension irrespective of a hypertensive family history. While the data are far from complete on this matter, these findings suggest that low levels of HR reactivity may be associated with a suppression of the SBP reactivity that might be expected in the offspring of hypertensive parents. Low heart rate reactivity may also be associated with lower casual BPs and perhaps a lower rate for developing future hypertension in this same population.

The relationship between essential hypertension and cardiovascular reactivity during cognitive stress has also been evaluated by assessing the blood pressure reactivity among established hypertensives. If reactivity has some bearing on the development of hypertension, then one might expect hypertensive patients to be more reactive to environmental stressors than normotensives tested under the same conditions. For example, Schulte and Neus (1983) studied 10 mild hypertensives (BP > 140/90 mm Hg), borderline hypertensives (120/80 – 140/90 mm Hg) and normotensives (120/80 mm Hg or less), during both resting and mental maths conditions. All groups significantly increased in systolic blood pressure and mean arterial pressure, from resting to stress conditions. The hypertensives showed the strongest rise in systolic and diastolic pressure (15–17 mm Hg) as well as stroke volume. In a related study, Schulte *et al.* (1984) evaluated 30 hypertensives and 13 normotensives in separate relaxation baseline and stress sessions. The stressor involved mental maths, performed under time pressure and 90 dB noise distraction. The results showed that SBP variability during the relaxation baseline correlated significantly with SBP reactivity between the stressor, and the pre-stress baseline assessment conducted on the same day. The hypertensives were also more variable at rest and more reactive during stress than the normotensives. This work extends and confirms previous findings suggesting that reactivity to cognitive stressors among high normotensives is highly correlated with variability in blood pressure measures obtained outside the laboratory (Manuck *et al.*, 1979). It should be noted, however, that there is some question regarding the exact relationship between reactivity and resting BP variability among established hypertensives. Some studies have reported that established hypertensives may not be more variable in resting BP (Julius *et al.*, 1983) than non-hypertensives. In comparison to normotensives, we may expect a higher proportion of hypertensives to be abnormally reactive (Schulte *et al.* 1984). Resting BPs, however, may not be more labile among the hypertensives, except for those subjects in which high levels of reactivity can be demonstrated.

In a study designed to directly assess the reactivity of labile hypertnesives, Steptoe *et al.* (1984) evaluated 12 male normotensives (BP <120/80 mm Hg), 12 labile hypertensives (see below) and 12 mild hypertensives: (175/105 – 145/90 mm Hg at rest). Blood pressures were obtained in and out of the laboratory environment. After the initial screening, some subjects also self-monitored their blood pressures. The labile hypertensives were subjects whose blood pressures exceeded 145/90 mm Hg at initial screening, then dropped below this limit during subsequent self-monitoring and resting assessments. The Stroop Color Word Test (Stroop, 1935), a challenging video game (i.e., 'pong') and a stressful film were presented to all subjects. The results showed that mild hypertensives experienced significantly more SBP reactivity (+ 23 mm Hg) than normotensives (+ 17 mm Hg) to the video game and the Stroop, but not to the film. The film was considered a passive stress condition and may not have evoked sympathetic arousal sufficient enough to sustain large blood pressure changes. Labile hypertensives also showed the greatest reactivity in diastolic blood pressure, heart rate and pulse transit time: a measure which is positively correlated with SBP during β-adrenergic driving (Obrist *et al.*, 1979). Thus, in at least three separate studies, exaggerated cardiovascular reactivity has been identified among borderline (labile) and established hypertensives during the presentation of a cognitive stressor. It would also appear that an elevated casual BP is not necessarily indicative of enhanced lability in reacting BPs. However, BP reactivity to stress may be positively correlated with resting BP lability.

3. Psychophysiological relationships of reactivity and hypertension

It is intriguing to think that essential hypertension may proceed to established hypertension though an imposition of psychological factors on the proper biological substrate. A major assumption behind this reasoning is that the episodic psychological stress can impact significantly on the pathophysiology of hypertension. As yet, this assumption is only beginning to receive support in the epidemiological literature. Prospective studies of high and low reactors, which target important features of hypertensive pathophysiology, have not yet been done. However, the endocrine and psychophysiological concomitants of reactivity may indeed influence several of the known pathogenetic mechanisms related to hypertension. For example, the pressor effects of acute stress could have implications for altering vessel morphology. The work from Folkow's laboratory (Folkow, 1977) suggests that repeated pressor episodes may lead to arteriolar hypertrophy and to changes in the wall to lumen ratio—altering geometry and rendering the vessels yet more responsive to future pressor stimuli. In time, a positive feedback loop may be established, through which vascular hypertrophy and pressor responsiveness are increased, resulting in increased peripheral resistance and blood pressure. This is an extremely important point since it helps to explain how the excessive cardiac output seen in the high reactor may be related to the enhanced peripheral resistance, characteristic of the established hypertensive. Acute reactivity in the pre-hypertensive state may directly influence the process of normalizing cardiac output in the hypertensive, while producing long-term elevations in peripheral resistance (Julius *et al.*, 1983). Reactivity tied to psychological stressors has the potential of producing frequent and pervasive elevations in cardiac performance. The reactivity appears unique to situations which have some behavioural significance and is not a ubiquitous feature of hypertension. This idea is supported by the fact that borderline and mild hypertensives are not uniformly more labile in resting BP, nor are they excessively responsive to exercise or cold pressor testing (cf. Julius *et al.*, 1983, for an extensive review). Thus, the possibility may be entertained that individuals predisposed to develop hypertension are not generally hyperresponsive, but may be more frequently exposed to pressor stimuli, which have pathognomonic consequences.

The most frequently occurring class of these pressor stimuli which may have significance for the pathophysiology of hypertension may indeed be psychological in nature. Both the magnitude and the extent (frequency) of a person's reactivity may be directly related to the risk of a hypertensive disorder (Manuck *et al.* 1978). The reactivity data of Falkner *et al.* (1979, 1981) are particularly interesting in this regard, since enhanced SBP hyperresponsiveness to a psychological stressor, e.g., mental stress, was demonstrated among normotensive and hypertensive offspring of hypertensive parents. As indicated above, subjects hyperresponsive to mental stress show a higher likelihood of being hypertensive at a 5-year follow-up than subjects low in reactivity

(Falkner *et al.*, 1981). The enhanced BP observed for the air traffic controllers (Jenkins *et al.*, 1984) during aircraft direction may possibly be related to the psychologically stressful components of this activity. It will be recalled that the risk of hypertension in the controllers was positively correlated with the magnitude of work-related reactivity. Light and Obrist (1980) also found enhanced heart rate and BP reactivity to mental stress (reaction time) among borderline hypertensives, while Hollenberg *et al.*, (1981) found normal BP but an excessive renal vasoconstriction to a cognitive stressor (maths) among similar groups.

Presumably, more frequent exposure to an event producing reactivity, e.g., adrenergically mediated psychological stress, results in a higher likelihood of cardiovascular damage and the development of hypertension. The importance of reactivity in the development of hypertension may he highlighted by the fact that only 27% of individuals in the upper quartile of all known hypertension risk factors develop hypertension 5 years into the future (Julius *et al.*, 1983). It has been suggested that factors related to psychological alertness or mental engagement could result in chronic elevations in sympathetic tone and a slow but persistent rise in BP (Julius *et al.*, 1983). Alteration in vascular smooth muscle morphology has been proposed as one consequence of elevated sympathetic activity (Folkow, 1977). However, other related hypotheses have been proposed to explain the pathophysiology of hypertension. Each hypothesis emphasizes different physiological processes. However, converging lines of evidence may link psychologically based changes in reactivity to the mechanisms normally regulating BP.

The patterns of sympathetic arousal produced during psychological (behavioural) stress have been extensively studied. Most of the stress induced elevations in cardiac performance have been related to enhanced β-adrenergic stimulation (e.g., Glass *et al.*, 1980, 1981; Obrist, 1981). For example, studies of normotensives (Obrist *et al.*, 1979) experiencing psychological stress (threat of shock) have shown an increased sympathetic influence on the myocardium, e.g., raised cardiac contractility, and heart rate. These effects like the cardiac output increases observed in some borderline hypertensives may be abolished by β-blockade (Obrist, 1981; Julius *et al.*, 1983). Thus the contention that reactivity and hypertension share a strong neurogenic component is supported.

Excessive sympathetic drive has also been noted among coronary-prone individuals (Type A) during certain types of psychological stress. Research on the salient features of the Type A–environment interaction further implicate adrenergic hyperresponsiveness in the pathophysiology of cardiovascular disease. For example, Type A's have shown enhanced reactivity during mental stress in measures of blood pressure, heart rate, forearm blood flow, catecholamine and cortisol secretion (*see* Matthews, 1982; Cinciripini, 1984). Epidemiologically, the Type A pattern has not been consistently related to hypertension (Jenkins *et al.*, 1984) but it has been related to atherosclerosis (Bloom and Herd, 1983), and electroconductive disturbances, which may be the sequelae of acute hypertensive episodes.

Psychological stress could also play an important role in the aetiology of hypertension, through its effect on the regulation of water and sodium balance. For example, Guyton and Coleman (1969) propose that, under normal circumstances, increased blood pressure leads to diuresis, lowered blood volume and subsequently reduced blood pressure. Hypertension may result from an increased threshold for renal pressure diuresis, such that higher and higher pressure levels are required in order to initiate a volume correction. Initially, the higher threshold may be associated with volume expansion and/or increased venous return which results in elevated cardiac output. The elevations in cardiac output may set in motion a process of autoregulation, whereby vascular resistance increases in order to protect the tissues from overperfusion (Obrist, 1981) resulting from delivery of oxygen in excess of metabolic demand. The work of Obrist and his colleagues (Obrist, 1981; Light and Obrist, 1983) suggests that conditions characterized by active coping with a mental stressor, e.g., control over the delivery of aversive shocks by speedy reaction time, may be likely to raise cardiac output levels high enough to trigger autoregulation. This idea has particular appeal from the standpoint of cognitive induced reactivity since numerous studies have demonstrated that clear and, in some cases, sustained increases in cardiac output, may result from exposure to psychological stress (*see* Glass *et al.*, 1980; Bloom and Herd, 1983; Krantz and Manuck, 1985; McKinney *et al.*, 1985). Such changes in cardiac output have the potential for triggering autoregulation, subsequent vasoconstriction, and enhanced blood pressure.

It should be noted that Julius *et al.* (1983) have questioned the applicability of the concept of autoregulation to the development of essential hypertension. They note that the time constant for the development of volume expansion is variable, and among boderline hypertensives, relative, but not absolute, hypervolaemia can be demonstrated. This is contrary to the expected increase in blood volume which might be predicted if autoregulation was taking place in the borderline, or pre-hypertensive state. Julius *et al.* (1983) have also criticized the evidence supporting increased renal thresholds, suggesting that borderline and established hypertension may show increased diuresis, but the blood pressure increases expected in response to volume loading are not consistently observed.

As an alternative to the autoregulation hypothesis, Julius *et al.* (1983) have suggested that a disruption in the autonomic control of the cardiovascular system may also be important in the development of hypertension. The work of Julius *et al.* (1983) has involved studies of borderline patients in a hyperkinetic state. These hypertensive patients show increased cardiac output, and increased β-adrenergic driving. Increased sympathetic discharge is suggested as the key factor in the conversion from the stages of early to established hypertension (Julius *et al.*, 1983). As previously discussed, the early phases of hypertension may be characterized by an increased cardiac output. Established hypertension, however, involves a normokinetic state, characterized by increased peripheral vascular resistance and an absence of excessive pressor episodes. Julius *et al.* (1983) suggest that excessive sympathetic stimulation, without autoregulation or volume expansion, may result in the down-regulation of adrenergic receptors in the myocardium. Combined with structural changes in the cardiac tissue (hypertrophy), the reduced sensitivity of cardiac β-adrenergic receptors results in a return to normal cardiac output. In the arterioles, down-regulation of the α-receptors is offset by the structural changes in the vessel wall (hypertrophy) brought about by an increase in the wall to lumen ratio. Julius proposes that a positive feedback loop develops in which less and less sympathetic stimulation is required to initiate the same level of vasoconstriction. In effect, the level of SNS tone is enhanced. Julius contends (Julius *et al.*, 1983) that excessive sympathetic drive (reactivity) to the heart and increased parasympathetic inhibition results from an abnormal central integration of cardiovascular autonomic tone, which is probably related to behavioural factors, e.g., recurrent episodic stress.

4. Conclusion

There are several possible avenues through which a hyperresponsiveness to mental stress can be implicated in the development of hypertension. This process may involve direct influence on the sympathetic nervous system, function and cardiovascular performance, and the renal regulation of water and sodium balance. The data suggest that reactivity may be more important that static BP measures in determining who develops hypertension, and that the frequency of pressor episodes may be related to psychologically induced stress. Highly reactive individuals may be at greater risk of developing hypertension, since they may potentially be exposed to a higher frequency of pressor episodes and the pathogenetic sequelae which follow.

Acknowledgements

Preparation of this manuscript was supported in part by grants to the author from National Institute for Occupational Safety and Health (# 84–257) and the Texas Affiliate of the American Heart Association (# G–337), the Forman Research Fund (507 RR 07205).

References

Bloom, F.E. and Herd, A.J. (1983). Physiologic and neurobiologic mechanisms in arteriosclerosis. In J.A. Herd and S.M. Weiss (eds), *Behavior and Arteriosclerosis* (New York: Plenum), pp. 33–43.

Cinciripini, P.M. (1984). Applications of behavioral medicine with children I: Epidemiology of coronary heart disease. In M. Hersen, R. Eisler and P. Miller (eds), *Progress in Behavior Modifications*, Volume 17, (New York: Academic Press), pp. 73–110.

Devererex, R.B., Pickering, T.G. and Harshfield, G.A. (1983): Left ventricular hypertrophy in patients with hypertension: Importance of blood pressure response to regularly occurring stress. *Circulation*, **68**, 470–476.

Falkner, B., Onesti, G., Angalakos, E.T., Fernandes, M. and Langman, C. (1979). Cardiovascular response to mental stress in normal adolescents with hypertensive parents. *Hypertension*, **1**, 23–30.

Falkner, B., Onesti, G. and Hamstra, B. (1981). Stress response characteristics of adolescents with high genetic risk for essential hypertension. A five year follow-up. *Clinical and Experimental Hypertension*, **3**, 583–591.

Folkow, B. (1977). Role of vascular factor in hypertension. *Contributions to Nephrology*, **8**, 81–94.

Glass, D.C., Krakoff, L.R. and Finkelman, J. (1980). Effect of task overload upon cardio-vascular and plasma catecholamine responses in Type A and individuals. *Basic and Applied Social Psychology*, **1**, 199–218.

Guyton, A.C. and Coleman, T,G. (1969). Quantitative analysis of the pathophysiology of hypertension. *Circulation Research*, **24–25**, Suppl. 1, 1–19.

Hollenberg, N.K., Williams, G.H. and Adams, D.F. (1981). Essential hypertension: abnormal renal vascular and endocrine responses to a mild psychological stimulus. *Hypertension*, **3**, 11–17.

Hewitt, J.K., Carrol, D., Last, K.A., Turner, J.R. and Sims, J. (1982). A twin study of cardiac reactivity and parental hypertension. Presented at *14th Annual Meeting of the Behavior Genetics Association*, Bloomington, IN: May.

Jenkins, C.D., Hurst, M.W., Rose, R., Anderson, M.C. and Kreger, B.E. (1984). Bio-medical and psychosocial predictors of hypertension in air traffic controllers. In C.D. Spielberger, I.G. Saroson and P.B. Refars (eds), *Stress and Anxiety*, Volume 9 (New York: McGraw-Hill), pp. 231–239.

Julius, S., Weder, A.B. and Egan, B.M. (1983). Pathophysiology of early hypertension. Implication for epidemiologic research. In F. Gross and T. Strasser, (eds), *Mild Hypertension: Recent Advances* (New York: Raven Press), pp. 219–236.

Krantz, D.S. and Manuck, S.B. (1984). Acute psychophysiologic reactivity and risk of cardio-vascular disease: a review and methodologic critique. *Psychological Bulletin*, **96**, 435–464.

Krantz, D.S. and Manuck, S.B. (1985). Measures of acute physiologic reactivity to behavioral stimuli assessment and critique. In A. Ostfeld and E. Eaker (eds), *Measuring Psychosocial Variables in Epidemiologic Studies of Cardiovascular Disease*, (Bethesda, MD: National Institute of Health).

Light, K.C. and Obrist, P.A. (1980). Cardiovascular reactivity to behavioral stress in young males with and without marginally elevated causal systolic pressures. *Hypertension*, **2**(6), 802–808.

Light, K.C. and Obrist, P.A. (1983). Task difficulty, heart rate reactivity and cardiovascular response to an appetitive reaction time task. *Psychophysiology*, **20**, 301–312.

Manuck, S.B., Corse, C.D. and Winkelman, P.A. (1978). Behavioral correlates of individual differences in blood pressure reactivity. *Journal of Psychosomatic Research*, **23**, 281–288.

Manuck, S.B., Giordani, B., McQuaid, K.J. and Garrity, S.J. (1981). Behaviorally induced cardiovascular reactivity among sons of reported hypertensive normotensive patients. *Journal of Psychosomatic Research*, **25**, 261–269.

Matthews, K.A. (1982). Psychological perspectives on the Type A behavior pattern. *Psychological Bulletin*, **91**, 293–323.

McKinney, M.E., Miner, M.H., Ruddell, H., McIlvain, H.E., Witte, H., Buell, J.C., Eliot, R.S. and Grant, L.B. (1985). The standardized mental stress test protocol: test-retest reliability and comparison with ambulatory blood pressure monitoring. *Psychophysiology*, **22**(4), 453–463.

Obrist, P.A. (1981). *Cardiovascular Psychophysiology: A Perspective* (New York: Plenum).

Obrist, P.A., Light, K.C., McCubbin, J.A., Hutchenson, J.S. and Hoffer, J.L. (1979). Pulse transit time: Relationship to blood pressure and myocardial performance. *Psychophysiology*, **16**, 292–301.

Perloff, D., Sokolow, M. and Cowan, R. (1983). The prognostic value of ambulatory blood pressures. *Journal of the American Medical Association*, **249**, 2792.

Rose, R.M., Jenkins, C.D. and Hurst, M.W. (1978). *Air Traffic Controller Health Change Study*, FAA-AM No. 78-39 (Washington, DC: NTIS).

Schulte, W. and Neus, H. (1983). Hemodynamics. *European Heart Journal*, **4**, 803–809.

Schulte, W., Neus, H., Thones, M. and von Eiff, A.W. (1984). Basal blood pressure variability and reactivity of blood pressure to emotional stress in essential hypertension. *Basic Research in Cardiology*, **79**, 9–16.

Steptoe, A., Melville, D. and Ross, A. (1984). Behavioral response demands, cardiovascular reactivity, and essential hypertension. *Psychosomatic Medicine*, **46**(1), 33–48.

Stroop, J.R. (1935). Studies of interference in serial verbal reactions. *Journal of Experimental Psychology*, **18**, 643–662.

12

Self-Reports and Physiological Measures in the Workplace

James W. Pennebaker and David Watson

1. Introduction

The measurement of stress levels in the workplace poses a number of difficult problems for the researcher, employer and employee. Because of time and cost factors, most projects designed to assess individuals' perceptions of job stress have been limited to questionnaires handed out *en masse* at one time to employees of selected companies. Although simple surveys are cost-effective, a number of potential problems exist that may bias the results by artificially inflating or deflating levels of self-reported stress. Many physiological measures that are collected at only one time are also subject to systematic and substantial error due to a number of psychological variables.

The purpose of this chapter is to examine the perceptual and physiological correlates of self-reported stress, physical symptoms and health. Our primary focus is on the individual in the workplace who is earnestly interested in evaluating his or her symptoms, emotions and physiological levels. Our approach, then, ignores the often powerful impact of political and policy considerations within and outside the organization. This approach also assumes that self-reports and physiological measures are not consciously distorted by the employee in order to curry favour with management.

The chapter is divided into three sections. We will first evaluate the nature of self-reports of stress, symptoms and health in the light of commonly accepted principles of perceptual processes. As with vision or hearing, the perception of bodily states can be distorted easily by situational and personality variables. The second section of the chapter focuses on non-invasive physiological measures of job stress. As will be seen, self-reports of physiological activity correspond poorly with objective measures of physiology. Reasons for, and implications of, poor stress perception are discussed in detail. The final section describes methodological designs best suited to self-report and objective measures of stress. Recent findings based on within-subject studies using multiple measures will be evaluated. We will illustrate that by adopting idiographic methods, the researcher can pinpoint specific aspects of a job that may be most stressful and/or rewarding.

2. Self-reports and the perception of stress

Before we can discuss the measurement of job stress, we must briefly outline some of the definitions. As many researchers have noted, stress is a vague and general concept that encompasses physiological, perceptual and behavioural components (*see* Mason, 1975; Horowitz, 1976; Selye, 1976). To best understand each component, we must consider each of the following:

1. Objective and perceived stimulus situations that precede and evoke stress responses.
2. Individual differences that predispose the organism to cope in certain ways.
3. The cognitive and perceptual processes involved in evaluating stressors and one's own stress responses.
4. Physiological responses to stress.
5. Overt behaviours that change as a result of stress.
6. The interactions of each of the above systems over time (*see* Lazarus *et al.*, 1985 and Dohrenwend and Shrout, 1985 for discussions of these components).

Although each component is important in order to understand stress, we will focus on the ways that individuals perceive and report feelings of stress.

By way of an introduction, most individuals feel under stress or perceive stress from time to time. These perceptions may cause the person to change his or her work habits, seek medical attention, alter social behaviour at work or at home, etc. The perception of stress—irrespective of its objective base—is of critical interest to the researcher. Here, we shall address three related issues. The first question concerns the components of self-reported stress. That is, when individuals report being under stress, to what degree does this perception reflect increases in physical symptoms and negative emotions? The second related issue concerns how the various components of stress can best be measured. The final issue involves the perceptual processes underlying the experience and reporting of stress. As will be seen, certain settings, beliefs and feelings can powerfully affect reports of stress, even when physiological status remains constant.

Components and correlates of perceived stress

Several years ago, the first author asked 412 undergraduates to rate the degree to which they felt each of the following during 'the average day': under stress, sad, guilty, angry, frustrated, headache, upset stomach, dizzy, racing heart, tense muscles. As might be expected, self-reports of stress correlated $+0.40$ to $+0.70$ with each of the other items. This and later surveys continued to suggest that perceptions of stress are highly related to both negative emotions and physical symptoms (*see* Pennebaker, 1982, and Watson and Pennebaker, in press, for reviews). Indeed, the magnitudes of the relationships were sufficiently high to suggest that the items all represented the same underlying construct.

In an extensive review of the mood literature, the second author demonstrated that a variety of mood and anxiety questionnaires were all highly intercorrelated and thus reflected the same underlying construct of Negative Affectivity, or NA (Watson and Clark, 1984). This conclusion was reached from a review of dozens of studies that had included such measures as the Multiple Affect Adjective Checklist (Zuckerman and Lubin, 1965), the Beck Depression Inventory (Beck *et al.*, 1961), the Taylor Manifest Anxiety Scale (Taylor, 1953) and the State–Trait Anxiety Inventory (Spielberger *et al.*, 1970), as well as various measure of repression/sensitization, neuroticism, defensiveness, ego strength, social desirability and general maladjustment. Watson and Clark (1984) argue that high NA individuals are more likely to experience discomfort at all times and across situations. Further, high NA subjects tend to be more introspective and apparently dwell on the negative side of themselves and the world (*see* also Watson and Tellegen, 1985).

More recently, we asked over 150 healthy adults to complete measures of NA and stress reactions (e.g., the Multidimensional Personality Questionnaire by Tellegen, 1982), reports of physical symptoms (e.g., the PILL from Pennebaker, 1982) and general mood measures. Again, we found that self-reports of physical symptoms, stress reactivity and negative moods were highly intercorrelated (approximate mean intercorrelation among measures = $+0.50$). In other words, the domains of stress, symptoms and negative moods overlap considerably. The overlap is sufficiently high to suggest that perceptions of stress, symptoms and negative moods represent the same affective state.

Implications for the measurement of stress

That self-reports of stress, physical symptoms and negative moods reflect a common psychological state is both reassuring and disquieting. On the one hand, it is comforting to know that the researcher can use any of several stress-relevant measures and need not be overly concerned that one might be 'better' than another. By the same token, we can draw on the larger body of research data when analysing specific phenomena. On the other hand, the problems that surround such a broadly based concept are multifaceted. First, there are large individual differences in NA. These individual differences apparently have a heritable component (Scarr *et al*, 1981) and are stable over time and situation. In other words, measures of presumed transient job stress can be expected to correlate strongly with NA measures. Any simple between-subjects surveys that compare different groups will have to be large enough to overcome the individual variation in NA. By the same token, high NAs may be selectively drawn to different types of jobs than low NAs. If differential employment cannot be evaluated, the researcher must rely on random assignment or pre/post-designs when studying job stress.

A second disquieting feature of the NA concept for the researcher studying job stress concerns the general problem of causality. As an example of the problem, consider the following common sense causal model. Some aspect of a job is extremely frustrating and so causes undue stress. Over time, according to our simple causal model, this stress will cause health problems that can be measured by symptom reports. The NA findings argue that such a model is not tenable without very careful testing. That is, perceptions of frustration, stress and physical symptoms all reflect the same construct. To say that one of the three constructs—frustration, stress or symptoms—causes the other (without independent measurement of all three at three different points in time) simply has no meaning.

A particularly relevant example of this problem is evident in the current popularization of the Hassles Scale (Kanner *et al*, 1981). According to the authors of the scale, perceptions of minor irritants in one's daily lives (e.g., waiting in line, being in traffic) are highly predictive of stress. Over time, these accumulated hassles are causally related to health problems. In testing this, Delongis *et al.* (1982) and, more recently, Lazarus *et al.* (1985) note that the measurement of hassles is related to reports of physical symptoms. Based on our discussion, it should be clear why this claim cannot be validated. The process related to the perceptions of hassles is the same process related to the perception of symptoms. In short, a person who feels bad will perceive hassles and symptoms as well. To some extent, both probably cause the other; surely, causality in this instance cannot be simply or easily discerned.

Given the overlap of reports of stress, emotion and physical symptoms, it is important to examine the processes of perception and reporting in greater detail. When, for example, are people likely to report these feelings? When might these reports be biased?

The perception of internal state

Perhaps the most fundamental question that we must address concerning the self-reports of stress is on what is the perception of stress based? That is, if a person reports feelings of stress, physical symptoms or negative emotions, to what extent do the feelings reflect physiological activity, the setting or other perceptual factors? To get a better understanding of the factors underlying self-reports of stress, we must first examine the perceptual process.

A basic assumption of our research is that the perceptual processes involved in the awareness and reporting of sensations, symptoms, moods and stress represent the same rules of perception that dictate our perceptions of sights, sounds and smells (Leventhal, 1975; Brener, 1977; Pennebaker, 1982). Consequently, by examining biases and distortions in the perception of external environmental events, we can get a better understanding of conceptually similar biases that affect our perception of internal cues. To illustrate some of the basic perceptual rules involved in both processes, imagine the following scenario:

> You are driving down an isolated highway in your 10-year old car listening to a favourite song on the radio. As soon as the song is over, you detect a slight shaking in the steering wheel. Knowing the repair record of your car, you first touch the key in the ignition to see if it is hot. Because the key is warm and you suspect an electrical short, you immediately stop the car and jump out, fearing that it may explode at any time.

There are three important perceptual principles and sources of bias in this vignette. The first principle, based on *focus of attention*, concerns when you noticed the shaking in the first place. The second, which we refer to as *schema and selective search*, involves the role of the prior beliefs and how they cause us to search selectively for information that validates these beliefs. The third principle, based on *inference* processes, assumes that people make logical guesses about their environments. Each of these principles will be discussed below as to how they relate to both your car and stress.

Focus of attention and competition of cues

In an excellent summary of his and others' work on focus of attention, Berlyne (1960) noted that people were more likely to orient naturally to certain types of stimuli than others. Visual arrays that were unique, complex and displayed motion were far more likely to be attended to than similar arrays that were redundant, simple or stationary. If we assume that people can process only a finite amount of information at any given time (e.g., Navon and Gopher, 1979), it is clear that the more that we attend to one stimulus, the less we can attend to others. Orienting, then, is a function of the stimulus properties as well as the degree to which competing stimuli are being processed at the same time.

Over the years, we have derived an attentional principle to predict when internal sensory cues will be processed relative to external environmental cues. At any given time, the more we process external cues, the less likely it is that we will notice internal cues. All stimulus cues—whether internal or external—compete for attention. Referring back to our car example, we are more likely to notice the shaking of the steering wheel when we are not listening to music than when the music is on. By the same token, we would be more likely to notice or attend to a headache in a boring environment than in an interesting one.

Without going into detail, we have conducted several studies that demonstrate that settings lacking in external information are associated with increased reporting of internal states—such as physical symptoms and negative emotions. In one study, for example, students ran faster and reported less fatigue when their exercise environment was interesting than if it was boring (Pennebaker and Lightner, 1980).

In a test of Person–Environment Fit (Caplan *et al*, 1975), laboratory subjects worked on a task at either a very slow, a moderate or a very fast speed. Those in the very slow and the very fast conditions reported a high number of symptoms relative to those in the moderate condition. Interestingly, only those in the very fast cell evidenced significantly elevated heart rates (*see* Pennebaker, 1982 for discussion of this and related studies). Consistent with the competition of cues idea, underworked individuals have very little external information on which to focus, thus increasing the probability that they will notice and dwell upon internal cues. Those in moderately-paced tasks focus almost exclusively on external information, since there are virtually no competing internal cues to notice. Those in fast paced jobs have a great deal of external and internal information to process. The reporting of stress and symptoms, then, depends on the relative magnitude and salience of the various sources of information.

Schemas and selective search

The focus of attention perspective represents only one portion of the perceptual process. Whereas focus of attention implies a relatively passive perceiver, work on schemas and selective search assumes that the organism actively searches for information in order to better understand the world (Gibson, 1978). Depending on one's preferred terminology, we all hold certain beliefs, hypotheses, sets, expectations, scripts, templates, interpretations, attitudes, labels, cognitions, schemata or schemas. These organizational frameworks—which we will call schemas—direct the ways by which we search for and ultimately find information.

Referring back to the example of your car, if we believe that your make of car is prone to explosions, we will look for explosion-relevant information. Hence, when we sense that the car is shaking, we will look for further validation of this explosion hypothesis. Although this is an efficient and adaptive strategy, two major types of bias may occur. First, people tend to look for schema-relevant or schema-consistent information at the expense of information that is irrelevant or inconsistent with existing beliefs (Taylor and Crocker, 1981). Hence, you may not notice that the shaking is due to road conditions, or even an earthquake. Second, the more ambiguous the information the more likely the person will think that the schema is correct. Recall that your car key was ambiguously warm, which was interpreted in this instance as evidence for an electrical short.

Beliefs play a particularly powerful role in the interpretation of bodily state because of the ambiguity of physical symptoms and sensations associated with stress. In a series of studies, for example, we have induced people to believe that specific environmental stimuli (e.g., bogus ultrasonic noise) caused either vasodilation or vasoconstriction. As would be expected based on our knowledge of schemas and selective search, subjects selectively attended to sensations indicating an increase (vasodilation) or decrease (vasoconstriction) in skin temperature—when, in fact, their skin temperature was both increasing and decreasing (from Pennebaker and Skelton, 1981).

Particularly vivid examples of schemas and selective search can be seen in cases of mass psychogenic illness (Colligan *et al*, 1982). Specifically, when individuals in the workplace are under stress, they are especially prone to the adoption of disease-relevant schemas through watching and talking with others. A person under stress who sees another get visibly sick (e.g., vomiting, fainting) is much more likely to label his or her stress symptoms as disease symptoms.

Inference processes

Competition of cues, schemas and selective search are concerned with the direct perception of internal state. A third cognitive/perceptual bias, however, is based on an educated guess. That is, people often infer that they are feeling something even though they are not directly experiencing it. Again using the example of your car, if a researcher asked you after you had just jumped out of the car whether you recalled smelling any smoke, you would probably infer that you had.

Note that the inference process is particularly likely to occur when the individual is reporting on an incident (or body state) that has already occurred. Indeed, this phenomenon is similar to Loftus' (1979) findings on reconstructive memory, in which an eye-witness gives an honest and sincere account of a previous incident that has been altered by the questions that others ask about the event, or even by logic. It must be emphasized that an eye-witness or a person giving retrospective accounts of stress is not lying or trying to deceive. Rather, memory of the events has been subtly and permanently changed.

One of the most common forms of inference in the reporting of physical symptoms concerns people's reactions to loud, aversive noise bursts. Almost without exception, subjects assume that when they hear these loud bursts that their heart rate and blood pressure levels increase. Ironically, even though self-reports suggest an increase, we and others have consistently found decreases in both heart rate and blood pressure in response to noise (Libby *et al*, 1973; Pennebaker, 1980; Pennebaker *et al*, 1982).

Perceptual implications for the measurement of stress

Self-reports of stress, symptoms and moods are based on perceptual processes. Individuals' reports of internal state are subject to the same biases that exist in visual or auditory perception. The researcher who is attempting to collect objective reports of stress must be aware of the impact of environmental factors, beliefs and individual differences on the perceptual and reporting process. Even when physiological status is constant among prospective subjects, variations in self-reports of stress, symptoms or moods can be found and are attributable to any of the following:

1. Stress, symptoms and moods reflect negative affectivity, or NA. There exist stable and pervasive individual differences in NA. Because stress, symptoms and negative moods are highly interdependent, one cannot assume simple causal links among them.

2. Self-reported stress, symptoms and moods will tend to be higher when individuals are in environments lacking meaningful stimulation. Jobs characterized by social isolation, tedious or repetitive tasks, or that otherwise force the person to attend to his or her own body will be associated with higher reports of stress.

3. The cultural, community or office milieu can directly influence self-reports by affecting group- and individually-held beliefs or schemas related to health. Beliefs about chemicals, viruses or stress in general may result in the selective search for, and reporting of, sensations.

4. The way the researcher asks questions or presents research may inadvertently bring about different symptom search patterns or inference strategies. A person who learns that a specific aspect of the job was particularly hazardous after the fact tends to infer logical levels of symptoms or stress when interviewed later.

3. Non-invasive physiological measures and self-reports

The discerning reader might have noted that the previous section dealt with self-described physiological status without ever referring to objective physiological measures. Rather than reflecting an oversight, this distinction between self-reported and actual physiological activity is central to our approach. Here we will discuss four issues. The first addresses the relationship between physiological activity and one's perception of that activity. In other words, to what degree can people accurately report on their physiological levels in the real world? The second issue involves the broader question of the origins of stress perceptions. Since specific autonomic measures are poorly correlated with their corresponding self-reports, do more generalized physiological levels reflect general self-reports? The third issue concerns the psychological meaning of different physiological and physical states. Further, some physiological measures are more clearly and directly related to self-reports than others. The final issue within this section addresses problems associated with the measurement of physiological variables in the workplace. This will serve as an introduction to our final issue: between-subjects versus within-subject designs.

Correspondence between self-reports and physiological measures

A common misconception among stress researchers is that self-reports are highly correlated with physiological measures of stress. This view dates back to early conceptions within psychophysics which demonstrated a one-to-one correspondence between stimulus intensity and perception of intensity when all extraneous variables are constant (Stevens, 1975). Unfortunately (for physiologists) or fortunately (for psychologists), this correspondence is not maintained in the real world. As is discussed below, regardless of how self-reports or physiological variables are measured, the two are only weakly related.

From a series of between-subjects projects conducted by ourselves and others, it has become clear that the correlation between specific self-reported and actual physiological measures averages around +0.30. For example, in samples ranging in size between 30 and 200, the correlation between self-reported fast pulse or racing heart and actual heart rate averages 0.21. Correlations between skin conductance levels and self-reported sweaty hands averaged 0.28. Average correlations between perceived and actual finger temperature are around 0.36 (*see* Pennebaker, 1982 for a review of the studies).

Broader self-report variables, such as ratings of fatigue, anxiety, or stress, correlate even more poorly with specific autonomic measures such as heart rate, blood pressure and skin conductance (Mihevic, 1981). Although the between-subjects correlations range between 0.10 and 0.50, the average value across over a dozen or more studies is only 0.20–0.30.

An eager methodologist who reviews these relationships might conclude that between-subjects correlations are inappropriate for various reasons. For example, baseline physiological and self-report levels differ greatly across individuals, and their patterning is highly idiosyncratic. It would follow that if self-reports and physiological measures were collected from the same people on a number of occasions in a variety of settings, then the measures would correlate more highly. Nevertheless, within-subject correlations tend to be as low, if not lower. In studies where self-reported and actual heart rate, skin conductance, finger temperature, breathing rate, blood pressure and/or blood glucose levels were measured a minimum of 40 times per subject, the average self-report correlates approximately 0.25 with its physiological referent (for specific details of the various studies, *see* Pennebaker, 1982; Pennebaker *et al.*, 1982; Pennebaker and Epstein, 1983; Pennebaker *et al.*, 1985).

Additional information concerning the correspondence between self-reports and physiological state is useful. Most importantly, the ability to detect internal cues is not unidimensional. In other words, someone who is accurate at detecting heart rate is no more or less likely to be able to detect breathing rate. With one possible exception, no stable individual difference variables are related to accuracy. The single exception may be sex. In highly controlled laboratory studies, males appear to be better at detecting heart rate, blood pressure, blood glucose levels and stomach contractions (Katkin *et al.*, 1982; Whitehead and Drescher, 1980; Pennebaker and Hoover, 1984; Pennebaker *et al.*, 1985). Interestingly, a number of studies indicate that males and females are equally accurate in detecting physiological changes in the natural environment (*see* Pennebaker *et al.*, 1985 for discussion).

General versus specific physiological indicators of stress

Taken together, the various findings paint a rather dim picture of the correspondence between self-reports and autonomic measures. These findings would suggest that self-reports and autonomic variables—both of which are presumed to be indicators of the same stress construct—are in fact virtually independent of one another.

Fortunately, recent investigations offer some promising new directions. Recall that most previous studies have relied on highly specific autonomic measures, such as heart rate, breathing rate, finger temperature, skin conductance and muscle tension. Although they are easily measured, indexes such as these do not reflect the general bodily state. Further, one reason that people are so poor at perceiving these autonomic measures is that it is not necessary, nor particularly adaptive, for them to know what their current levels of heart rate, skin conductance, and so on, might be.

From a self-regulatory and adaptive perspective, organisms are better off knowing about general physiological changes that could affect their survival on a minute-to-minute or day-to-day basis. Any organism must know if it is suffering from a lack of food or oxygen, or if it is about to collapse from fatigue, disease or lack of sleep. If we are to tap the perception of these general changes, we must examine physiological changes that affect the entire organism. Fortunately, there are a few promising physiological candidates: blood glucose levels, blood pressure, blood oxygen and lactate levels.

Over the last few years, we have used a within-subject design wherein subjects report the degree to which they were feeling each of several moods and symptoms. We have also collected simultaneous blood pressure and/or blood glucose data. In these studies we have consistently found high within-subject correlations among selected symptoms and moods and the blood pressure or glucose data. Indeed, in laboratory studies with college students and adults we have found that most normotensives exhibit significant and high correlations ($r > 0.50$) with systolic blood pressure fluctuations (e.g., Pennebaker *et al.*, 1982), and that diabetics have comparable correlations with their blood glucose changes (Pennebaker *et al.*, 1981; Gonder-Frederick, 1985).

Although subjects demonstrate that they have physical symptoms and sensations that covary strongly with blood pressure or glucose, the correlated symptoms are unique from person to person. Further, these symptoms are usually not labelled by the subjects themselves as blood pressure or blood glucose. In other words, massive physiological changes are associated with a general feeling, but this feeling does not have a general name in the subject's eyes.

Work on perceived exertion among exercise physiologists has evolved in comparable ways. For example, feelings of fatigue are poorly related to heart rate, muscle tension, and skin conductance. However, fatigue is highly correlated with more general measures of oxygen consumption and blood lactate levels (Mihevic, 1981). Similarly, hunger perception has been shown to be poorly related to specific changes such as stomach motility (Stunkard and Fox, 1971) but strongly related to blood glucose levels (Pennebaker *et al.*, 1981).

Based on these and related studies, we would predict that the most fruitful approach to stress perceptions is to first define what aspects of stress are most relevant to behaviour. For example, how would a naturally-behaving human respond when stress levels were too high? Such a person would probably reduce their rate of behaviour, sleep, and so on. If these behaviours are appropriate, we then would need to identify the signals that dictate slower behaviour or sleep. Epinephrine levels, chemical changes associate with sleep or fatigue, and perhaps even immune system changes would be good measures to examine.

Psychological meaning of physiological measures

The above data suggest that specific autonomic changes are not always directly reflected in self-reports. Unfortunately, those channels that may be the most sensitive to general feelings of stress may also be the most invasive and difficult to measure in the natural environment. This raises two questions. First, is it always necessary to collect autonomic measures that are highly correlated with self-reported stress? Second, do the easier-to-measure non-invasive autonomic channels have psychological meaning? We believe the answers are 'no' and 'yes' respectively.

We have shown that self-reports of symptoms, moods and stress are poorly correlated with specific autonomic measures, but that these self-ratings may be more highly correlated with general physiological changes. It is important to emphasize that the self-ratings, in and of themselves, represent an important source of information. If people report that they have headaches, are depressed, and under stress, we can assume that there will be some bahavioural implications—whether or not blood chemistry corroborates their perceptions. Hence, the collection of physiological data is not necessary for an interpretation of self-reports.

By the same token, even if highly specific autonomic indices (e.g., heart rate, skin conductance) are not strongly related to self-reports, such measures may still have psychological value. That is, they may measure processes that self-ratings cannot capture. Two common classes of psychophysiological measures are particularly promising—cardiovascular measures such as heart rate and blood pressure, and skin conductance levels. Because of the scope of this literature, we can merely summarize some of the recent findings.

Heart rate and related cardiovascular measures (systolic blood pressure, vaso-constriction and vasodilation as measured by finger temperature) are clearly linked to somatic activity. If the organism moves or anticipates moving, heart rate typically increases (Fowles, 1980; Obrist, 1982). Similarly, heart rate and blood pressure rise when people talk.

As a general rule, heart rate and systolic blood pressure rise when the individual attempts to screen out external information. Hence, when people are attempting to think, or are faced with a chronic level of aversive stimulation, cardiovascular activity increases (Lacey, 1956; Cohen *et al.*, 1980). On a more psychodynamic level, Graham *et al.*, (1962) provide evidence suggesting that when a person holds a psychological attitude of 'being on guard against attack', heart rate and blood pressure rise.

Skin conductance may be particularly interesting in that it apparently reflects behavioural inhibition and/or psychological conflict (Fowles, 1980). Skin conductance levels are lowest among individuals who are poorly socialized or are impulsive and uninhibited (Hare, 1978; Waid and Orne, 1982). Skin conductance rises when people attempt to hold back information—such as when they are induced to deceive another (Waid and Orne, 1981; Pennebaker and Chew, 1985). Finally, when a person expresses emotion, or in some way immerses him- or herself in an emotion, skin conductance drops (Pennebaker, 1985).

Although the psychological meanings of such autonomic measures as heart rate and skin conductance are still being investigated, these findings suggest that they may be of great value to the stress researcher. We should interject that measures such as blood pressure are also externally valid as predictors of stroke and heart disease.

Some practical considerations in the use of autonomic measures

Many stress researchers measure blood pressure or other physiological variables in order to make their research appear more 'scientific'. Vague or contradictory findings among the various self-report and physiological measures are then dismissed on technical grounds, or ignored altogether. Here, we will briefly point to some of the difficulties that we have encountered in measuring blood pressure, heart rate, skin conductance and other autonomic levels in the laboratory, the office and in the person's natural environment.

The setting in which autonomic readings are taken is extremely important. Certain settings associated with anxiety, unpredictability, evaluation or threat will artificially increase most autonomic levels. For example, in a clever study by Hansell *et al.* (1982), unattractive male individuals were found to have higher blood pressures than those rated as attractive. Not surprisingly, the blood pressure measurements were taken by females.

Anxiety associated with blood pressure measurement can also result in gross mis-classification of individuals as hypertensive or normotensive. In a recent study with 81 university employees, we found that blood pressure measurements taken in medical and work settings seriously overestimated an individual's blood pressure in many cases. For example, based on initial medical and/or work readings, 13 employees were classified as mild hypertensives; of these, five (38.5%) proved to be normotensive when measured a number of times (45 assessments per employee) in our laboratory. Multiple measurements, based on their greater reliability, can help to eliminate other types of classification errors as well. For example, of those who were initially classified as normotensive on the basis of their initial readings, 12% were later found to be hypertensive when assessed in the laboratory. As a general rule, multiple measures obtained in a low anxiety setting will produce the most reliable and valid autonomic measures.

It should be emphasized that large individual differences also exist with respect to skin conductance, finger temperature and other measures. Moreover, some individuals habituate quickly in the laboratory so that their autonomic levels stabilize rapidly; others, however, adjust more slowly. In fact, across individuals the habituation time may vary from five minutes to over an hour.

A number of common sense difficulties must also be watched out for. Time of day influences the blood pressure and heart rate of many subjects. Outdoor and room temperature can strongly affect skin temperature and skin conductance. Even time of year has marked and reliable effects on autonomic activity. In addition, drugs, alcohol, nicotine and other substances may influence physiological levels in idiosyncratic ways. Finally, as many researchers have warned, it is critical that the personnel who collect the measures are well-trained, and the measurements must be collected and coded in uniform ways (for general discussions about common problems, *see* Andreassi, 1980; Cacioppo and Petty, 1983).

4. Research design: between-subjects versus within-subject

As we have already suggested, there are a host of problems associated with simple between-subjects designs when studying real-world stress. Self-reports vary tremendously from person to person irrespective of transient stress levels. As the research on negative affectivity indicates, stable and pervasive individual differences will markedly influence self-reported symptoms, negative moods and stress levels. In order to assess the impact of stress from a particular job, then, it behoves the researcher either to collect data from a tremendously large population or to collect multiple measures over time.

Physiological measures also fail to lend themselves to simple between-subjects designs. Baseline autonomic levels are highly variable. A single, one-time assessment of blood pressure or other autonomic indexes may tap social or evaluative anxiety more than job stress. Finally, the correspondence between self-reports and physiological measures can only be assessed on a within-subject basis. As noted earlier, this is particularly important because self-reports tend to covary with physiological measures in idiosyncratic ways; simple between-subjects designs tend to wash out any relationships that may appear using within-subject methods.

We are currently involved in a large-scale research project that allows us to evaluate stress levels of employees, both at home and at work, on a within-subject basis. In the study, 54 adults completed a 12-item questionnaire and then measured their own blood pressure approximately once every 30 minutes during their waking hours, over a period of 3–5 days. Each subject's data were analysed separately. Among other things, we were able to evaluate the degree to which being at home or being at work was associated with increases in systolic or diastolic blood pressure, as well as negative moods and physical symptoms.

Preliminary analyses point to some striking relationships that vary considerably from person to person. For example, 19% of the subjects have significant positive correlations between being at work and blood pressure (either systolic or diastolic); another 8% show negative correlations. Indeed, those who have negative relationships would be classified as 'workaholics' in that they spend a disproportionate amount of time at work immersed in their jobs. Comparable analyses in looking at blood pressure at home show that 4% had positive correlations whereas 21% had a negative relationship between blood pressure and being at home.

Interestingly, somewhat different patterns appear when examining self-reports. Overall, 33% of the subjects evidenced significant negative correlations between being at home and reports of symptoms and negative moods. For none of the subjects was the relationship positive. By the same token, over 25% of the subjects reported more symptoms and moods at work than when not at work. Only one subject evidenced the opposite pattern. Inspection of the self-report and physiological data clearly show that the two types of measure tap very different types of information. Indeed, the researcher interested in assessing subjective well-being would come away from this project with different results than the researcher studying the physiological correlates of work and home settings.

Although a within-subject approach such as this can be time-consuming and expensive, one could use it to examine an employee's physiological and self-report levels from one aspect of the job to another. Recently Csikszentmihalyi and Larson (1984) have reported a masterful series of studies using a technique wherein individuals carry a 'beeper' around with them during a 1—2-week interval. The beeper beeps approximately 8 times a day at random times. On hearing the beep, subjects are required to complete a short questionnaire. Using this technique, one can evaluate where and how individuals spend their time, the quality of the time spent, and other parameters of people's daily lives.

5. Conclusions

This chapter attempts to provide a brief overview of the potential problems and advantages of using self-reports and physiological measures to assess stress in the workplace. Although our discussion has been brief, we can summarize the major points:

1. Self-reports of stress, negative moods, and physical symptoms reflect a common underlying dimension of negative affectivity, or NA.

2. Caution must be exercised when interpreting self-reports in a causal manner. For example, to say that stress causes physical symptoms may be meaningless or circular.

3. Self-reports of internal state reflect basic perceptual processes.

4. People tend to notice and report symptoms and emotions when in low-stimulation environments.

5. Prior beliefs greatly influence how people search and report their bodily state. That is, we are very suggestible when it comes to labelling and reporting stress levels, symptoms and moods.

6. People are notoriously inaccurate at perceiving specific physiological changes. In other words, there is no one-to-one correspondence between self-reported symptoms and physiological measures.

7. General physiological measures (e.g., blood glucose levels, blood pressure, blood lactate) more accurately reflect self-ratings than highly specific physiological measures such as heart rate or skin conductance.

8. Even though highly specific physiological indices are not directly related to self-reports, they may still have great psychological significance. Cardiovascular measures reflect somatic activity; skin conductance covaries with conflict or inhibition.

9. Within-subject designs lend themselves particularly well to measuring stress in the workplace. Between-subjects designs can be both misleading and inefficient when using self-reports and physiological measures, either alone or in combination.

References

Andreassi, J.L. (1980). *Psychophysiology: Human Behavior and Physiological Response* (New York: Oxford University Press).

Beck, A.T., Ward, C.H., Mendelson, M., Mock, J. and Erbaugh, J. (1961). An inventory for measuring depression. *Archives of General Psychiatry*, **4**, 561–571.

Berlyne, D. (1960). *Conflict, Arousal, and Curiosity.* (New York: McGraw-Hill).

Brener, J. (1977). Visceral perception. In J. Beatty and J. Legewie (eds), *Biofeedback and Behavior* (New York: Plenum Press).

Cacioppo, J.T. and Petty, R.E. (1983). *Social Psychophysiology: A Sourcebook* (New York: Guilford Press).

Caplan, R.D., Cobb, S., French, J.P.R., Harrison, R. and Pinneau, S. (1975). *Job Demands and Worker Health* (Washington, DC: US Government Printing Office).

Cohen, S., Evans, G., Krantz, D.S. and Stokols, D. (1980). Physiological, motivational, and cognitive effects of aircraft noise on children: Moving from the laboratory to the fields. *American Psychologist*, **35**, 231–243.

Colligan, M.J., Pennebaker, J.W. and Murphy, L. (1982). *Mass Psychogenic Illness: A Social Psychological Analysis* (Hillsdale, NJ: Lawrence Erlbaum).

Csikszentmihalyi, M. and Larson, R. (1984). *Being Adolescent* (New York: Basic Books).

Delongis, A., Coyne, J.C., Dakof, G., Folkman, S. and Lazarus, R.S. (1982). Relationship of daily hassles, uplifts, and major life events to health status. *Health Psychology*, **1**, 119–136.

Dohrenwend, B.P. and Shrout, P.E. (1985). ''Hassles'' in the conceptualization and measurement of life stress variables. *American Psychologist*, **40**, 780–785.

Fowles, D.C. (1980). The three arousal model: Implications of Grays two-factor theory for heart rate, electrodermal activity, and psychopathy. *Psychophysiology*, **17**, 87–104.

Gibson, J.J. (1979). *The Ecological Approach to Visual Perception* (Boston, MA: Houghton-Mifflin).

Gonder-Frederick, L.A. (1985). Relationships between moods, symptoms, and blood glucose level in insulin-dependent diabetic patients. Unpublished doctoral dissertation, University of Virginia, Charlottesville, Virginia.

Graham, D.T., Kabler, J.D. and Graham, F.K. (1962). Physiological responses to the suggestion of attitudes specific for hives and hypertension. *Psychosomatic Medicine*, **24**, 159–169.

Hansell, S., Sparacino, J. and Ronchi, D. (1982). Physical attractiveness and blood pressure: Sex and age differences. *Personality and Social Psychology Bulletin*, **8**, 113–121.

Hare, R.D. (1978). Electrodermal and cardiovascular correlates of psychopathy. In R.D. Hare and D. Schalling (eds), *Psychopathic Behavior: Approaches to Research* (New York: John Wiley).

Horowitz, M.J. (1976). *Stress Response Syndromes* (New York: Jacob Aronson).

Kanner, A.D., Coyne, J.C., Schaefer, C. and Lazarus, R.S. (1981). Comparison of two modes of stress measurement: Daily hassles and uplifts versus major life events. *Journal of Behavioral Medicine*, **4**, 1–39.

Katkin, E.S., Morell, M.A., Goldband, S., Bernstein, G.L. and Wise, J.A. (1982). Individual differences in heartbeat discrimination. *Psychophysiology*, **19**, 160–166.

Lacey, J.I. (1956). The evaluation of autonomic responses: Toward a general solution. *Annals of the New York Academy of Science*, **67**, 123–164.

Lazarus, R.S., Delongis, A., Folkman, S. and Gruen, R. (1985). Stress and adaptational outcomes: The problem of confounded measures. *American Psychologist*, **40**, 770–779.

Leventhal, H. (1975). The consequences of depersonalization during illness and treatment. In J. Howard and A. Strauss (eds), *Humanizing Health Care* (New York: John Wiley).

Libby, W. L., Lacey, B.C. and Lacey, J.I. (1973). Pupillary and cardiac activity during visual attention. *Psychophysiology*, **10**, 270–294.

Loftus, E.F. (1979). *Eyewitness Testimony* (Cambridge, MA: Harvard University Press).

Mason, J.W. (1975). A historical view of the stress field. *Journal of Human Stress*, **1**, 22–36.

Mihevic, P.M. (1981). Sensory cues for perceived exertion: A review. *Medicine and Science in Sports and Exercise*, **13**, 150–163.

Navon, J.D. and Gopher, D. (1979). On the economy of the human-processing system. *Psychological Review*, **86**, 214-255.

Obrist, P.A. (1982). Cardiac-behavioral interactions: A critical appraisal. In J.T. Cacioppo and R.E. Petty (eds), *Perspectives in Cardiovascular Psychophysiology* (New York: Guilford Press).

Pennebaker, J.W. (1980). Perceptual and environmental determinants of coughing. *Basic and Applied Social Psychology*, **1**, 83–91.

Pennebaker, J.W. (1982). *The Psychology of Physical Symptoms* (New York: Springer-Verlag).

Pennebaker, J.W. (1985). Traumatic experience and psychosomatic disease: Exploring the roles of behavioral inhibition, obsession, and confiding. *Canadian Psychology*, **26**, 82-95.

Pennebaker, J.W. and Chew, C.H. (1985). Inhibition and cognition: Toward an understanding of trauma and disease. In R.J. Davidson, G.E. Schwartz, and S. Shapiro (eds), *Consciousness and Self-regulation*; Volume 4 (New York: Plenum Press).

Pennebaker, J.W. and Epstein, D. (1983). Implicit psychophysiology: Effects of common beliefs and idiosyncratic physiological responses on symptom reporting. *Journal of Personality*, **51**, 468–496.

Pennebaker, J.W. and Hoover, C.W. (1984). Visceral perception versus visceral detection: A comparison of methods and assumptions. *Biofeedback and Self-Regulation*, **9**, 339–352.

Pennebaker, J.W. and Lightner, J.M. (1980). Competition of internal and external information in an exercise setting. *Journal of Personality and Social Psychology*, **39**, 165–174.

Pennebaker, J.W. and Skelton, J.A. (1981). Selective monitoring of bodily sensations. *Journal of Personality and Social Psychology*, **41**, 213–223.

Pennebaker, J.W., Cox, D.J., Gonder-Frederick, L.A., Wunsch, M., Evans, W.S. and Pohl, S. (1981). Physical symptoms related to blood glucose in insulin dependent diabetics. *Psychosomatic Medicine*, **43**, 489–500.

Pennebaker, J.W., Gonder-Frederick, L.A., Stewart, H., Elfman, L. and Skelton, J.A. (1982). Physical symptoms associated with blood pressure. *Psychophysiology*, **19**, 201–210.

Pennebaker, J.W., Gonder-Frederick, L.A., Cox, D.J. Hoover, C.W. (1985). The perception of general vs. specific visceral activity and the regulation of health-related behavior. *Advances in Behavioral Medicine*, **1**, 165–198.

Scarr, S., Webber, P.L., Weinberg, R.A. and Wittig, M.A. (1981). Personality resemblance among adolescents and their parents in biologically related and adoptive families. *Journal of Personality and Social Psychology*, **40**, 885–898.

Selye, H. (1976). *The Stress of Life* (New York: McGraw-Hill).

Spielberger, C.D., Gorsuch, R.L. and Lushene, R.E. (1970). *Manual for the State–Trait Anxiety Inventory* (Palo Alto, CA: Consulting Psychologists Press).

Stevens, S.S. (1975). *Psychophysics: Introduction to its Perceptual, Neural, and Social Prospects* (New York: John Wiley).

Stunkard, A.J. and Fox, S. (1971). The relationship of gastric motility and hunger: A summary of the evidence. *Psychosomatic Medicine*, **33**, 123–134.

Taylor, J. (1953). A personality scale of manifest anxiety. *Journal of Abnormal and Social Psychology*, **48**, 285–290.

Taylor, S.E. and Crocker, J. (1981). Schematic bases of social information processing. In E.T. Higgins *et al.* (eds), *The Ontario Symposium of Personality and Social Psychology* (Hillsdale, NJ: Lawrence Erlbaum).

Tellegen, A. (1982). Brief Manual for the Differential Personality Questionnaire. Unpublished manuscript, University of Minnesota, Minneapolis.

Waid, W. M. and Orne, M.T. (1981). Cognitive, social and personality processes in the physiological detection of deception. *Advances in Experimental Social Psychology*, **14**, 61–106.

Waid, W.M. and Orne, M.T. (1982). Reduced electrodermal response to conflict, failure to inhibit dominant behaviors, and delinquency proneness. *Journal of Personality and Social Psychology*, **43**, 769–774.

Watson, D. and Clark, L.A. (1984). Negative affectivity: The disposition to experience aversive emotional states. *Psychological Bulletin*, **96**, 465–490.

Watson, D. and Tellegen, A. (1985). Toward a consensual structure of mood. *Psychological Bulletin*, **98**, 219–235.

Watson, D. and Pennebaker, J.W. (in press). Health complaints, stress, and distress: Exploring the central role of negative affectivity. *Psychological Review*.

Whitehead, W.E. and Drescher, V.M. (1980). Perception of gastric contractions and self-control of gastric motility. *Psychophysiology*, **17**, 552–558.

Zuckerman, M. and Lubin, B. (1965). *Manual for the Multiple Affect Adjective Check List* (San Diego, CA: Educational & Industrial Testing Service).

13

Application of the Triangulation Strategy to Stress Research

John M. Ivancevich and Michael T. Matteson

1. Introduction

In the past decade the term stress has found its way into the medical and behavioural science literature. In fact, since the publication of the early stress research work of Selye (1936) and Wolf and Wolff (1943), it is estimated that over 100 000 publications dealing with the stress concept in biology, medicine and the behavioural sciences have appeared (Selye, 1977). With the possible exception of Darwin's theory of evolution, one is hard pressed to find another theoretical position that has been so productive of research and speculation in a multidisciplinary context.

The study of stress has traditionally presented methodological and conceptual challenges to scientists and professionals in every discipline. This chapter offers a brief overview of various biomedical and behavioural science research and measurement traditions that currently address stress. The available research is extensive and complex, extending through fields as diverse as behavioural medicine, clinical and applied psychology, medicine, epidemiology, sociology, ergonomics, psychosomatic medicine, and anthropology. This chapter is to be synoptic and integrative; it is therefore selective rather than exhaustive in its coverage. A contemporary stock-taking of stress measurement for theorists and researchers is overdue if more reliable, valid and meaningful studies of stress are to be conducted in field settings.

The focus here is on measuring stress responses associated with work within organizational settings. A review of major biomedical and behavioural science methods of measuring stress will be presented. Whatever measurement procedures are used to study stress there is a need to study organizationally relevant problems. Until researchers can provide organizations with reliable, valid and minimally disruptive measures of stress, field studies in organizational settings will be rare and constrained.

There is sufficient evidence that biomedical and behavioural science techniques can and should be concurrently used in organizational studies of stress. Many researchers have recognized the importance of simultaneous measurement of biological, psychological and behavioural responses to stress (Baum *et al.*, 1982; Lazarus, 1974; Mason, 1975; Gatchel, 1979). However, to date few organizationally based studies of stress indicate that a multi-level measurement approach has been attempted (Beehr and

Newman, 1978; Newman and Beehr, 1979; Schuler, 1980; Eden, 1982; Ivancevich *et al.*, 1982).

Biomedical researchers have been reluctant to admit that 'quantitatively soft' measures of stress have the same weight as more clearly physiological and biochemical measures. Biomedical research thinking has for years been dominated by models and methods of classical physics, chemistry and quantitative measurement. Accordingly, biomedically trained researchers have relegated the more qualitative or subjective models of stress measurement to inconsequential status. Unfortunately, biomedical stress researchers fail to realize that individuals who can provide permission to conduct longitudinal field studies and experiments do not typically understand nor are they overly impressed with measures of cortiocosteroids, catecholamines and blood pressure. In fact, representatives (those who grant admission to organizational sites and samples) of organizations are less inclined to permit biomedical measures to be taken than they are to allow more behavioural science oriented measures.

In this chapter, researchers are encouraged to examine, evaluate and develop methodological triangulation methods to measure stress responses. It is suggested that in order for organizational stress research to have any lasting and significant impact on the quality of work-life, productivity, health enhancement and societal values, biomedical and behavioural science theories, measurements and applications must be considered and used whenever possible in a complementary manner. Researchers must attempt to move away from a reductionist, single method model for measuring stress in work settings. The move towards using multiple assessment modalities can be enhanced by incorporating a triangulation strategy.

2. Triangulation methods

Triangulation is defined by Denzin (1978; p. 291) as "the combination of methodologies in the study of the same phenomenon". The triangulation metaphor is taken from navigation and military strategies that use multiple reference or citing points to locate an object's exact position (Jick, 1983). In the behavioural sciences, the notion of triangulation can be traced to the idea of multiple operationism (Campbell and Fiske, 1959). This idea suggested that more than one method should be used in the validation process to ensure that the variance reflected that of the phenomenon (i.e., trait, characteristic) and not of the method.

The between (or across) methods form of triangulation is the most popular. It is in essence a vehicle for cross-validation when two or more distinct methods are found to be congruent and yield comparable data. For stress researchers, this would involve the use of biomedical and behavioural science methods to examine the stress response. Multiple and independent measures, if they reach the same conclusions, provide a more complete portrayal of the particular stress responses being studied.

Triangulation can have other meanings and uses as well. There is the 'within method' type which uses multiple techniques within a given method to collect and interpret data. For biomedical methods, this could take the form of multiple methods focused on the same stress response (e.g., measuring blood pressure with two different procedures). For behavioural science methods, multiple scales or indices could be used to examine stress. In short, within method triangulation involves cross-checking for internal consistency or reliability, while 'between-method' triangulation investigates the degree of external validity (Jick, 1983).

The use of triangulation offers stress researchers something more than reliability and convergent validity checks. It can capture a more complete portrayal of the stress construct. That is, beyond the analysis of overlapping variance, the use of biomedical and behavioural science measures may also uncover some unique variance which otherwise may have been neglected by single method studies of stress.

The robustness of triangulation rests on the premise that the weaknesses in a single method will be compensated by the counter-balancing strengths of another. It is assumed that biomedical and behavioural science measures of stress do not share the same weaknesses or potential for bias. The variety of biomedical and behavioural science combinations to measure stress is so great that they should be viewed as complementary. Yet, research designs that integrate both methodologies are still rare.

Fortunately, there are already examples of stress research that use triangulation. For example, Kasl and Cobb (1970) longitudinally investigated the health, psychological and behavioural effects of job loss among 10 ex-employees and 74 controls. The researchers studied such factors as depression, anxiety/tension, self esteem, pulse rate, blood pressure, cholesterol and serum uric acid. Although this study had limitations it clearly shows the value of investigating the complexity of stress in organizational settings.

In another study using triangulation, Caplan and Jones (1975) studied the effects of the impending shutdown of a university computer. They measured subjective stress (self-report) and objective stress (heart rate) prior to the shutdown and five months later. However, contrary to prediction, subjective quantitative work-load stress declined an insignificant amount. Anxiety, repression, resentment and heart rate declined as predicted.

A study by Eden (1982) used triangulation and a quasi-experimental longitudinal design. A class of 43 first-year students, all women, in a hospital-affiliated nursing school participated. The researcher used self-reports, blood pressure, pulse rate, serum uric acid and cholesterol measures. He examined stress responses to patient care and student course examinations at five data points. A consistently confirmatory pattern of significantly rising and falling stress response was found for anxiety, systolic blood pressure and pulse rate; qualitative overload and serum uric acid changed as predicted four times out of five.

These three research studies indicate that the triangulation strategy is already being applied by researchers. The use of triangulation is found in only a minority of studies, and most of them do not use longitudinal designs with samples drawn from organizations. In most investigations employing triangulation, college samples are used to biomedically and behaviourally study the stress responses of participants engaging in some form of simulation or anagram exercise. The generalizability of such research to real-world samples of managerial or operating employees in organizational settings must be seriously questioned.

3. Stress responses

One of the most well-developed Person–Environment (P–E) Fit stress models l
proposed by French and his associates at the University of Michigan. The fou........tion
of the French job stress model (French and Kahn, 1962) is based on the theoretical
work of Lewin (1938) and Murray (1938). A central hypothesis in the model is that
when there is a lack of fit (discrepancy) there is likely to be a significant stress response.
The stress response may be physiological, psychological, behavioural, performance,
health–illness, or some combination.

Stress responses may be inferred in five ways:

1. By noting the individual's physiological conditions and responses.
2. By noting the individual's overt behaviour.
3. By noting the conditions or situations which the individual perceives psychologically as stressful.
4. By examining performance changes.
5. By noting health–illness episodes.

These five ways of viewing stress can be categorized as offering physiological,
behavioural, psychological, performance and health–illness views of stress responses.
For example, an assay of the catecholamine titre could be used to measure the physiological response. An on-the-job observation of a person's work behaviour could
provide a measure of overt behaviour. A self-report scale could yield a perceptual
measure. Examination of performance records over time would yield information on
increase, decrease or no change. Finally, the number of somatic complaints or doctor's
visits could provide a measure of the health–illness stress response. Each of these
measures examines a possible stress response mode.

Despite the sometimes overwhelming nature of job stressors or the likelihood that
they will be appraised as threatening, stress cannot be measured without reference to
the responses made by the person. Stress responses that have been the subject of
measurement and interpretation come in a variety of forms. A well publicized and
debated type of stress response is that originally described by Selye (1956) as the
General Adaptation Syndrome (GAS). The GAS explanation and measurement of the
stress response focuses on physiology. It pays little, if any, attention to understanding
the psychological or sociological aspects of stress. Also, Selye's explanation of the stress
response paid little attention to the stimulus (antecedent causative agents). He failed to
specify with sufficient clarity the conditions that are necessary to activate the stress
mechanism and the response.

A secondary category of stress responses can be called fight/flight behaviour. Once
the alarm stage of the GAS is put into motion the behavioural response can be either to
fight or flee. Consider the situation where the mail carrier's path to the mail box is
blocked by a large, growling dog. There seems to be two courses of action—run to the
box and deliver the mail or leave the scene. Either response will normally be characterized by excessive physical activity and if successful, will remove the stressor (and, by
the way, relieve the mail carrier's stress).

Less vivid, but more interesting to organizational researchers is when the situation one faces is symbolic rather than physically present. Consider, for example, the steelworker in Gary, Indiana who is threatened with the loss of his job. His autonomic nervous system may be activated, but neither a fight or flight response is appropriate. The predicted behaviour pattern may one of helplessness. The sequential steps in the pattern may be verbal aggression, frustration and finally helplessness.

Another category of stress response is referred to as long-term performance decrement. This is appropriately the category that managers of organizations have the most direct interest in. There are numerous organizational and individual causes of performance decrement—lack of skill, poor management procedures, inappropriate reward systems, politics, fatigue.

Each of these stress response categories can provide useful information to researchers. Unfortunately, there is an undeveloped measurement base available to those interested in conducting rigorous and practical organizational stress research of these and other stress responses. The reasons for this undeveloped state may lie in the facts that:

1. Biomedically trained researchers refuse to accept quantitatively soft measures of stress.

2. The biomedical basis of stress response measurement is not understood by behavioural science researchers, who are generally more familiar with their own preferred measurement techniques.

3. The behavioural science research base of stress response has relied disproportionately on self-report assessments that have paid little attention to validity and reliability issues.

4. Biomedical and behavioural science researchers fail to communicate with each other about organizationally specific measurement needs and practices.

4. Biomedical measurement of the stress responses

Recent advances in technology and electrophysiology have increased the reliability, availability and the unobtrusiveness of biomedical measures. However, biomedical measures are still not used to any significant degree in organizationally based and oriented studies of stress responses. This is unfortunate since biomedical measures of physiological stress responses can be incorporated in many organizationally based studies. Examples of biomedical technology and procedures can be used to illustrate the kind of measures that can be more widely used in organizational research.

Cardiovascular measures

Heart rate is a popular physiological measure used in studies of stress. It is possible to count beats of the heart while keeping track of elapsed time with a stopwatch. In some situations, a stress electrocardiogram (EKG) can be taken to measure heart rate. There are wide individual differences in heart lability, a feature that is especially useful where changes in environmental load (e.g., number of activities to perform on the job) have been correlated with heart rate.

An important question to consider when using heart rate or any other physiological measure is: what does a change in heart rate mean? Lacey and Lacey (1974a, b) based their research findings on the claim that a lowered heart rate (HR) reflects a 'taking-in' attitude and a greater sensitivity to stimuli, whereas, a raised HR will facilitate a 'rejection' attitude and cognitive manipulation.

The blood pressure measure of the cardiovascular system is also of interest in stress research. In routine medical tests, blood pressure is usually measured by means of an indirect method using a sphygmomanometer. A person that is experiencing stress often shows an elevation above his or her normal blood pressure readings. A rise in blood pressure is necessary during the stress response in order to force the blood quickly to the active muscles. Blood pressure has been used to index responses to loss of employment, chronic exposure to aircraft noise, and a number of other stressors (Kasl and Cobb, 1970; Cohen *et al.*, 1980).

The measurement of cardiovascular or other physiological functions can be useful but must be carefully conducted. Such measurement requires sensitive instrumentation which is diffcult but not impossible to apply in work situations. Collecting data often requires subjects to remain still and to tolerate having electrodes attached to them. This is uncomfortable, but is not an insurmountable problem since advances in instrumentation design and telemetry permit subjects to act more naturally while being monitored while performing job activities (McNamara, 1979; Tuttle, *et al.*, 1979; Sime *et al.*, 1980).

Corticosteriod measures

The research of Selye (1936), Mason (1974, 1975) and others have established that endocrine function is a part of the stress response. Hormones released when a person is stressed include adrenaline (epinephrine), noradrenaline (norepinephrine) and the corticosteriods. A widely used measure of stress response in biomedical research studies is 17-hydroxycorticosteriod (17-OHCS) hormone. 17-OHCS is measured by assessing blood or urine samples. It has been related to both experimental and naturally occurring stressors (Bieliauskus, 1980; Mason, 1974).

Researchers have found elevated 17-OHCS in pilots and crewmen after long flights (Hale, 19765), post-operative surgical patients (Thomasson, 1959), and dental patients routinely scheduled for simple extraction or oral surgery for impactions (Shannon, *et al.*, 1961). Schwartz and Shields (1954) reported a positive correlation between estimates of tension and 17-OHCS in medical students taking final examinations.

Researchers in a field study examined 200 male NASA employees in administration, engineering and science. Subjects were grouped by an index of quantitative work-load. It was found that high work-load subjects had higher 17-OHCS levels over the course of the working day than did the low work-load subjects (Caplan, *et al.*, 1979). The researchers noted that the high work-load subjects showed lower than normal morning 17-OHCS and that the expected decrease in hormone levels from morning to afternoon did not occur. Thus, they suggested that hormones have a circadian rhythm that must be considered when interpreting results.

Rose *et al.* (1979) studied 416 air traffic controllers for three years. Their main goal was to determine the nature and extent of health changes in the air traffic controllers. While the air traffic controllers were on the job actually separating aircraft, endocrine measures were taken. Over the course of the study, blood was drawn to assay on-the-job levels of cortisol and growth hormones. A total of 16 792 samples of blood were withdrawn from the participants by use of a small non-thrombogenic catheter in the air traffic controller's forearm. Radio-immunoassay was used to determine cortisol and growth hormone levels. The researchers' findings indicated that the controllers as a group were secreting more cortisol than other groups reported in the literature and that there was a tendency for maximum levels of cortisol to be higher when the samples were taken during actual work activities. It was also found that growth hormone secretion for the controllers was so small as to be undetectable.

Catecholamines

Catecholamines are secreted by the adrenal medulla rather than by the adrenal cortex, and reflect activation or response of a different system than, for example, 17-OHCS levels. Research has found an increased secretion of catecholamines, namely epinephrine and norepinephrine, to such conditions as cold, failure, loss, threat and uncertainty (Euler, 1966; Frankenhaeuser, 1972; Levi, 1972; Lundberg and Frankenhaeuser, 1978; Eliot, 1979).

There are some studies in organizational settings that have examined catecholamine responses to stressors. For example, one study focused on the control which workers have over their pace of work. A group of workers that worked on machine-paced or structured jobs was compared to a group of workers who controlled their own work-pace. The machine-paced group had higher catecholamine levels than the self-paced group (Johansson *et al.*, 1978).

In a series of studies, Froberg *et al.* (1970) examined how work conditions affect endocrine reactions. In one study 12 female invoicing clerks were studied for four consecutive days while performing job activities. On the first and third day they were paid piece wages in addition to their base salary. The second and fourth days were controlled days when the rate of pay was the base salary. During the second and fourth days, mean excretion of epinephrine and norepinephrine (the catecholamines) was 5.5 and 18.5 mg respectively. During the piece-work days, the catecholamine levels rose by 40% and 27% respectively—these are significant increases that were interpreted by the researcher to imply the presence of stress.

Measurement of catecholamine levels has also been used to examine differential responses of people. It has been determined that individuals characterized by the Type A behaviour pattern exhibit higher catecholamine levels than do individuals classified as Type B when exposed to challenge, harassment and work overload (Glass *et al.*, 1980).

5. Behavioural Science Measurement of the Stress Response

In the behavioural sciences, the measurement of stress responses is typically obtained via self-reports, behavioural measures and interview response content analyses. A major difference in the measures of stress responses collected by biomedical versus behavioural scientists involves the assessment of physiological and biochemical variables instead of the collection of cognitive/affective variable measures. The behavioural scientist has typically focused stress response measurement on probing perceptions, emotions, feelings and behaviours.

Self-report measures

At present only limited standardization across self-report measures exists so that subjective reports of occupational stress responses remain incomparable from study to study. Even worse, the metric of most available scales is not known, so that, for example, the failure to find differences on a measure of stress reported by two presumably differentially stressed work groups may represent an actual lack of differences in the self-reports, unfortunately, at an insensitive part of the scale. Attitudinal or subjective stress responses are not unitary and the magnitude of the obtained response on a self-report scale often varies as a function of deceptively simple changes in the working of the eliciting questions or of the scale (Berglund *et al.*, 1977). One reason for the dominance of the life events approach in behavioural science measurement is the difficulty of studying the stress response in more sophisticated and complex ways, such as considering the subjective significance of a life event change (Horowitz *et al.*, 1979) or taking into account individual differences (Andrew *et al.*, 1978). In the absence of an alternative or better metric, listing and cumulating major life events seems to be a method that will continue to be used to measure stress.

For the most part, the self-report scales to assess stress and stress responses have involved the use of life event scales or rating scales. Recently, Lazarus and colleagues have constructed a hassles and uplifts scale which they offer as a better way to measure stress (Kanner, *et al.*, 1981; Lazarus, 1981). Hassles are defined as the irritating, frustrating or distressing incidents that occur in everyday life. They can take the form of disagreements, accidents or surprises. They range from getting stuck in a traffic jam to a dispute with a colleague at work. The impact of hassles on a person's physical and mental health depends largely on their frequency, duration and intensity. A person's response to a hassle depends on a variety of factors: personality, coping style, how the rest of the day has gone, etc.

In the development work to assess hassles, Lazarus and colleagues considered the effect of uplifts, their positive psychology counterparts—pleasant, happy or solving a difficult problem. Just as hassles can result in negative responses such as being depressed, uplifts are assumed to serve as positive responses which can buffer physical and mental problems.

The Hassles Scale consists of a list of 117 hassles such as misplacing or losing things, trouble relaxing, concerns about job security, dislike of fellow workers, filling out forms and financial security. The Uplifts Scale is a list of 135 uplifts such as using skills well, relaxing and spending time with families. To measure the effect of hassles and uplifts, Lazarus (1981) used a health status questionnaire, the Hopkins Symptom Checklist, a 58-item scale. Research findings indicated that the hassles score was a better predictor of concurrent and subsequent physiological symptoms than were life events scores. Uplifts were found to be positively related to health symptoms for women, but not for men.

Some researchers propose that at the present state of measurement sophistication it is more economical and practical to use purely self-report data to examine organizational stress. They argue that impressive findings from well-constructed self-report data, when replicated and extended, are likely to encourage other investigators to test them with other controlled methods (Lazarus and Folkman, 1984).

Behavioural measures

Behavioural assessment has been a topic of much theoretical and empirical research (Hersen and Bellack, 1976). For purposes of utility in behavioural science stress research, the behaviour of an individual is conceptualized as influenced by stimuli (stressors), conditions within the person, such as physiological state, thoughts and feelings, and the consequences of certain actions.

A variety of techniques are used to gather behavioural measures of the stress response. These techniques have evolved from behavioural analysis-based research and include the behavioural interview, behavioural observation and self-monitoring. The behavioural interview consists of a systematic probing for information regarding trhe development of stress. Through a series of questions, the interviewer prepares assumptions and propositions about the nature of the stress problem. In a high-blood-pressure education programme, Chadwick *et al.* (1977) implemented the behavioural interview strategy. Individuals were interviewed as to specific problem areas. Following these interviews, treatment goals were established and behaviourally based change interventions were designed.

Directly observing, say, an air traffic controller or police officer on the job can be another source of information. Inter-observer checks on the reliability of the observation is certainly important in this measurement approach. Self-monitoring of target behaviours has also been used in the area of stress asessment and management (Zorn *et al.*, 1977). In general, opportunities for research exist when feasible behaviour can be evaluated under stimulus conditions (stressors) that are assumed to contribute to the target problem (high blood pressure). Evaluating and modifying target problems would probably be undertaken in more organizational settings if researchers became more involved in using a combination of biomedical and behavioural science measures of stress responses.

Self-monitoring

It is reasonable to hypothesize that individuals will be able to report their cognitive and behavioural reactions to stressors more accurately after they have just encountered these stimuli than while filling out a self-report questionnaire or answering an interviewer's questions. Furthermore, it would also appear that the accuracy of self-reports will be enhanced when the phenomena individuals are asked to report are specific and highly discriminable. These two notions coalesce in the concept of self-monitoring, a methodological approach that has been used to assess stress responses. In self-monitoring, the individual is asked to keep a written record of discriminable behaviour, feelings or emotions. Self-monitoring is useful in assessing behaviour, cognitive and perhaps even physiological manifestations of stress.

Self-monitoring has the advantage of providing data on individual responses to stressors soon after they have been encountered in the work setting. Despite the apparent benefits of self-monitoring, it has only rarely been used in studying organizational stress. The reliability and reactivity of self-monitoring, however, has been used to investigate smoking, eating and study behaviours (Johnson and White, 1971; Nelson *et al.*, 1974).

Despite the seeming applicability and simplicity of self-monitoring, there are some potential problems. First, it is frequently tedious and requires regular interruptions in the natural sequence of activity and thought. Second, it can be potentially embarrassing if the recording process is visible in inter-personal situations. Third, individuals differ in the extent to which they are characteristically aware of their own behaviour. Fourth, Kazdin (1974) and Lipinski and Nelson (1974) have demonstrated that self-monitoring records are not highly accurate. Thus, self-monitoring problems such as these must be minimized if this measurement technique is to become more widely used.

6. Using biomedical and behavioural science measures of stress

As any review of the literature points out, there is no shortage of methods to measure organizationally based stress responses. However, an apparent problem with much of the research to date is that the majority of research efforts attempt to measure one or a few stress responses instead of examining multiple responses via a triangulation methodology. Although the setting, the population and the circumstances will, at times, severely limit the number of stress response channels which can be measured (self-report, hormone secretion, physiological, behavioural, self-monitoring, performance, health–illness) it is important to assess as many of the different proposed responses concurrently that will be permitted by the host organizaiton. The use of biomedical and behavioural science measures of stress will permit tests to determine whether and in what ways self-report data on stress are associated with physiological and behavioural stress responses.

The detailed examination of the relationship between physiological and psychological indicators of stress responses is beyond the scope of this chapter. However, it should be noted that researchers have found that many physiological and psychological measures are quite independent (Gal and Lazarus, 1975). For example, there has typically been no direct relationship found between levels of adrenocortical excretion and psychologically based self-report measures of anxiety (Fox *et al.*, 1961). In other studies only moderate to weak relationships have been found between physiological and psychological measures of stress. However, it is premature to conclude that researchers should forget about further research on stress, use a single-method bio-

medical or behavioural science paradigm or assume that physiological and psychological measures of stress are simply not convergent.

Researchers have much to gain by incorporating biomedical measures of stress
response in their organizationally based research. First, the availability and use of biomedical technology and assays to examine various physiological, autonomic and
hormone responses is possible. The fact that behavioural and attitudinal reactions are
so individually based makes the availability of a physiological or hormonal marker an
important tool for calibrating the magnitude of the effects of the stress. Second, the
physiologically based theories of stress suggest mechanisms by which stress can be
additive (across different stressors), cumulative (across time) and interactive (Singer,
1980). A theoretical basis suggesting why these mechanisms should operate offers
practical and heuristic help in understanding stress responses. Third, the biomedical
approach offers technology to monitor internal states of a person while he or she is
actually performing an interpersonal or job activity. This knowledge can help an
organizational researcher determine the impact of a particular event (e.g., receiving
feedback on performance, jointly setting goals with a superior) within a person (e.g.,
brain waves, gastrointestinal, blood pressure, heart rate).

On the other hand, the behavioural science approach to stress response offers the
biomedical researcher some unique benefits. First, cognitive processes are un-
equivocally involved in all individual stress. The organizational stress response is
modified by a person's appraisal and interpretation of the stressors. The behavioural
science approach provides some clues about how the appraisal occurs. Second, a
problem of biomedical measurement of stress response is, although improvements have
been made in instrumentation, the obtrusiveness of acquiring measures. Thus, in any
field study only a limited number of biomedical measures could be used. The
behavioural science measures are generally less obtrusive and easier to acquire. Third,
one of the major problems of simply collecting biomedical measures of the stress
response is that they offer no explanation of the obvious role that organization
environment stressors play in physiological reaction.

7. The triangulation approach: a demonstration

The use of a triangulation approach would incorporate biomedical and behavioural
science measures in studies of stress. A brief demonstration is provided here to illustrate
how triangulation could be utilized in organizational research. The introduction of
new technologies in organizations such as computer systems, robots or automation
have created anxiety, stress and concerns about job security among some employees
(Goodman, 1982). How can the stress response(s) associated with the implementation
of new technology be measured? Researchers could ask the employees directly, ask
colleagues who work with the employee, observe the person's behaviour over a period
of time, or assess physiological reactivity. Each of these types of measure has both
strengths and weaknesses. Since no one method is error-free and perfectly accurate, the
most appropriate strategy might be triangulation.

The triangulation strategy can be designed to examine the stress responses of employees affected by a major technological change. A number of techniques can be used to measure stess responses at a series of data points. The participants can be interviewed and asked directly about the stress associated with the change. The participants can also be systematically observed and various biomedical measures obtained at a number of data points.

A representative sample of employees can be monitored over a 24-month or 36-month period. A series of psychological, physiological, behavioural and performance observations can be obtained from the employees influenced directly by the change, as well as matched counterparts who are not affected by the change. For example, a baseline set of observations could be taken from groups that are about to initiate change and the matched groups of controls. Interviews, self-report surveys, biochemical, psychophysiological and performance measures used in combination and implemented by experts would provide useful longitudinally-based information on stress responses.

The combined administration of biomedical and behavioural science techniques would generate a comprehensive longitudinal picture of stress responses. It would be interesting to determine if the various techniques yield a set of convergent results. Or perhaps if stress responses are found in some modalities and not in others, researchers would have an opportunity to develop feasible explanations. Divergence does not mean that the results of triangulation methodology are useless. It may in fact illustrate that a technological change has a more pronounced impact in one stress response modality and no identifiable effect in other stress response categories. Triangulation provides researchers with an opportunity to uncover either convergence, divergence or neutral results.

The results of this type of triangulations study could then be combined with economic cost savings analysis data to provide a more complete picture of the impact of the technological change. This type of thorough questioning and analysis can be applied to many other organizational interventions that are purported to be in some way linked to increased stress or reduced stress. For example, do time management procedures, relaxation or cognitive stress management training, structural changes, personnel changes, mergers, career counselling, goal setting, incentive pay plans and performance appraisal increase or decrease stress? Which stress response modality is influenced by these techniques and events? What type of individual indicates the most or least responsivity to the techniques and events?

8. Research to fill some gaps

The demonstration example of studying technological change and stress responses and economics is only one of many traingulation strategy research possiblities. In a society that is struggling to improve productivity it is important to examine more closely job design, stress vulnerability, personal characteristics and vocational placement. Although theoretical models for these factors already exist, we know little about how stress response co-varies with productivity across a range of responses. Is it possible to place individuals with dysfunctional stress response tendencies in the potentially least stressful jobs? Is it possible to place individuals with dysfunctional stress response tendencies in the most compatible work environment for their tendencies?

Also, more triangulation strategy research is needed on the influence of various stress conditions on stress response. For example, how does the duration of a particular stressor affect stress response? Systematic research is needed on the kinds of organizational stressors and the intensity of stress on the stress response. Is the major response to a particular kind or configuration of stressors primarily physiological, psychological, behavioural or performance? What are the after-effects of such responses (e.g., decreased job performance for an hour, a day, a week, or more)? How do the after-effects of the stress response affect an employee's ability to adapt in the future?

There is also a need to examine, via the triangulation strategy, stress response difference across sex. Are there sex differences in the stress response? What types of differences? Do any differences in response affect job performance or career advancement? Since larger numbers of women are moving into work, these types of issues need to be examined.

Are there occupational differences in stress response? Do air traffic controllers and police officers display more pronounced psychological, behavioural or physiological responses on the job than construction workers, computer programmers and sales personnel? What type of differences in these stress responses are associated with ill health and psychosomatic disorders? These questions, when answered, could provide knowledge which is fundamental to developing organizationally sponsored intervention programs to minimize the negative consequences of stressful occupation-oriented circumstances.

There are a variety of work related events that are seemingly pleasant yet presumably stressful, such as receiving a sudden job promotion, receiving a performance recognition award, or being selected to attend a special training programme. Little is known about the stress response of pleasant events. Some theories of stress imply that a stress response of such pleasant stressors should not differ from negative stressor induced responses. Are these theories correct, partially correct or incorrect? The recent work of Lazarus (1981) on hassles and uplifts could be expanded using the triangulation strategy to include biomedical assessments of responses to hassles (negative stressors) and uplifts (pleasant or positive stressors). This would permit organizational researchers to compare the stress response associated with negative and positive stressors.

There is much measurement work yet to be done before the assessment of stress responses is considered scientifically and practically acceptable. It is the contention in this chapter that triangulation methods and the expertise of biomedical and behavioural science theorists, researchers and measurement specialists is needed to accomplish greater precision and insight. The answers to important organizational, individual and societal questions about stress responses, health, illness and productivity await the efforts of those researchers who adopt triangulation measurement procedures that incorporate both biomedical and behavioural science measures of occupational stress.

References

Andrew, G., Tennant, C., Henson, D. and Schonnel, M. (1978). The relation of social factors to physical and psychiatry illness *American Journal of Epidemiology*, **108**, 27–35.

Baum, A., Grunberg, N.E. and Singer, J.E. (1982). The use of psychological and neuro-endocrinological measurements in the study of stress. *Health Psychology*, **1**, 217–236.

Beehr, T.A. and Newman, J.E. (1978). Job stress, employee health, and organizational effectiveness: A facet analysis, model, and literature review. *Personnel Psychology*, **31**, 665–699.

Berglund, B., Berglund, V., Jonsson, E. and Lindvall, T. (1977). On the scaling of annoyance due to environmental factors. *Environmental Psychology and Nonverbal Behaviour*, **2**, 83–92.

Bieliauskus, L.A. (1980). Life events, 17-OHCS measures, and psychological defensiveness in relation to aid-seeking. *Journal of Human Stress*, **6**, 28–36.

Campbell, D.T. and Fiske, D.W. (1959). Convergent and discriminant validation by the multitrait-multimethod matrix. *Psychological Bulletin*, **56**, 81–105.

Caplan, R. and Jones, K.W. (1975). Effects of workload, role ambiguity, and Type A personality on anxiety, depression, and heart rate. *Journal of Applied Psychology*, **60**, 713–719.

Chadwick, J.H., Chesney, M.A. and Jordan, S.C. (1977). High blood pressure education in an industrial setting. Paper presented at the Annual High Blood Pressure Education Research Program Meeting, Washington, D.C.

Cohen, S., Evans, G.W., Krantz, D.S. and Stokols, D. (1980). Physiological, motivational and cognitive effects of aircraft noise on children: Moving from the laboratory to the field. *American Psychologist*, **35**, 231–243.

Denzin, N.K. (1978). *The Research Act* (New York: McGraw-Hill).

Eden, D. (1982). Critical job events, acute stress, and strain: a multiple interrupted time series. *Organizational Behavior and Human Performance*, **30**, 312–329.

Eliot, R.S. (1979). *Stress and the Major Cardiovascular Diseases* (Mt. Kisco: Futura).

Euler, V.S. (1966). Twenty years of noradrenaline. *Pharmacological Review*, **18** 29.

Fox, H.M., Murawski, B.J., Bartholomay, A.F. and Gifford, S. (1961). Adrenal steroid excretion patterns in eighteen healthy subjects: Tentative correlations with personality structure. *Psychosomatic Medicine*, **23**, 33–40.

Frankenhaeuser, M. (1972). Experimental approaches to the study of catecholamines and emotion. *Report from the Psychological Laboratories, University of Stockholm*.

French, J.R.P., Jr and Kahn, R.L. (1962). A programmatic approach to studying the industrial environment and mental health. *Journal of Social Issues*, **18**, 1–47.

Froberg, J., Carlsson, C.G., Levi, L., Lidberg, L. and Seeman, K. (1970). Conditions of work: psychological and endocrine stress reactions. *Archives of Environmental Health*, **21**, 789–797.

Gal, R. and Lazarus, R.S. (1975). The role of activity in anticipating and confronting stressful situations. *Journal of Human Stress*, **1**, 4–20.

Gatchel, R.J. (1979). Biofeedback and the modification of fear and anxiety. In R.J. Gatchel and K.P. Price (eds), *Clinical Applications of Biofeedback: Appraisal and Status* (Elmsford, NY: Pergamon).

Glass, D.C., Krakoff, L.R., Finklemen, J., Snow, B., Contrada, R., Kehoe, K, Mannucci, E.G., Isecke, W., Collins, C., Hilton, W.F. and Elting, E. (1980). Effect of task overload upon cardiovascular and plasma catecholamine responses in Type A and B individuals. *Basic and Applied Social Psychology*, **1**, 199–218.

Goodman, P. (ed.) (1982). *Change in Organizations*. (San Francisco, CA: Jossey-Bass).

Hale, H.B. (1965). Plasma corticosteroid changes during space-equivalent decompression in partial-pressure suits and in supersonic flight. *Hormonal Steroids, Biochemistry, Pharmacology, and Therapeutics*, **2**, 527.

Hersen, M. and Bellack, A.S. (eds) (1976). *Behavioral Assessment* (New York: Pergamon).

Horowitz, M., Wilner, N. and Alverez, W. (1979). Impact of event scale: A measure of subjective stress. *Psychosomatic Medicine*, **41**, 209–218.

Ivancevich, J.M., Matteson, M.T., and Preston, C. (1982). Occupational stress, Type A behavior, and physical well being. *Academy of Management Journal*, **25**, 373–391.

Jick, T.D. (1983). Mixing qualitative and quantitative methods: Triangulation in action. In J. Van Maanen (ed.), *Qualitative Methodology* (Beverly Hills, CA: Sage).

Johansson, G., Aronsson, G. and Lindstrom, B.O. (1978). Social psychological and neuro-endocrine stress reactions in highly mechanized work. *Ergonomics*, **21**, 583–599.

Johnson, S.M. and White, G. (1971). Self-observation as an agent of behavioral change. *Behavior Therapy*, **2**, 488–497.

Kanner, A.D., Coyne, J.C., Schaefer, C. and Lazarus, R.S. (1981). Comparison of two modes of stress measurement: daily hassles and uplifts versus major life events. *Journal of Behavioral Medicine*, **4**, 1–39.

Kasl, S.B. and Cobb, S. (1970). Blood pressure changes in men undergoing job loss: a preliminary report. *Psychosomatic Medicine*, **32**, 19–38.

Kazdin, A.E. (1974). Effects of covert modeling and model reinforcement of assertive behavior. *Journal of Abnormal Psychology*, **83**, 240–252.

Lacey, B.C. and Lacey, J.I. (1974a). Studies of heart rate and other bodily processes in sensorimotor behavior. In P.A. Obrist, A.H. Glack, J. Brener and L.V. DiCara (eds). *Cardiovascular Psychophysiology*. (Chicago, IL: Aldine).

Lacey, J.I. and Lacey B.C. (1974b). On heart rate responses and behavior: A reply to Eliot, *Journal of Personality and Social Psychology*, **30**, 1–18.

Lazarus, R.S. (1974). Cognitive and coping processes in emotion. In B. Weiner (ed.), *Cognitive Views of Human Motivation* (New York: Academic Press).

Lazarus, R.S. (1981). Little hassles can be hazardous to health. *Psychology Today*, **15**, 58–62.

Lazarus, R.S. and Folkman, S. (1984). *Stress, Appraisal, and Coping* (New York: Springer).

Levi, L. (1972). Stress and distress in response to psychosocial stimuli: laboratory and real life studies on sympathoadrenomedullary and related reactions. *Acta Medica Scandinavia*, Suppl., 528.

Lewin, K. (1938). *The Conceptual Representation and Measurement of Psychological Forces* (Durham, NC: Duke University Press).

Lipinski, D. and Nelson, R. (1974). The reactivity and unreliability of self-recording. *Journal of Consulting and Clinic Psychology*, **42**, 118–123.

Lundberg, U. and Frankenhaeuser, M. (1978). Psychophysiological reactions to noise as modified by personal control over noise intensity. *Biological Psychology*, **6**, 51–59.

Mason, J.W. (1974). The integrative approach in medicine: implications of neuroendocrine mechanisms. *Perspectives in Biology and Medicine*, **17**, 333–347.

Mason, J.W. (1975). A historical view of the stress field. *Journal of Human Stress*, **1**, 22–36.

McNamara, J.R. (1979). Behavioral psychology in medicine: an introduction. In J.R. McNamara (ed.), *Behavioral Approaches to Medicine* (New York: Plenum Press).

Murray, H. (1938). *Explorations in Personality* (New York: Oxford University Press).

Nelson, R.O., Lipinski, D.P. and Black, J.L. (1974). The effects of expectancy on the reactivity of self-recording. *Behavior Therapy*, **6**, 335–349.

Newman, J.E. and Beehr, T.A. (1979). Personal and organizational strategies for handling job stress: a review of research and opinion. *Personnel Psychology*, **32**, 1–45.

Rose, R.M., Jenkins, C.D. and Hurst, M.W. (1979). *Air Traffic Controller Health Change Study*. Federal Aviation Administration contract, Department of Transportation (Washington, DC: Government Printing Office).

Schuler, R.S. (1980). Definition and conceptualization of stress in organizations. *Organizational Behavior and Human Performance*, **25**, 184–215.

Schwartz, T.B. and Sheilds, D.R. (1954). Emotional tension and excretion of corticoids and creatinine. *American Journal of Medicine*, **16**, 608.

Selye, H. (1936). A syndrome produced by diverse nocuous agents. *Nature*, **138**, 30–32.

Selye, H. (1956). *The Stress of Life* (New York: McGraw-Hill).

Selye, H. (1977). Introduction. In D. Wheately (ed.), *Stress and the Heart* (New York: Raven).

Shannon, I.L., Prymore, J.R., Hester, W.R., McCall, C.M. and Isbell, G.M. (1961). Stress patterns in dental patients: 1. Serum free 17-hydroxycorticosteroid, sodium, and potassium, in subjects undergoing local anaesthesia and simple exodontic procedures. *Journal of Oral Surgery*, **19**, 486.

Sime, W.E., Buell, J.C. and Eliot, R.S. (1980). Cardiovascular responses to emotional stress (quiz interview) in post-myocardial infarction patients and matched control subjects. *Journal of Human Stress*, **6**, 39–46.

Thomasson, B. (1959). Studies of the content of 17-hydroxycorticosteroids and its diurnal rhythm in the plasma of surgical patients. *Scandinavian Journal of Clinical Laboratory Investigation*, *11*, Suppl. 42.

Tuttle, W.C., Davis, J.G. and Green, E.R. (1979). Development of an automated stress/duress detection system. *Biomedical Sciences Instrumentation*, **15**, 37–44.

Wolf, S. and Wolff, H.G. (1943). *Gastric Function: An Experimental Study of a Man and his Stomach* (New York: Oxford University Press).

Zorn, E.W., Harrington, J.M. and Goethe, H. (1977). Ischaemic heart disease and work stress in West German sea pilots. *Journal of Occupational Medicine*, **11**, 762–765.

Index